MYLENE FARMER
THE SINGLE FILE

by

Steve Cabus

Grosvenor House
Publishing Limited

All rights reserved
Copyright © Steve Cabus, 2011

Steve Cabus is hereby identified as author of this
work in accordance with Section 77 of the Copyright, Designs
and Patents Act 1988

The book cover picture is copyright to Steve Cabus

This book is published by
Grosvenor House Publishing Ltd
28-30 High Street, Guildford, Surrey, GU1 3HY.
www.grosvenorhousepublishing.co.uk

This book is sold subject to the conditions that it shall not, by way of
trade or otherwise, be lent, resold, hired out or otherwise circulated
without the author's or publisher's prior consent in any form of binding or
cover other than that in which it is published and
without a similar condition including this condition being imposed
on the subsequent purchaser.

A CIP record for this book
is available from the British Library

ISBN 978-1-908105-78-3

Mylène Farmer: The single file

Contents

Introduction	1
Part 1: Cendres De Lune	**5**
1/ Maman A Tort - 2/ My Mum Is Wrong	7
3/ On Est Tous Des Imbéciles	15
4/ Plus Grandir	20
5/ Libertine	25
6/ Tristana	33
Part 2: Ainsi Soit Je... / En Concert	**39**
7/ Sans Contrefaçon	41
8/ Ainsi Soit Je...	49
9/ Pourvu Qu'Elles Soient Douces	54
10/ Sans Logique	61
11/ A Quoi Je Sers...	68
12/ Allan Live - 13/ Plus Grandir Live	74
Part 3: L'Autre... / Dance Remixes	**81**
14/ Désenchantée	83
15/ Regrets	94
16/ Je T'Aime Mélancolie	100
17/ Beyond My Control	107
18/ Que Mon Coeur Lâche -	
19/ My Soul Is Slashed	114
Part 4: Anamorphosée / Live à Bercy	**123**
20/ XXL	125
21/ L'Instant X	133

22/ California	139
23/ Comme J'Ai Mal	148
24/ Rêver	153
25/ La Poupée Qui Fait Non (live) -	
26/ Ainsi Soit Je...(live)	159

**Part 5: Innamoramento / Mylènium Tour /
Les Mots / Remixes** — **165**

27/ L'Âme-Stram-Gram	167
28/ Je Te Rends Ton Amour	175
29/ Souviens-Toi Du Jour	183
30/ Optimistique-Moi	190
31/ Innamoramento	198
32/ Dessine-Moi Un Mouton (live)	203
33/ L'Histoire D'Une Fée, C'Est...	208
34/ Les Mots	212
35/ C'Est Une Belle Journée	219
36/ Pardonne-Moi	225

**Part 6: Avant Que L'Ombre... / Avant
Que L'Ombre...à Bercy** — **231**

37/ Fuck Them All	233
38/ Q.I.	244
39/ Redonne-Moi	250
40/ L'Amour N'Est Rien...	256
41/ Peut-Être Toi	261
42/ Slipping Away (Crier La Vie)	269
43/ Avant Que L'Ombre...(live) -	
44/ Déshabillez-Moi (live)	274

Part 7: Point De Suture / No 5 On Tour — **281**

45/ Dégénération	283
46/ Appelle Mon Numéro	294

MYLENE FARMER — THE SINGLE FILE

47/ Si J'Avais Au Moins...	301
48/ C'Est Dans L'Air	308
49/ Sextonik	314
50/ C'Est Dans L'Air (live) -	
51/ Paradis Inanimé (live)	324

Part 8: Bleu Noir — 329

52/ Oui Mais...Non	331
53/ Bleu Noir	344
54/ Lonely Lisa	351
55: ???	352
Thank You	353
Mylène Farmer, the singles: a crazy bonus French "poem"	355

Introduction

She may sing mostly in French, and be widely known to the general public only within Francophone countries, but yet Mylène Farmer can, paradoxically, be called an international star. Not only because of the levels of her fame and her unusual career trajectory, more in line with that of a worldwide pop sensation than that of the average French pop artist. Not only, either, because of her easy association with globally renowned musicians: although the bulk of her work of course stems from her long-time collaboration with her legendary composer Laurent Boutonnat, Mylène Farmer is unusual amongst French artists in that her reach and influence have grown enough over the years that she can now afford to call on the biggest international names in the business for the needs of her discography.

But more to the point, Mylène Farmer can be called an international star precisely because she has managed to gain fans from all corners of the globe: websites to the glory of the star exist of course in French, but also in English, German, Italian, Russian, and other languages besides. What's more, the extraordinary devotion of which she is the object in the French-speaking territories has somehow managed to cross over, undiminished, into the hearts and minds of fans from all over the world, be it in China, the USA, the UK or Saudi Arabia, to name but a few: and this, in spite of the obvious stumbling block that the language barrier would at first appear to represent. It is hard to pinpoint exactly what it is that makes the singer so special in the eyes of so many, but one thing at least is for sure: whatever it is, it cannot be contained by mere linguistical barriers. It is not necessary to speak much French, or indeed any at all, to fall under her spell: the Mylène Farmer magic operates on a level that is beyond words. A strange thing, too, when words occupy such a prize place within the Farmer universe...

Curiously, it is only comparatively recently that I truly became aware of the extent of Mylène's reach with fans from all across the world: for this, I must thank the MFInternational website, whose members have shown me that it is indeed possible to converse about my favourite singer in a language other than my native French, and with just as much passion and attention to detail as can be expected from French fans. Although I have been speaking pretty much exclusively English for the last 23 years, I am nevertheless grateful for my Gaul heritage, if only for one reason: I have never had to try too hard to understand what it is that Mylène is singing about. (Of course, understanding her precise meaning is often a different story, even for a Frenchman, but you know what I mean.) As such, I feel very lucky: and even more so, when it comes to the star's biography. Countless books have been published about Mylène, approaching the subject from every possible angle; but the one thing these books all have in common is that they are all, without exception, written in French. After over a quarter century of incomparable success, this seems a little strange, and must certainly feel unfair, not to say frustrating, to those non-French speakers who also happen to be Mylène Farmer fans. And so, after waiting (fruitlessly) for many years for someone to redress the balance at last, I have decided to take matters into my own hands. I won't pretend that I'm the best writer in the world: that, I am not. But, I know my Farmer stuff, and I can promise you that what follows is nothing but accurate facts, put together in a way that is informative and, hopefully, entertaining to read. Quite often I have also included rumours, because in a way they are also a part of the story, and they are fun, but these are always clearly indicated as such. I had a lot of fun writing this book: I sincerely hope that you find some enjoyment reading it too.

Part 1: Cendres De Lune

1/ Maman A Tort - 2/ My Mum Is Wrong

Most Mylène Farmer fans will never forget the very first time they were exposed to her music, and I am no exception. Indeed, unlike other "first times" in my life, I can still remember this one very clearly. One day in early 1984, the whole family was gathered for dinner over at my grandparents' house in Brest, in the Britanny region of France. As usual, the TV was blaring away in the corner, ignored for the most part as we concentrated on our half-dozen snails and artichoke hearts for starters. And yet, I suddenly found my attention temporarily diverted from my food. On the tiny screen, without so much as a warning, a pretty brunette woman wearing not much more than a flimsy nightie was now demurely letting the whole table know of her fondness for the forbidden and impolite pleasures. I wasn't the only one to notice, of course: I can still remember the gradual hush that descended over the assembled family members, the forks stopping in mid-air, as the words coming from the TV set finally registered: did this woman just declare her love for...another woman? Did she really just say that her nurse's singing does things to her? I could suddenly sense my grandmother's gaze fixed on us kids, entranced as we were by the pretty-looking lady and her catchy song that almost sounded like an innocuous nursery rhyme. I was 14 at the time and no longer quite a child, but my cousins were little and as young as three, and the sudden sight of the singer's head offered on a plate for consumption by a group of children was finally too much for our grandmother, who got up and walked over to the television (this was before remotes, of course), to change the channel. "That's unhealthy..."

Did I know that day I had just had my first glimpse of a singer whom, over the following years, I would come to practically worship? No, of course not. Although "Maman a tort" definitely struck a chord with me on first listen, as it was no doubt doing at the same time with thousands of other kids throughout the country, I did not yet realise just how much of an impact this singer would turn out to have on my life. In fact, as Grandma turned the channel over, I wasn't even that upset: a little annoyed, perhaps, but I forgot all about it within seconds. In any case, little did I know that I would get to see that video again very soon, for the first of what would be hundreds of times. And counting.

The impact of "Maman a tort" and the accompanying video upon its release in March 1984 cannot be overstated. Although not a huge hit by the standards of the time -around 100,000 copies sold, a moderate success- its influence will be felt in more subtle ways. The French musical landscape of the time was, of course, safe and bland, with, for the most part, no themes that could be considered challenging, at least not in the mainstream. "Maman a tort" will only really meet with success from the summer onwards, after Mylène's first manager, Bertrand Le Page, has come on board and shaken things up with, amongst other things, a new colour sleeve for the single. It is around this time that I renew my acquaintance with Ms. Farmer (and finally get to see the video in its entirety.) A few months is a long time when you're 14, and my interests have recently got a whole lot broader. Lately I've been noticing my friends' bodies in ways I hadn't before. As "Maman a tort" begins to get some heavy rotation on French radio, I'm reminded of that very first time a few months earlier, prematurely interrupted by my morally-preoccupied grandmother. Already, back then, something about those "plaisirs impolis" had rung a bell inside my head, faint but clear, but not yet urgent enough to engage me fully. As the summer comes around, however, as me and my friends go from one "boum" to another, those innocent after-school discos usually supervised by one or more parents, there are two songs in particular we keep hearing again and again: the first is Dead Or Alive's "You spin me round", the second is "Maman a tort" by a certain Mylène Farmer. And this time round, as Mylène declares her taste for what is forbidden, I understand her a whole lot better.

My experience was far from unique, of course. Up and down the country, countless others were seduced by the song and its gently twisted narrative, by the almost childlike subversion it brought into our homes at a time when French "variété" could always be relied upon to play it safe. Even in the case of someone like Jeanne Mas, at the time *the* huge success and seen as daring and bold, the music, and especially the lyrics, were, in retrospect, fairly bland and generic, and not likely to cause offense with anyone. Any sense of Jeanne being "out there" was, perhaps, due more to her outrageous use of make-up and striking dress sense than to any specific message delivered through her songs. (This assessment is based purely on the early, massively successful period of her career, or the first two albums: not knowing anything about the artist or her music thereafter, I recognize that this may well have changed over time.) Mylène, on the other hand, wore a lot less make-up, was light-years away in terms of confidence and stage presence, and yet her message seemed somehow more sincere, more substantial. Although the lyrics to "Maman a tort" were penned not by Mylène but by her early collaborator Jérome Dahan, it is surprising to see how very fitting they turned out to be as an introduction to the universe yet to be born, as if the song had been written with Mylène specifically in mind.

And yet that wasn't the case at all. In the very beginning, co-composers Dahan and Laurent Boutonnat have a teenage girl in mind for the song, but her age at the time (15 or 16, according to various reports) brings up a whole lot of complex legal issues. The teenage singer is therefore let go. In the meantime, however, Jérome has introduced a friend of his, a certain Mylène Gautier, to Laurent, who falls under her spell right away. He is immediately smitten

MYLENE FARMER — THE SINGLE FILE

by her "psychotic" appearance, and is convinced she is the one. Nevertheless, a casting has been arranged for "Maman a tort", and Mylène must submit to it just like any other candidate. Luckily, she impresses on the day, and is eventually selected. Hard today to imagine the outcome having been any different! In view of Laurent's initial "psychotic" impression of the young woman, it is interesting to note that she will shortly go on to dedicate her first single to two distinct characters from different eras, both afflicted with mental health issues in the course of their lives: on the back of the "Maman a tort" sleeve, Mylène has written a couple of short dedications: "à Louis II de Bavière...à Frances..." King Louis II, "Le Roi fou", was sent to a mental institution in his later years; as for "Frances", the lack of a surname cannot hide the fact that this is a reference to the Hollywood star Frances Farmer, famously institutionalized against her will by her own mother, and from whom Mylène got her stage name. With these uncommon dedications, the singer sets the tone early on...

The "Maman a tort" video holds the distinction of being one of the cheapest music videos ever made (with a budget of about €750 in today's money), although Laurent Boutonnat initially had a far more ambitious vision in mind. A storyboard, partially reproduced in the '89 Tour programme, shows tantalizing glimpses of what could have been: a black and white short set in an orphanage, where a young girl bereft of maternal love attempts to transfer her affections onto the nuns entrusted with her care. The clip would have ended on a suicide as the girl jumped from a height in order to escape her misery. Had this video been shot, it would apparently have been both in french and english, so as to assist with the "My mum is wrong" promotion. Unfortunately, the estimated budget of around 450,000 francs was, at the time, out of reach for a team only just starting out.

There will be numerous TV prestations of "Maman a tort" in 1984, thanks in large part to Bertrand Le Page's efforts. Not only on prime-time shows like Michel Drucker's "Champs-Élysées", which introduces Mylène to the great public for the very first time, but also on countless regional broadcasts, where the budding singer can be seen performing her song in glorious 80's outfits, all big jumpers and shapeless skirts. Even this early on, Mylène gets her first taste of censorship: her performance of the single on the children's show "Le club des Mickeys" is vetoed, as the song is deemed a tad too ambiguous for impressionable young minds. Some music programmes also take it upon themselves to show the clip only partially, the sequence with Mylène's head on a dish being judged a little disturbing by some. Some early TV appearances now come across as slightly surreal: on one particular show, "Les jeux de 20h", a staple of saturday night broadcasting at the time, Mylène performs the song in what appears to be a town square, right on the cobbles, with the only mildly interested audience sat on plastic chairs just inches away, close enough to touch her. There is no screaming, of course, not a single hysterical "Mylèèèène!" to be heard. To be fair, who then could have guessed what was to come? Though Mylène's performance on the night is adequate and professional, there is no hint yet of the charismatic, enigmatic superstar we will all come to know and love. The Mylène of the day is still in her embryonic stage: she doesn't know it yet, but it will take another two attempts, two more singles, before the magic really begins.

For the time being, anyway, the "Maman a tort" promotion period continues. In September of the same year, an english version, "My mum is wrong", is released, although curiously it will only ever come out in France. It must be said that releasing a "version anglaise" of your latest "tube" is all the rage at the time, and fairly common practice for anyone who's had a sizeable hit. On this occasion, the english translation comes courtesy of one FR David, who has just enjoyed a huge hit in France with his song "Words". Sadly, this updated version will fail to make much of an impact, and sales are negligible. This, of course, will later on turn the 7" single into a real collector's item, not to mention the promo-only 12" featuring an extended mix not available anywhere else! At its peak market value, the "My mum is wrong" 12" single will command over £400 from an England-based mail-order company. Having passed over the 7" in my local record store on many an occasion at the time, I will have many chances to rue my lack of clairvoyance in the years to come. Indeed, I will never even hear "My mum is wrong" until the mid-90's, when I finally manage to acquire a copy for a sum close to €100, a bargain compared with the above-mentioned company's asking price of £225.

The "Maman a tort" promotion period comes to an end with the single's release in Canada, in January 1985. Laurent Boutonnat is credited as "Boutannat" on the label, not a good omen, and the single fails to take off in Mylène's childhood home. Not to worry: with a respectable success under their belt, the team have taken their first step, and Mylène has achieved the initial exposure she needed. It is now time to move on to the next phase.

3/ On Est Tous Des Imbéciles

In an interview with "Boys and Girls" magazine in 1984, Mylène offers some information regarding the continuation of her career. We are told that the new, second single will be released sometime in the autumn, and that it will be called "Bip Be Bo" (also known as "Bip Be Bou Rock n' Roll (L'amour au téléphone)", according to alternate sources). Mylène also lets slip that she has recorded a song called "I do love you". These songs, or in any case any songs by those names, will never be heard from again. Concerning "I do love you", it is tempting to speculate that this may have been an early version of "La ronde triste", which features on the "Ainsi soit je..." album, although this is of course nothing but speculation! In the end, it is "On est tous des imbéciles" which will act as follow-up. Released in January 1985, slightly later than originally announced, the second single is entirely Jérome Dahan's composition. He also signs the lyrics. Just like "Maman a tort", the song was actually written before the encounter with Mylène had taken place, and was therefore not written with her in mind. Originally, Jérome, who also nursed ambitions of being a singer, had planned to record the track himself.

Musically quite similar to its predecessor, "On est tous des imbéciles" takes a gentle, sarcastic swipe at the world of show-business and all its inherent pretensions.

During a TV interview for the now-defunct Antenne 2 channel in February 1985, Mylène reiterates the idea, stressing the importance of doing things well while not taking yourself too seriously. Some have cited the song's theme as one of the reasons for its ignoble flop: maybe it was a little too early on to start poking fun at the industry, they suggested. Of course, this may have had absolutely nothing to do with it: it could simply be that the song flopped because not enough people liked it, and nothing more than that. And flop it did: with a mere 40,000 copies sold, a catastrophically meagre amount at the time, "On est tous des imbéciles" is a resounding failure. This is in spite of generally agreeable reviews, and some fairly generous radio airplay, as well as some serious and sustained promotional effort on Mylène's part: in all, she will perform the song no less than 14 times on TV, treating us to that unforgettable "pouet!", sometimes delivered with a cross-eyed, dorky look on her face.

Much like "My mum is wrong", the poor sales of "On est tous des imbéciles" will ensure that in later years, the 7" and accompanying 12" will become real collectors' items. Especially as the song will be effectively dropped from Mylène's répertoire therafter, never to feature on any album or ever be performed again. It will become the ultimate "lost" Mylène song, and many fans who missed it first time round will have to wait a long, long time to finally make its acquaintance. It goes without saying that the single will fetch high sums at specialized stores and record fairs over the following years. This is even truer for the "promo" version of the 7": although not an actual promo in the strict sense of the word, the copies sent out to the media did feature a little something extra: a little insert in red paper, of dimensions only slightly smaller than the record sleeve, on which were printed, in white letters, the words: "Mylène Farmer est une imbécile. Et vous?"

But if the record became of such interest to collectors later on, it is not only because of the title track, but also because of what is featured on the B-side. "L'Annonciation" is the very first published track in Mylène's career to be solely composed by Laurent Boutonnat, who also takes care of the lyrics. A dark tale of rape and abortion, with religious overtones and sinister strings (plus some unsettling laughter from Mylène towards the end for good measure), the song almost acts as a precursor to the dark universe that is only just around the corner, with its recurring themes of sex, death and religion, to name just a few. Through its rarity and unavailability, the song will attain almost mythical status in the eyes of some fans. Not yet a committed enough fan myself at the time, "On est tous des imbéciles" did indeed completely pass me by in 1985, and I do not have any recollections of it at the time of release, and in fact only became aware of its existence several years later, in1990. Once again I was lucky, scoring a dog-eared copy of the 7" from a private collection for around €90, rather than paying the £200+ expected by mail-order companies. It will take another ten years before I can listen to the extended version for the very first time. Of course, this was all in the days before the emergence of the internet: nowadays, anyone curious can just click their way to an instant listen of whatever song or version tickles their fancy, but back then there was a genuine sense of achievement to be gained from finally getting your hands on a long yearned-for hard copy! (and also a definite sense of having a lot less money in your pocket than you did before.)

Another reason for "On est tous des imbéciles" having made much less of an impression than the preceding single is, no doubt, the fact that there was never an accompanying video, making the song the first of (to date) three such "orphan" singles, the other two being "L'Histoire d'une fée, c'est..." and "Sextonik". With music videos still very much an emerging format at the time, proceedings were made even more difficult by the disagreements between TV stations and video producers as to who the rights should belong to. It's tempting to try and imagine what could have been, even if the song does not easily lend itself to visualisation. Would the infamous cross-eyed "pouet" have been immortalized on celluloid? What's more, unlike in the case of "Maman a tort", the imagination is further restricted (or freed, depending on your viewpoint) by the fact that there never was a storyboard or concept in the first place (at least none that ever became public knowledge), let alone an alternate one.

The failure of "On est tous des imbéciles" will mark the end of two working relationships: that of Mylène Farmer with RCA, who chooses not to renew her contract, and also, more significantly, the end of the collaboration between the Farmer/Boutonnat tandem and Jérome Dahan. Already, a divergence of opinion is becoming apparent between Boutonnat and Dahan: while the former wants to carve out an all-conquering, outstanding career for his muse, Jérome thinks Mylène is more suited to a low-key, laid-back niche in the style of someone like Françoise Hardy. Unable to envision Mylène as a "Jeanne Mas to the power of 10", as he put it, Jérome Dahan departed, taking with him the songs Mylène was about to record. Fast-forward 25 years: on 16th October 2010, it is revealed that Jérome Dahan has died, following a long illness. Although no longer amongst his inner circle, Mylène will take the time to pay him a final visit. Since then, rumours have been circulating about a possible 25th anniversary re-edition of "Cendres de lune", possibly featuring previously unreleased Dahan compositions. Whether this is truth or rumour should soon be known in any case, the date of the 25th anniversary being less than two months away at the time of writing.

As for the break with RCA, it could have been disastrous and brought everything to a premature end, had Alan Lévy at Polydor not seen the artistic and commercial potential of the young singer. He signs Mylène to his label for a three-album contract, throwing her the lifeline that will enable her to record her next single and get one step closer to realising her (and Laurent's) dream.

4/ Plus Grandir

"Plus Grandir", the third single proper, brings with it many firsts. It is Mylène's first single for Polydor, her new record company, to whom she has remained faithful to this day. It is the first 100% Farmer/Boutonnat collaboration to be committed to vinyl. It is also the first time Mylène signs the lyrics to a track, something she will of course carry on doing with incredible success: how amazed Laurent must have been, upon discovering the singer's incomparable lyrical talents... "Plus Grandir" is also the first of Mylène's songs to benefit from an elaborate videoclip, more in line with a short film than the usual pop promos of the day. The video for "Maman a tort", though undoubtedly fascinating, comes across as somewhat amateurish in comparison. This is no doubt why it was relegated to the "bonus" section of the Music Videos I DVD. But now, for the first time, Laurent Boutonnat has a sizeable budget at his disposal, somewhere in the region of 300,000 Francs, to put images to his and Mylène's song. Shooting takes place over five days, one day on location at the Saint-Denis cemetary and four days on set at the Sets Studios in Stains.

The first impression upon seeing the video for the first time was one of unexpected surprise, on two different levels: on the one hand, surprise at the singer's unsuspected depth and versatility: could this really be the same artist who, barely a few months ago, was singing

MYLENE FARMER — THE SINGLE FILE

her sweetly perverse nursery rhyme of a song, displaying a charming smile on the single's (second) cover? Although there is of course a fair amount of darkness to "Maman a tort", it was a lot less explicit, perhaps somewhat concealed behind the song's cute, almost childlike exterior. Of course, it could also be a question of perception on the part of this particular viewer: as stated earlier, an adolescent at 14 and then at 15 will often be two very different persons. Some thematics will not be picked up on so easily. But here, in any case, the darkness makes no apologies, and, rather than insinuate itself gently, whacks you square on the side of the head. Such a direct approach to subjects not usually considered appropriate for public discussion was new and exciting, and unlike anything else in the country's musical landscape of the era. What was also extremely surprising, on the other hand, was to see a video of such quality, and length, coming from a French artist: at the time, this felt like a bolt from the blue. French promos of the era were unvaryingly awful and cheap-looking, more often than not little more than the singer or group bouncing around in front of a superimposed background; expensive-looking endeavours with a cinematic feel were usually the preserve of American superstars such as Michael Jackson.

And yet, the evidence was right there on our screens, right in front of our eyes: opening titles, foreboding background music, as Mylène glumly pushes her pram along, navigating her way through the headstones before finally coming to a halt in front of what appears to be her own. The action then moves on indoors, where Mylène is working out some anger-related issues on her doll prior to being violated by a dark brooding stranger in the middle of the night. (The actor playing the role of the rapist is none other than Rambo Kowalski, now better known as Hervé Lewis, to this day the star's personal trainer.) Having given in to sin, Mylène is duly chastised by the attending nuns, who nevertheless did appear to be getting some kind of vicarious thrill out of spying in on her during the act. With her innocence lost, there is nothing left for Mylène to do but rapidly grow old, and possibly a little mad too, while spinning around in the net curtains, occasionally looking out for pigeons. (It took Mylène three hours in make-up, and three professional make-up artists, to be transformed into her elderly counterpart.) The picture moves back to Mylène in the cemetary, standing before the headstone engraved with her name and the words "Plus Grandir". With an almost disdainful look on her face, she tosses some flowers on the grave before walking away, as the shot pans out to show us her long-suffering doll, apparently still in one piece, giving us a knowing, slightly evil wink. And to top it all off, full film-style credits roll on afterwards. Pure class.

Death, partial nudity, religion, despair: what's not to like? The clip obviously creates an immediate sensation, and is even shown in avant-première at the Kinopanorama cinema in Paris on 13th November. Of course, it isn't long before censorship puts in its two cents: in an interview with Starfix magazine, Laurent Boutonnat reveals how the video was rejected by an American company that was at the time putting together a compilation of the best videoclips from around the world. Not that they weren't seduced by the final product: on the contrary, they loved it, but couldn't even go anywhere near it because of the religious elements. As they told Laurent, religion was the one thing you did not mess with! Cold feet and censorship aside, the video receives a generally very positive reception from the media, not surprisingly as it is easily heads and shoulders above its contemporaries of the time in terms of quality and presentation. With the "Plus Grandir" clip, Mylène and Laurent set the early foundations to their complex universe, and Mylène once more gets talked about, even if the song itself, in the end, is not quite the hit one could have hoped for. With sales of around 80,000 copies, a modest amount half-way between flop and success, it does not even manage to integrate the recently-created Top 50.

"Plus Grandir" may have sold twice as much as "On est tous des imbéciles", but that is not to say the single will be twice as easy to come across over the following years, far from it. Indeed, after over two decades of hardcore collecting, it will remain the one Mylène single I could never get a hold of, in any format. A copy of the 12" was glimpsed once, long ago, in a shop window in Lille in northern France, but the eye-popping asking price meant I had to make do with merely glancing at it longingly for a few minutes. Even on specialized websites, the "Plus Grandir" single, for some reason, seems to remain one of the most elusive to track down to this day. Thankfully, there are now other, easier ways to finally get to hear the six-minute version: there is something strangely melancholy about listening at last to a previously-unheard extended version after close to 25 years of waiting: the price of not being fan enough, quickly enough. Although, once again, there were no promotional supports as such for "Plus Grandir", the 7" sent out to radios did feature an interesting little something extra: the single came housed inside an A4-sized cream-coloured folder, with a cropped version of the sleeve photo and the Polydor logo on the front, and a beautiful, blue-tinged shot of the pram from the clip on an enclosed sheet, complete with lyrics and Mylène Farmer signature. No doubt any surviving copies would fetch a small fortune today. In Canada, in place of "Plus Grandir" as the first single to be taken from the soon-to-be-released "Cendres de lune" album, it is "We'll never die" that gets a single release, on the Trafic label, in February 1986. No picture sleeve release appears to exist, merely a plain cut-out white paper sleeve. Sales were insignificant and "We'll never die" did not chart, but once again the item has acquired a value far above the original, and must surely qualify as one of the scarcest Mylène releases around.

They may not have scored the big hit they were hoping for -indeed, "Plus Grandir" was not the team's first choice, but a decision imposed upon them by their record company- but Mylène and Laurent have certainly earned themselves an awful lot of critical acclaim, and there is suddenly much interest and high expectations in the (still) brown-haired singer. What the tandem now needs is a genuine, bona fide smash in order to consolidate their position. Their next release might just be the exact thing they need...

5/ Libertine

When "Libertine" is first released in April 1986, in the same week as the "Cendres de lune" album, there are at first no obvious signs that it will become any more of a hit than the previous single. Radio and the public in general are slow to pick up on the track, in spite of the previous media interest generated by Mylène, and for a while it looks as though the new single is headed for an unremarkable destiny. Indeed, the track itself has been failing to make an impact for quite a while already: composed way back in 1984 by Jean-Claude Dequéant, the song, then called "L'Amour Tutti Frutti", has already been turned down time after time by various record companies. Originally a rock track with totally different lyrics, something about the song nevertheless appeals to Laurent Boutonnat, and a deal is made to enable Mylène to record it as her own. Laurent goes to work on the song, re-arranging it into a poppy, bubblier version, discarding the original lyrics along the way and replacing them with his own. Displaying his talents as a writer, he comes up with a text that is full of sexual innuendos, and manages to namecheck the album in the opening line. Though Mylène will not play the part of lyricist in this case, she does contribute slightly during rehearsals, when she sings the first thing that comes into her head, "Je suis une putain" ("I am a whore"). This will later on be amended to "catin" ("harlot") by Laurent, an old-fashioned expression more in keeping with the spirit of the song and, more importantly, of the upcoming video.

For there are, of course, two central elements that will turn the fortunes of "Libertine" -and those of Mylène, too- around: a change of hair colour, and a video. On the sleeve of the very first "Libertine" pressing, Mylène strikes a pose in an orange outfit; but more importantly, her hair is still brown, and pretty much similar to the "Plus Grandir" cover permed style. Nothing very striking, no "hook" to grab the public's imagination. Encouraged by, amongst others, her manager Bertrand Le Page (himself a natural redhead), Mylène takes the plunge and undergoes a radical transformation. The results are stunning, and, with hindsight, pretty much self-evident. Although Mylène was clearly a beautiful woman before, the new hair colour fits her like a glove and further sublimates her beauty. But more than merely cosmetic, the change is also a huge step forward in terms of Mylène finding her own visual and artistic identity, and from that day on there will be no going back: although the shade will vary over the following years, Mylène stays and will stay a redhead for good, with one exception, much later in the mid 90's. Around that time, Mylène, in temporary self-exile in the USA following the "Giorgino" debacle, dyes her hair platinum blonde, instantly making herself almost unrecognizable, no doubt her intention. Or perhaps she simply couldn't stand being

"Mylène Farmer" anymore, and saw this as a good way to take a break from herself. In any case, it all goes to show just how much her hair colour became linked to her persona, and what an essential role it has played in the forging of her musical identity.

And then there was, of course, that video. Although Laurent had already strongly hinted at his talent with the "Plus Grandir" clip, "Libertine" will constitute a veritable revolution in the audio-visual landscape of the time, leaving most observers slack-jawed with astonishment. It is probably fair to say, without any disrespect to the composer, that the song would have struggled to achieve the same iconic status had it not been so inextricably entwined with Laurent Boutonnat's artistic vision. Once again, as for the previous single release, the video benefits from a storyboard treatment and a full cinematographic sensibility, although on this occasion the director has really gone all out to outdo himself. Shot over a period of four days in the château de Ferrieres for the main part (the bath scenes were filmed elsewhere, in the château de Brou), "Libertine" draws from various references including Stanley Kubrick's "Barry Lyndon" as well as the back-stabbing shenanigans of 18th century nobility in order to deliver a masterpiece of short film. From the opening duel scene (with another appearance from Rambo Kowalski, this time as Libertine's doomed opponent) until the blood-soaked finale, the viewer feels they are watching, more than a mere pop promo, a real cinematic, historical drama. Not surprising, when the scenario, written by Mylène and Lauren, manages to pack in intrigue, sex, death and generous lashings of violence within the 10 minutes 53 seconds running time. Extreme care is also paid to historical accuracy and to sets design, right down to the smallest details. Add to this a full team of actors and technicians comprised of around fifty people, all under the helm of the maestro Boutonnat, and it's easy to see how "Libertine" came to leave its competition trailing in the dust. Just like "Plus Grandir", "Libertine" will earn itself an avant-première showing, this time at the Mercury cinema on the Champs-Élysées on 18th June '86. Something it amply deserved, in view of the quality and crafstmanship of the finished product.

And yet, one of the most surprising things about the whole affair is that "Libertine" was made on a relative shoestring. With a budget of around €75,000, less than that of a lot of other videoclips of the era, Laurent and his team deliver the ultimate lesson in getting value for your money. No doubt motivated by the director's enthusiasm, and the sense of being part of something special, a lot of the cast and crew are reported to have offered their services for free. The young court ladies who come join Libertine in the tub for some bath frolics, for instance, were supposedly secretaries with Movie Box, the advertising company who co-financed the clip along with Laurent Boutonnat. Mylène also throws herself into the part with gusto: although a stand-in will be used for some of the more complicated fight scenes, she decides to suffer for her art, and so, for the sake of realism, she has no problem with being slapped across the face, for real, by her "rivale".

Sophie Tellier has become something of a cult figure in Farmer history, and for good reason: her deliciously evil rivale, that she plays to perfection, is the ideal counterpart to Mylène's heroine figure. Wronged, boiling mad and finally avenged (or was she?), her character is like the ultimate movie villain: mad, bad and definitely dangerous to know, we nevertheless wait for them to appear with some anticipation, and delight in their wickedness when they finally do. Mylène first meets Sophie at the Juan-les-Pins film festival in 1984, and it isn't long before a working relationship develops, with Sophie becoming her personal choreographer. As well as teaching Mylène some moves, Sophie Tellier will also make two further appearances in later videos, as well as reprising her rivale role for the stage during the '89 Tour, where she is one of the singer's backing dancers. Originally from the world of dance, Sophie will go on to become a celebrated actress in France, on the screen and on the stage. Another familiar name also makes a surprisingly early appearance on the set of "Libertine": François Hanss, who will of course in later years go on to direct several of Mylène's videos as well as the "Avant que l'ombre...a Bercy" and "Stade de France" films, is assistant-director.

As the video finally hits TV screens in the summer of '86, the effect on sales is immediate: the single integrates the Top 50, not to depart until January of the following year. Climbing steadily, it reaches its peak position, number 9, and will shift around 280,000 copies in all, a huge jump in terms of sales, and exactly what the Farmer/Boutonnat tandem needed. Finally, Mylène is a star. She suddenly finds herself in high demand, and performs the song on numerous TV shows, no less than a total of 22 times in the later part of the year. One of the most memorable performances must be the one where Mylène sings poolside in front of two slightly camp men who dance while wearing nothing but tight swimming trunks: we thought nothing of it at the time, although it's true that the sequence has become gloriously kitsch over the years. But it's not only on TV that Mylène is popular: in nightclubs everywhere, the reaction is the same: as soon as the first notes of the "Remix spécial club" ring out, people rush to the dancefloor. At the time, perhaps because Mylène has only just become seriously famous, and those who do not like her can still hope she might just fade away quietly soon, there is not yet the sense of snobbery that will develop towards her music in later years from some quarters. Although less likely to apply in other countries, this certainly holds true within France, where some view a career that mixes pop with success as incompatible with the idea of artistic merit. Most Mylène fans in France will have stories of being looked down upon or made fun of for liking her and her music. Sometimes the derision will even come from totally unexpected quarters: many years ago, I came across the "L'Autre..." collectors' box-set in a small record shop in Nancy, eastern France. The shop owner's first reaction to my enquiry about the price was not to tell me what he was charging, but to let me know, in no uncertain terms, what he thought of the artist: "Mylène Farmer? But it's crap!" Not the greatest sales technique, and yet it worked, as I left with the precious box. Of course, his dislike for Mylène did not stop him from putting a fairly high price on the object, but as it was still within reasonable limits, and the box-set was ever so tempting, I had no option but to swallow my pride. But in 1986, at any rate, no-one is afraid to admit that they like "Libertine", and the track is everywhere: on the radio, in clubs, in "boums", and of course on TV, even if often in a shortened version, although that is quite natural as most music shows' time constraints make it impractical to show a ten-minute long video in its entirety every time. The shot of Libertine lying nude on the bed after her amorous encounter (the first time an artist offers full frontal nudity in a music video) is also often either excised or re-touched, so as to avoid offending sensibilities.

As befits the single's success, "Libertine" will benefit from quite a few more formats than the preceding singles. In addition to the early "orange dress" releases, by now mostly gone from the shops, a new 7" is published to capitalize on the song's new-found success. Not surprisingly, the new sleeve picture is a still from the video, showing Libertine with pistol aloft, ready to fire, and, not to be forgotten, with red hair. A new 12" is also released, in a totally different sleeve, a black background with white titles and a tiny picture of Mylène, the same as the one that graces the "Cendres de lune" album cover, right in the middle. (The "version longue" presented on the original release has now been replaced by the "Remix spécial club"). And for the first time in Mylène's career, it is not just one, but two 12" singles that are made available. The second version, subtitled "Bande originale du clip", features the entire video soundtrack, and glorious, large picture labels -a truly beautiful object, that will rise in price accordingly through the years. The single is also released in Canada, once again on the Trafic label, inside a plain white paper sleeve. The first truly promotional items since the "My mum is wrong" 12" also make their appearance: an "Avant Première" 7", with custom "searchlights" pink and yellow sleeve, of interest for its promotional value, though perhaps less for its aesthetic one. There is also a promo Maxi 45 Tours (12"), more appealing as it has a Mylène-specific sleeve, slightly different from that of the commercial release as the tiny picture of the singer in the centre has disappeared.

"Libertine" will also be performed live several times: a full theatrical version on the '89 Tour, with Sophie Tellier once again playing the part of the rivale; in 1996, with a rockier sound and slight oriental/arabic overtones on the chorus; as part of a medley during the Mylènium Tour, and in full rock-on mode for the Stade de France and 2009 Tour concerts. It has also been remixed several times, most recently on the 2003 "Remixes" album, where Y-Front deliver a fun, colourful electro-pop version. "Libertine" will also be covered on several occasions, most notably by the serial Mylène-cover-act Kate Ryan in 2003. There also exists an English version, "Bad girl", never released and long buried deep within Polydor's vaults, both in single and extended versions. After years of unavailability and even speculation as to its actual existence, "Bad girl" finally surfaced online a few years ago, to the delight of countless fans.

With the astonishing success of "Libertine", Mylène and Laurent have succeeded in making the big impression they were after, but this is no time to be resting on their laurels: Laurent, especially, must show that he can stand on his own as a songwriter. Thousands of newly-acquired fans (and detractors) are eagerly awaiting to see what comes next: the pressure is on.

6/ Tristana

With the amazing success of "Libertine", Mylène and Laurent now find themselves in an awkward position: Mylène is now a bona fide star, and interest in the "Cendres de lune" album is renewed, but all potential singles from it have already been exploited. (It was at one time briefly believed that "Au bout de la nuit" might become a single, after a prestation of the song on a TV show: that was not to be the case, however.) To wrap up the album's promotion at this point would be to miss on a golden opportunity, and would feel somewhat premature: before moving on to the next phase of the adventure, it is felt that at least one more hit single is needed in order to keep Mylène fresh in the public's mind. Thus "Tristana" is born, and a new edition of the album sees the light of day. The "Cendres de lune" first pressing will of course become a very much sought after item in no time, especially as the inner sleeve originally featured a black and white photograph, rarely seen since, of a pensive-looking Mylène wearing a long overcoat that will be replaced by a colour shot, more in line with "80's glamour Mylène", for the new edition. As "Tristana" makes its debut in February 1987, sales of the newly-expanded album begin to rise considerably.

But more than a simple marketing ploy to capitalize on the singer's new-found fame, "Tristana" represents most of all a very personal challenge to Laurent, one he has no choice but to meet head-on. The composer now needs to show the world that "Libertine" was no fluke, and that its success can be repeated with original compositions of his own! Already some are foreseeing the end of Mylène's career, and the term "one-hit wonder" is being bandied about. (Although to be fair, her detractors did not always wait that long: already, around the time of the release of "Maman a tort", a radio commentator had proclaimed on air: "Mylène Farmer? There's another one who'll have one hit and then never be heard from again!") Thankfully, the song is an immediate hit upon release. Entering the Top 50 in 33rd place, it will go on to rise to its highest chart position of number 9, selling somewhere in the region of 250,000 copies, earning itself a silver classification. Musically, "Tristana" is vintage Farmer/Boutonnat stuff, an immediately catchy melody with melancholy overtones that takes residence in your brain on the first listen. Mylène further demonstrates her lyrical skills, setting her plaintive words, full of unresolved longing, to Laurent's energetic pop construction. Once again, the track becomes a huge hit in nightclubs, the "Remix Club" making a particularly big impression: as soon as the abrupt intro kicks in, followed by the few notes on the flute, people get up and rush to the dancefloor. It has to be said that Laurent's remixing skills are now being complimented and enhanced by those of the sound engineer Thierry Rogen, another key name in the Farmer story, who joins the team around this time. His approach to sound and tight editing fit the era perfectly, offering a sound that is, at the time, fresh, new and exciting.

The "Tristana" video, with a budget of around 900,000 Francs, is shot in April 1987, over approximately five days for the outdoor scenes sections. The Vercors region of France acts as substitute for Russia, and the crew, mostly the same as for the "Libertine" video shoot, works hard, putting in 15-hour shifts, with filming starting at 6am and going on until 9pm. The interior shots of the tsarine's castle and the dwarves' cottage were filmed later on at the Sets studios in Stains, previously used for the "Plus Grandir" clip. The video introduces two elements that will soon become emblematic of the Farmer universe: snow-covered landscapes, and wolves. Indeed, one of the factors that contributed to the Vercors region being picked as the location was the nearby presence of a "wolf farm", where manageable animals could be hired for the scenes where the evil tsarine gets her just desserts. Once again, Sophie Tellier returns to play the villain, delivering another deliciously twisted performance as the demented tsarine who cannot accept that another woman should be fairer than she is, and sets out to kill her, first via her henchmen, and then, when this fails, by setting out to do the job herself with the help of a good old trusty poisoned apple. "Tristana" is, of course, loosely based on the Snow White story, the first time Laurent Boutonnat will revisit the world of fairytales through Mylène's videos. Though similar, the story is not identical: the action is relocated to Russia, with accompanying Russian dialogue and French subtitles, another exciting innovation. Mylène is at a slight advantage here, as she studied Russian as a second foreign language while still in education. This nod to Russia will not be forgotten, as Mylène will become extremely popular there over the following years, to the extent that she will even bring her live shows to Moscow and St Petersburgh on two occasions, first for the Mylènium Tour and also for the 2009 Tour. The Russian actor Vladimir Ivtchenko, who played the part of Rasoukine, Tristana's love interest, was so overcome with nerves during the filming of some scenes (notably the kiss scene) that he would sip vodka before the takes! Laurent Boutonnat will also differentiate his work from the classic fairytale by incorporating archive stock images from the October 1917 Russian revolution into the video footage. A portrait of Karl Marx can also be spotted hanging on the walls of the dwarves' cottage, adding an extra dimension to an already multi-layered work. This is the second time that a real historical character is referenced in a Mylène video, a picture of Sigmund Freud appearing briefly at the end of "Maman a tort", three years previously. Mylène once again implicates herself totally during filming, performing all her own stunts, including the scene where she falls down a snowy hillside while attempting to escape her pursuers. She also shows she has a sense of humour by bursting out laughing after landing on her backside on the floor when one of the chairs used in the dwarves' cottage scenes breaks under her weight. Mylène will dedicate the "Tristana" video to her father, who passed away the preceding year.

Another avant-première showing for "Tristana", this time at the UGC Normandie Champs-Élysées cinema on May 6th. Mylène won't skimp on her promotional efforts, performing her new single on TV no less than 26 times. For the first time in her career, she is accompanied for her prestations by two backing dancers, Sophie Tellier and Dominique Martinelli. Some of those TV performances will become some of the rare occasions where Mylène will sing live on a TV show, shortly afterwards gaining enough clout to be able to afford to impose her own conditions.

On stage, the song will only ever be performed during the '89 Tour, and never again after that, at least so far: some rumours would suggest it is not one of Mylène's personal favourites. She was allegedly surprised to hear that "Tristana" was one of the songs some members of the public would most like to see performed on the stage again. According to the same rumours, it now only "gets on her nerves".

In shops, "Tristana" is made available as a 7" single, with "Au bout de la nuit" on the B-side. Once again, there will be two separate "Maxi 45 Tours" to choose from (or both buy, more often): a regular edition featuring the "Remix Club" and "Wolf Mix", with a painted sleeve depicting a wolf howling at the moon casting its light over a snowy landscape; and, as for "Libertine", a "Bande originale du clip" edition, featuring the entire video soundtrack and a still from the video shoot on the cover. Sadly, this will be the last time that such a "Bande originale du clip" format is issued, but at least it is sent off with a bang as a promo copy is also produced, mostly similar in appearance but also including a small cinema-style "Tristana" poster. Two more commercial releases also see the light of day: a Canadian 7", again on the Trafic label, and once again in a plain white paper sleeve. It does, however, have the interesting distinction of featuring "Maman a tort" on the B-side in place of "Au bout de la nuit". The last object is one of the most interesting in the Farmer discography, as it is a completely unique format: there will be further cassette singles later on in Mylène's career, but this particular 4-track cassette is totally different in its presentation, presented mounted inside a 12" sized cardboard support featuring a large colour photograph and white and red titles, with the added mention "special price!" Of course, the price is likely to be very special indeed nowadays, as this short-lived format, extremely hard to find today, is one of the rarest around. In 2010, the Israeli DJ Offer Nissim will produce a brand new remix of "Tristana", but this has, as of yet, not been made available commercially or even on any promotional support.

Thanks to the early hits, in particular "Libertine", and a second edition featuring the new single and added remixes, "Cendres de lune" will eventually go on to sell somewhere in the region of 600,000 copies, a more than respectable figure for a first effort. Not surprisingly for a debut album, there were no collectors' versions available, although a promo vinyl album was sent out to the media, inserted inside a huge cardboard sleeve featuring the front cover image on both sides.

With "Tristana" having proved itself as a more than adequate follow-up, Mylène and Laurent can now turn the page on the "Cendres de lune" era, and move on to the next. With the next single only nine months away, time enough for the duo to give birth to it, it won't be too long before the fans can find out what's in store for them next: they will not be disappointed.

Part 2: Ainsi Soit Je... / En Concert

7/ Sans Contrefaçon

With two huge hits under her belt and one successful album already, Mylène is nevertheless very much aware that the hardest part is yet to come. Traditionally difficult to navigate for any artist, the second album's success or failure can mean the difference between ephemeral stardom or longevity. Hard at work crafting songs for the next opus, Laurent Boutonnat initially intends to propose as first single a cover of Juliette Gréco's classic, "Déshabillez-moi". Events will decide otherwise. In August 1987, Mylène invites the photographer Elsa Trillat to spend some of the summer holiday in a house that she and Laurent have rented in La Garde Freinet, in the south of France. The two women have only known each other a few weeks but already get on like a house on fire. A lot of their time is spent driving around in Elsa's car. Elsa is a huge Sylvie Vartan fan and plays her hit "Comme un garçon" over and over, prompting Mylène to tell her friend of how, as a young girl with short hair, people always used to mistake her for a boy, something she would play on by stuffing a handkerchief down her trousers in order to further the illusion. Later on, Elsa asks Mylène whether she has any new songs in the pipeline, to which the singer replies that she has, if not yet a new song, at least a title, which should please Elsa no end given her obsession with Sylvie Vartan: "Sans contrefaçon, je suis un garçon". Soon, Mylène invites her friend to witness first-hand how a song is created. Sat by the pool with a rhyming dictionary by her side, Mylène has fun playing around with synonyms and rhymes until, not much more than a couple of hours later, the final text is done. That very evening, Laurent sees the lyrics, and after just a few minutes of playing around on his portable synthesiser, he comes up with the hook, as Elsa and Mylène look on. The song title will eventually be shortened, and just like that, a future classic is born. The "Dis maman, pourquoi je suis pas un garçon?" that opens the song is the result of a private joke between Elsa and Mylène: when doing their grocery shopping in the small nearby town, Elsa would dare the somewhat shy Mylène to ask for their vegetables and other foodstuffs in the voice of a five-year-old; which the singer did, to great hilarity.

Sensing they are now sitting on a potentially huge hit, Mylène and Laurent put aside the "Déshabillez-moi" cover for now and concentrate their efforts on "Sans Contrefaçon". The song is recorded in Paris in September, and released as a single on 16th October with a brand new track on the B-side, "La ronde triste". The single is off to a slow start on French radio, which does not sit well with Mylène: she issues her manager Bertrand Le Page with a challenge: if he is as good a manager as he claims to be, he will get her twice the daily plays on NRJ! Not an easy task, but one Bertrand manages to accomplish somehow. At the same time, Mylène will take care of TV promotion, performing "Sans Contrefaçon" a total of 16 times between November 87 and February 88. (She will also perform the song on Swedish and Italian TV.) One prestation in particular will be much commented upon:when Mylène performs the song at the "Oscars de la mode", a live TF1 show in November, she accidentally exposes a breast: she was later said to be "livid" over the wardrobe malfunction. In any case, the hard work soon pays off: on 5th December, the new single enters the Top 50 at number 21, and will climb steadily until it reaches its peak position of second place. (It is Sabrina and her "Boys, Boys, Boys" that will deny Mylène the top spot.) Certified gold, "Sans Contrefaçon" will go on to sell half a million copies, becoming Mylène's biggest hit yet. In the end, the song's rapid success overtakes even Mylène and Laurent: when it first charts on 5th December, music channels are unable to broadcast a video for "Sans contrefaçon", as it is not yet finished!

Of course, that is not to say that the duo have been idle in this respect. As early as October, Mylène and Laurent begin work on the scenario, the first time Mylène is involved in this aspect of their work: unconfirmed rumours state that the singer initially wanted the video to be set in a concentration camp. On the 19th, she has a cast of her face made so that work on making the clip's puppet may start: the puppet will be created by Benoit Lestang, who will later go on to direct the "Q.I." video in 2005. For "Sans Contrefaçon", Laurent Boutonnat once again finds his inspiration in the world of fairytales, in this case revisiting the Pinocchio story. A wandering puppeteer stumbles across a travelling circus (interestingly named "Giorgino Circus"), where he and his wooden companion are met with a less than warm welcome by the frankly sinister resident clowns, who sneakily jump him and then proceed to play catch with the unfortunate marionnette. Luckily, a mysterious woman clad all in black wades in to save the day, running off with the puppet she rescues from the clowns' evil clutches. Following after her, the puppeteer is greeted with an unbelievable scene, as his puppet is brought to life under the guise of an achingly beautiful young woman, of course incarnated by Mylène. With their game of pattycakes interrupted, the woman in black runs off, leaving the puppeteer to enjoy a few too-short moments with the beautiful young woman, before she cruelly turns back into a lifeless wooden marionnette. The actor who plays the part of the puppeteer, Frédéric Lagache, will be seen again in 1992 in the "Beyond my control" video, as Mylène's unfaithful lover. As for the mysterious woman in black, the part was played by the extraordinary actress and cult performance artist Zouc. An intense, complex personality, this video will be one of Zouc's last ever public appearances before she withdraws from the limelight in order to deal with severe mental health issues. Zouc had been invited by Mylène onto the set of "Mon Zénith a moi" on 10th October, making a strong impression on the singer. With an estimated budget of around €55,000, shooting for the "Sans Contrefaçon" video will take place over the course of four days on the beaches of Cherbourg in northern France, under cold, wet weather conditions. Once again, François Hanss will be on hand as assistant-director on this clip that, while not as long in its duration as the two previous ones, still comes in at an impressive almost-nine minutes. By the time the video is finally sent out to TV, in January 1988, "Sans Contrefaçon" is already a huge hit.

It would be impossible to evoke the success of "Sans Contrefaçon" without mentioning the impact of the song within the gay community. Though the theme of homosexuality is not itself directly approached in the song, the lyrics do deal with notions of sexual ambiguity, of difference and of being rejected for it. The "Sans Contrefaçon" puppet is itself highly ambiguous, as its gender is not clearly specified. And by referencing the Chevalier D'Éon, a legendary historical figure whose true gender was (and still is, to some) the object of much speculation, Mylène further increases her appeal with all those, boys and girls, who feel somewhat out of sync with the still relatively conservative values of the time. While French society in 1987 no longer regards homosexuality as a crime or mental illness, long-held prejudiced views are still deeply entrenched: it is therefore not surprising that the gay community of the time should have felt a natural affinity, a form of gratitude even, with a singer who so unequivocally proclaimed the right to be yourself, even if this self happens to be outside of what is considered "normal". The release of "Sans Contrefaçon" will bring about the consecration of Mylène as gay icon, a label that is still valid today. In 1994, it will become the theme song to the movie "Pédale douce", a gay-themed film by the director Gabriel Aghion, who will even later on rename his production company "Sans Contrefaçon Productions".

But a label is only a label, of course, and it would be restrictive to try and paint Mylène's career as being geared exclusively towards the gay community, especially when we know Mylène's dislike for labels and attempts to box her in into a specific niche. "Sans Contrefaçon" was a genuine popular hit, reaching across all sections of society, as evidenced by the sales figures and its omnipresence in 1987 and '88. It was nigh on impossible, at the time, to go to any party or any kind of social gathering where music might be played without hearing the song at least once. In clubs too, gay or straight, the track goes down a storm, with two different versions available, the Boy or Girl remixes, in keeping with the sexually ambiguous spirit of the song. Reflecting on its huge popular success, "Sans Contrefaçon" will become the only Mylène song to be performed during all of her concerts, albeit as part of a medley for the Mylènium Tour. During the '96 Tour, Mylène sends another wink to her gay fans by surrounding herself with drag queens for her performance, while the 2009 Tour version sees the song being given a new rockier arrangement, complete with air guitar choreography. When Mylène first performs "Sans Contrefaçon" on the '89 Tour, it is one of the most eagerly anticipated songs, and, very quickly, something of a tradition is born: when she gets to the word "chaméléon", Mylène lets the audience sing in her place, something they are more than willing to do. It is unlikely she can ever sing that particular line herself again, even if she should wish to! The song will also be covered numerous times over the years, by artists including Lorie, Julie Zenatti or also Les Enfoirés, demonstrating its status as a modern-day classic.

There will be a fair few supports made available commercially to promote "Sans Contrefaçon": a 7", 12", and, for the first time in Mylène's career, a CD single, a new format then still in its infancy. All three formats will also benefit from a European pressing, for distribution mostly in countries such as the Netherlands or Germany. Strangely, and, some may have felt, somewhat frustratingly, it is only the European Maxi 45 Tours that features both the "Boy remix" and "Girl remix". The French edition foregoes the second remix in favour of "Déshabillez-moi", although both mixes are available on the CD single. A "45 Tours" (or 7") is also released in Canada, through Polydor and with a full picture sleeve this time. In addition, three promotional items will be issued within France: a 7" and a CD single, differentiated from the commercial releases by their so-called "gold" sleeves, in a highly-reflective, almost mirror-like material. There is also a promo 12", which this time features both remixes and no "Déshabillez-moi". "Sans Contrefaçon" will be released again in 2003, although not as a single proper, and only on a one-sided 12" featuring the JCA remix, taken from the "Remixes" album. This partial release will only be available online and in specialist record stores.

With the first single from the forthcoming new album such a resounding success, Mylène Farmer is now unquestionably one of the major names in French pop music, and she and Laurent have already managed to establish their own particular sound and style. But this is not the time to be reflecting on their emergent success, and there is not a moment to waste: already, it is time for the follow-up.

8/ Ainsi Soit Je...

When "Ainsi soit je..." is released on 4th April 1988, just a month after the album of the same name, it is the first time a ballad has been put forward as a Mylène single. A complete contrast to the upbeat energy of "Sans contrefaçon", the track is the perfect choice to demonstrate the album's broad palette, in terms of themes and colour. As is now obviously fast becoming the rule, Mylène signs the lyrics while Laurent takes care of the music: the duo have clearly hit their stride, with Boutonnat's sound and Mylène's words a guaranteed winning combination. The gentle, melancholy track, dealing with themes of solitude and isolation, will go on to sell around 150,000 copies, earning it its highest placing of number 12 in the Top 50. This will be one of the rare occasions where a Mylène single fails to integrate the top 10, and yet this will not stop the song becoming one of the classics of the Farmer répertoire, beloved by fans and generally recognized as one of Laurent's finest compositions. The song has become a standard in French music today, and is still played regularly on the country's radio network, more than twenty years after its release.

Mylène will perform "Ainsi soit je..." on TV on eight occasions at the time in the course of her promotional duties, although there will be further prestations of the song in later years. In 1997, when the track is once again released as the second single to be taken from the "Live a Bercy" album, she proposes a new, different version of the song on the "Les enfants de la Une" show on the TF1 channel. The song will once again be rearranged into an even purer, stripped down version for the "Encore une chanson" broadcast in 2010, where Mylène, looking stunning in an ultra-short dress, delivers a flawless rendition, her voice at times bordering on the operatic in its purity and clarity. She is accompanied for the occasion by the ever reliable Yvan Cassar on the piano. "Ainsi soit je..." is clearly not the easiest song to sing in the world, especially when it comes to the chorus, and it is interesting to contrast these later, artful performances with earlier renditions. When Mylène performs the song live for the first time during the '89 Tour, for instance, although her rendition is perfectly adequate, it is far less poised and precise than, say, the "Encore une chanson" version: proof of Mylène's ever-increasing mastery of her craft, and her already well-demonstrated commitment to always better herself as an artist and a performer. "Ainsi soit je..." will also be performed live during the '96 Tour, and also, briefly, at the 2006 Bercy concerts, although only on the first few nights: sadly, these performances will not be committed to disc or film, the song being thereafter replaced by "L'Autre...". By the time the 2009 Tour and Stade de France concerts come around, however, Mylène, as if determined to have the last word on the subject, delivers stunning performances that literally take the breath away, and without avoiding the high notes either: the definition of a true professional!

The videoclip gets its avant-première showing on the TF1 show "Les animaux du monde", on 22nd May, where Mylène is also present on the set. The video, once again directed by Laurent, is a far more sober affair than the previous extravaganzas, in keeping with the spirit of the song itself, and, with a running time of "only" a little over five minutes, is only half as long as the preceding epics. Shot in sépia tones, the clip places Mylène within a melancholy, snow-covered setting where she encounters various animal creatures such as a fawn or owl, in between some light nudity and a faceful of mud. Going back and forth on her swing, the singer is eventually overcome by her melancholia and meets a watery end, although whether this is deliberate or not is somewhat ambiguous and left to the imagination. The shooting of the video is also a much simpler affair: shot over two days in the Sets Studios in the Paris suburbs (the setting for the "Plus Grandir" clip), with more or less the same technical team, there are this time no casting or outdoor filming considerations to be taken into account. Regardless of the means, the video remains an accomplished piece of work, its simplicity and sobriety in perfect accord with the music itself.

While obviously without the dancefloor potential of its predecessors, "Ainsi soit je..." nevertheless does put in an appearance in nightclubs around the time of its release. Back in the '80's, clubs in France (at least in the provinces) dedicate around 20 minutes of playtime to ballads for every two or so hours of dance music. Thus, when the time for "les slows" comes around, the opportunity arises for couples to smooch their way through Mylène's latest offering. The lyrics may have been somewhat on the dark side for a night out, but the "Maxi remix" of "Ainsi soit je..." was nevertheless savoured in this way on many an occasion, with many a happy memory as a result.

There were six formats in all released to support "Ainsi soit je...": commercial releases within France consisted of a 45 Tours, maxi 45 Tours and CD single, the second in Mylène's career, all with a close-up shot of Elsa Trillat's album sleeve photograph (doll out of shot) as artwork: beautiful items for any collection. Another short-lived format puts in an appearance on this single's release: the "CD Vidéo", that will only enjoy a fleeting existence. As well as three versions of the track, this also includes the videoclip, and comes in a somewhat different sleeve than the standard issue. Because of its uniqueness and rarity, this item nowadays exchanges hands for somewhere in the region of one hundred Euros. Outside of France, and for the very first time in an official capacity, Mylène gets a single release in Japan, where a 3" CD single in special "pop-up" packaging sees the light of day. Complete with Japanese titles, the item is an interesting curiosity, and one much sought after by collectors. On the promotional side, things are rather quiet for "Ainsi soit je...": it will have to make do with a measly "Avant-première" 7" with custom "searchlights" sleeve. The song is repeated on both sides, with no credits besides the artist and song names.

The "Ainsi soit je..." video, in view of what had come before, may have seemed a little simplistic, but with the next single just around the corner, any fans worried about Laurent Boutonnat's creative efforts were about to breathe a collective sigh of relief. Indeed, with the imminent resurrection of a (not so old) friend, Mylène and Laurent were about to amaze France (and beyond) all over again.

9/ Pourvu Qu'Elles Soient Douces

Two years earlier, TV viewers had bid a sad farewell to the Libertine heroine as she and her lover lay dead in a field, covered in blood, fallen victims to the evil Rivale's machinations. In keeping with their romantic ideals, Mylène and Laurent had seen fit for their heroine to meet the only possible suitable end: a gruesome, bloody death at the hands of the crazed Rivale and her pistolet-toting minions. And yet, as Mylène's latest video makes its avant-première début at the UGC Normandie Champs-Élysées cinema on 6th October 1988, two young 18th century British soldiers wandering round a blood-soaked battlefield make a startling discovery: coming across Libertine's "corpse" -and at first unsure whether it is that of a young man or woman ("It's a boy! It's a girl!"), a clever wink to "Sans Contrefaçon" and its games around sexual identity- they are soon shocked to realise that far from being dead..."she's alive!"

Way back in March '88, when the album "Ainsi soit je..." is first released, one track in particular stands out as an obvious hit single: the ode to sodomy that is "Pourvu qu'elles soient douces". Though it will make way for the title track when second single time comes around, a perfect way for Mylène and Laurent to give a taste of the album's diversity, "Pourvu qu'elles soient douces" finally gets its turn under the spotlight as third single, and is released on 12th September '88, which also happens to be

Mylène's 27th. Quite the birthday present, as the new single will turn out to be another monster smash for Mylène, and her first ever number 1 hit. Even before the video is sent out to TV, the song -slightly rearranged for its single release, losing the endless choruses that close the album version- quickly ascends up the charts, unstoppable, until it finally reaches pole position, where it will remain for five consecutive weeks. (As if that wasn't successful enough, Mylène also bags the Christmas number 1 at the same time that year.) More than 700,000 copies of "Pourvu qu'elles soient douces" will be sold in total, easily earning it a gold disc certification. The single's huge success, not surprisingly, also boosts album sales, and "Ainsi soit je..." finally reaches number 1 in the album chart, further consolidating Mylène's position as the undisputed queen of French pop. To date, "Pourvu qu'elles soient douces" remains one of Mylène's biggest hits, and one of the undisputed classics within her répertoire. '

The videoshoot takes place towards the end of August '88, in the Rambouillet forest near Paris, over a period of eight days. The team follows a heavy schedule, with shooting starting at 5 in the morning and going on until 1am the following day! And yet, the whole enterprise almost never got off the ground: in an interview with OK magazine in October, Mylène told of a very topical problem that nearly scuppered her and Laurent's plans: with the French revolution bi-centenary just around the corner, several films and documentaries on the subject were already in production, and finding enough historically accurate costumes proved to be a logistical nightmare. The "Pourvu qu'elles soient douces" video will also be an exercise in beating your own previous records. With a budget estimated at close to four million Francs and a duration of almost 18 minutes, this is "Libertine" on an even grander scale. Billed "Libertine II" right from the opening credits onwards, it was indeed a stroke of genius on Laurent's part to once more pick up the story, further elevating Mylène beyond the status of mere singer, and into that of a mythical, fictional character: such a way of doing things was totally unheard of within France, and propulsed Mylène towards iconic status with amazing speed and efficiency. At the time, Mylène and Laurent's universe is at its most enticing, and their latest cinematic extravaganza enables us to dream like never before: over twenty years after it was initially released, the palpable sense of excitement and thrill that was felt when watching the video for the first time is still easily recalled. And with good reason, as the team certainly didn't do things by halves: with over 600 extras, chosen from the French military, a team of over 50 technicians and a historical consultant on hand throughout the shoot, "Pourvu qu'elles soient douces" transcends the pop promo medium with ease, coming across more as a film in feel and appearance. Historical action, bloody military conflicts on a grand scale, subtitles, everything contrives to make the enterprise far more than a simple music video. And that's without mentioning the interpersonal drama, the debauchery, the sex...although Libertine won't be making it easy for the English captain, it must be said: a pitcher to the side of the head will be the price he must pay to gain the young woman's affections, not forgetting a lash of the whip right in the face! Played by the British actor Yann Babilee, the captain's attitude towards the rebellious

Libertine nevertheless softens considerably after his somewhat rough treatment at her hands, a possible nod to sado-masochism, perhaps not so surprising in a song that namechecks the Kama Sutra in its opening lines...

The pre-established characters, whom we already love (and love to hate), also contribute enormously to the viewer's emotional involvement: impossible not to feel a wicked thrill as the Rivale makes her reappearance, eagerly clutching at the bag of coins proffered as payment for her latest evil scheme. The amazing Sophie Tellier returns to play to perfection a Rivale clearly determined to ruin Libertine's love life: not content with slaughtering her previous lover, she goes on to shoot the English captain in the back, unfortunately for her just as Libertine emerges from her tent in time to witness the heinous act. One of the greatest catfights in music video history ensues, as a clearly not amused Libertine gives chase to her arch-enemy while a ferocious battle rages all around them. La Rivale gives as good as she gets, but a moment of inattention in a watery ditch finally sees her getting a long-deserved bayonet to the gut. And although Libertine herself appears to get away with her life, her later reappearance, clad all in black atop her equally black horse, as a sinister voice-over draws a parallel between her and death itself, only serves to cast a dark veil of doubt over the issue: is she dead, or alive? Interestingly, this theme of uncertainty regarding the heroine's condition appears to be a feature of all of the previous videos so far: in "Maman a tort", Mylène's disembodied head on a plate nevertheless shows signs of life; in "Plus Grandir", a clearly alive Mylène comes face to face with her own grave; in "Libertine", the heroine is assumed to be dead, only to be later resurrected; the ending of the "Tristana" video is deliberately ambiguous, with Tristana herself unsure as to whether she is dead or not; the initially lifeless "Sans contrefaçon" puppet comes to life only to become inanimate again within minutes; and the "Ainsi soit je..." protagonist is seen going back and forth on her swing seconds after seemingly drowning. Perhaps another contributing factor to the making of the Farmer myth: in addition to the blurring of the lines between performer and character through his filmic videos, Laurent adds another layer of mystery by leaving us to question the heroine's very existence: with our imagination unfettered, we are even more curious...

Right away, and perhaps even more so than its predecessors, "Pourvu qu'elles soient douces" becomes a huge club hit, the "Remix club" sound going down a storm on the dancefloors, generating huge enthusiasm amongst party-goers. In the club where me and my friends hang out every saturday night, the DJ proudly displays his promo 12" cover in front of his decks as he spins the record; although he shouldn't have, as the clearly much- coveted item mysteriously vanished from his collection one particular weekend, to his great distress. Not only that, but it was all in vain, as the promo 12" only featured the single version in the first place, and he would actually be playing the plain old commercial release, the promo sleeve being there purely for show. Tough luck... But it was not only the A-side that got some heavy rotation (until the record was stolen, at any rate): when the time for "les slows" arrives, "Puisque", on the B-side, gets an outing too. On the TV front, Mylène will promote her new single with around nine prestations on French channels, as well as some further foreign performances, as far away in time as December '90 in the Netherlands and January '91 in Denmark, barely a couple of months before the release of "Désenchantée". On the stage, "Pourvu qu'elles soient douces" is first performed during the '89 Tour, obviously being an unavoidable choice at the time. It is then zapped for the '96 concerts, but reappears in medley form for the Mylènium Tour, before being left out once more during the "Live à Bercy" period. Finally, and for what is only the second time in Mylène's stage career, the song is performed in full during the 2009 Tour and Stade de France concerts, in what is one of the concerts' sexiest moments, with some memorably suggestive vocalizing from Mylène during the middle section.

France and Canada will both be able to enjoy the release of "Pourvu qu'elles soient douces": within France, a 45 Tours, Maxi 45 Tours and CD single are issued, with a seductively-dressed Mylène striking a sultry pose on the cover. A promo 12" with cut-out sleeve features plain titles artwork on the same cream-coloured background, with a shrunk-down picture of Mylène peeking out from the exposed label. As previously alluded to in the case of the unfortunate DJ, this item plays the single version only, on both sides. Canada also sees a release of the 7" and 12" formats, although there does not appear to have been a CD single. The success of "Pourvu qu'elles soient douces" is such that it creates waves of interest outside of France, and the single is also released in countries such as Scandinavia, Italy, Austria, and the Netherlands, with

Germany in particular giving it a warm welcome. To simplify matters in foreign territories, the song title, somewhat obscure for non-French speakers, is shortened to "Douces", and this release is also given a totally different picture sleeve, with a shot of a pensive-looking Mylène resting her chin on her hand. An interesting promo item also comes out of Japan, although there is some debate as to whether this is a promotional Mylène Farmer item as such: a Polydor 45 Tours featuring Mylène on the A-side and the British band The Beautiful South on the reverse with "Song for whoever", with both acts' photographs sharing the front cover. An extremely rare, and costly piece nevertheless.

With another huge hit under their belt, Mylène and Laurent are cresting a wave of incredible success; but already, the exploitation of the "Ainsi soit je..." album is nearing the end. Time for just one more single with which to conclude this glorious period...

10/ Sans Logique

Thanks to "Pourvu qu'elles soient douces", Mylène has achieved a significant first double in her career: a simultaneous number 1 single and album. With "Ainsi soit je..." one of the major successes of the year, the time now comes for the team to select the track that will serve as fourth and final single. The honour falls to "Sans Logique", another uptempo number with extremely dark lyrics that deal with issues close to schizophrenia. Conjuring up some fairly graphic images, such as a pair of eyes being stabbed with scissors, the song makes use of opposing concepts, like the satanic and the angelic, to illustrate the idea of a split-personality: a fitting choice, and one that fits the Farmer universe like a glove. Released on 20th February '89, the newly-remixed version being played on the radio is slightly shorter and musically punchier than the original album version, the most notable difference being the disappearance of the violins on the verses and a slightly beefier beat. Apart from this "Logical single mix", Laurent and legendary mixer Thierry Rogen also produce the "Illogical club remix" for the maxi version: according to legend, the "this is a blank formatted disket" message that punctuates the song at various points came about as a direct result of a slight mishap in the studio. Having spent a fair amount of time working on an early mix of the track, Laurent allegedly saw his hard work reduced to nothing because of a software compatibility issue, and as he tried to play back the track he had just been working on, was greeted with nothing more than a synthetic voice informing him that "this is a blank formatted disket".

"Sans Logique" is released with the brand new track "Dernier sourire" on the B-side, one of the most poignant songs in Mylène's répertoire, in which she addresses a terminally-ill individual seemingly confined within what appears to be a clinical setting. The song, widely assumed to be in memory of her father, will be released once again in 1992 in a brand new, specially re-recorded version for the "Urgences" compilation, a charity release with all profits going to support the fight against HIV/Aids. "Dernier sourire" will once again take centre stage during the Mylènium Tour concerts, in what is one of the setlist's most emotional moments, leaving Mylène (and the fans) visibly affected. And yet, originally, it was a totally different track altogether that was envisaged for the "Sans Logique" B-side: "Je voudrais tant que tu comprennes", a Marie Laforet original that will eventually be performed as encore for the '89 Tour concerts instead.

In 1989, Mylène finds herself forced to take legal action after a still from the "Sans Logique" video, specifically the shot where she wears white lenses that cover her irises to give her a demon-like appearance, is used without her permission. Led by Jacques Cheminade, the European Workers Party, at the time on the campaign trail for the European elections, uses the photograph on their posters and leaflets, with the accompanying caption: "They promote ugliness and drugs!" (The "they" in question being the media, whom the party accuse of promoting a sub-culture of decadence.) The party have obviously picked on the wrong person, and, particularly in view of the drugs reference, which may have given the false impression that she endorsed the use of such substances, Mylène has no choice but to take the matter to court. Justice will rule in her favour, and the party is ordered to destroy all tracts, posters and other materials featuring her likeness, thus learning the hard way that you don't mess with Mylène Farmer's image without serious consequences. Six years later, it is Jean-Marie Le Pen, leader of the widely despised extreme-right Front National party, who will attract the star's ire: during an electoral meeting in the French town of Toulon, the after-dinner entertainment comes under the guise of a Mylène Farmer lookalike, who performs "Sans Contrefaçon" and "Désenchantée". In no time at all, an incensed Mylène is on the phone from Los Angeles, speaking live on the France 2 evening news, declaring herself scandalized and deeply upset that any of those who like her may have thought, even for a second, that she approved of such politics as a result of the party's devious stunt. A drawn-out legal battle ensues, with the courts eventually finding in favour of the singer, who will receive damages from the party and settle out of court with the lookalike. Commenting on the affair, Jean-Marie Le Pen, sore loser and making no more sense than usual, had this to say: "Thanks to this lookalike, I became aware of Mylène Farmer, whom I had never heard of; she's not my cup of tea."

The "Sans Logique" video, directed by Laurent Boutonnat, a far less flashier affair than that of the preceding epic, and with a running time more in line with the usual pop promo (although, at around five and a half minutes, still on the generous side), is nevertheless a visually accomplished piece of work, and one that doesn't shy away from dealing with somewhat dark themes. The song is illustrated by a Mylène wearing a set of sharp, painful-looking metal horns with which she is made to engage in a deadly game of corrida with her lover (played by the actor Lila Dahli), with devastating results. As a small coin-tossing crowd looks on, amused and worried expressions alternating on their faces, the game turns tragic as an enraged Mylène suddenly flips out, taking on the behavioural characteristics of an angry bull and goring her surprised lover to death. As a heavy rain starts to fall, the men, women and children spectators hurriedly retrieve their tossed coins from the muddy ground before departing, leaving Mylène to contemplate the consequences of her actions, alone by her dying lover's side. The video, influenced by Francesco De Goya's "Aquelarre" painting, is filmed entirely indoors at the Arpajon studios in southern Paris. (The same studios will be the filming location for Luc Besson's "Que mon coeur lâche" clip in 1992.) Two tons of earth are brought in (and tinted), and a huge painted background simulating a heavy, cloudy sky is manufactured for the shoot, with rain simulators brought in for the final scenes. These filming conditions enable Laurent Boutonnat to give the video an otherworldly feel and look, almost painting-like in its composition. As such, the "Sans Logique" clip, while less ambitious in scale than other works, remains one of Mylène's most visually striking videos. It has also been noted that this was the first time Laurent Boutonnat used the word "Fin" at the end of one of Mylène's videos, perhaps signalling the end of an era...

TV prestations for "Sans Logique" will be comparatively few, only five in total. (Still a huge amount, by today's standards.) Around this time, Mylène will also give a televised performance of "Dernier sourire" on a show hosted by Jean-Pierre Foucault, where she also receives an award for over a million sales of the "Ainsi soit je..." album. At the time, she is still the only female singer, within France, to have accomplished such a feat. Not that she has much to say about it, aside from never-forgotten expressions of gratitude towards her public: already, Mylène's interviews are becoming less frequent, and she is noticeably less given to idle chat during her TV appearances: she is, by now, certainly light-years away from the playful, brown-haired young woman of the early days, willing to cover a TV show host's face in lipstick kisses for the sake of a comedy skit. On the stage, "Sans Logique" remains a discreet presence, and has so far only ever been performed during the 1989 concerts. Selling around 200,000 copies, the single will reach its highest placing at number 10 in the Top 50.

There were also relatively few formats for this fourth and final single. In France, a 45 Tours, Maxi 45 Tours and CD single saw the light of day, while Canada had to make do with the 7" and 12" only. The sleeve picture is courtesy of Marianne Rosenstiehl, a long-time collaborator, and shows Mylène crying a bloody tear, in what has become one of the many iconic photographs of the singer. The only other format available was a promo 12", of great interest to collectors not only for its unique sleeve with red titles on a black background, but also because it features the "Classical version" of "Sans Logique", unavailable anywhere else. A beautiful version, stripped of all percussion for its first half, all strings and heavenly voice until drum rolls, much harder to make out in the other versions, eventually kick in, followed by a couple of solitary castanets towards the end. This is only the second time in Mylène's career that a particular mix is available only on a promo format, but it will certainly not be the last.

Carried by huge hits such as "Sans Contrefaçon" and "Pourvu qu'elles soient douces", the "Ainsi soit je..." album turned out to be a phenomenal success, with sales in excess of 1.5 million, earning it a diamond certification. Sadly, as in the case of "Cendres de lune", there was no collectors' box-set edition ever made available. There was, however, an ultra-rare promotional "coffret" sent out to the media in Germany, England, Spain and Italy. The frankly gorgeous boxes included a copy of the album both on CD and cassette, a copy of the "Sans Contrefaçon" Maxi CD single, a video profile VHS (in the relevant language) featuring a Mylène documentary and the "Sans Contrefaçon" clip, a lighter, an '89 Tour programme, some "Mylène Farmer"-headed notepaper and a short biography in one of the four languages! Only 50 copies were made per country, and consequently this item has turned out to be one of the most sought-after by collectors. Although I was never personally able to afford the 1,000+ Euros the item now commands, a kindly shop-keeper in a specialized Parisian boutique once let me examine it to my heart's content, and it is indeed a beautiful object, one I regretfully had to put back on the shelf...

The "Ainsi soit je..." album period will also be the setting for another marking event in Mylène's career: the beginning of a cold war between the singer and the Victoires de la Musique. In November '88, she is nominated for best French female singer, an award she goes on to win. But the lack of her name or even category on the trophy, combined with the overwhelming hypocrisy she feels coming from those at the mostly business-orientated ceremony, leaves a bitter taste in her mouth, and Mylène refuses to perform on the night. Everyone is outraged, and Bertrand Le Page doesn't exactly assuage anyone when he declares that "Mylène does not sing with a ballroom orchestra"...Already, she is making clear her refusal to play by the rules, and the business will not forget: she will never again be nominated at the Victoires.

But clearly, Mylène's popular success is such that she can afford to remain unfazed. For the time being, the "Ainsi soit je..." exploitation period has come to an end, and it is time to move on to the next logical step in her career: the stage.

11/ A Quoi Je Sers...

By now one of the biggest names in French pop, and a huge star with devoted fans in their thousands, there is only one way to go for Mylène: it is time to bring her universe to the stage, and come face to face with her public at last. Debuting in May '89 at the Paris Palais des Sports, after an avant-première in Saint-Etienne, the tour will turn out to be a huge success, pulling in fans in their droves and proving, without a shadow of a doubt, that the singer can make as strong an impact on the stage as she has in the charts and on the small screen. Many were those who predicted she would fail to pass this particular test: accusing Mylène of being a "no-voice" singer, or even, incredibly in retrospect, a charisma-free performer, the singer's prestation will very quickly leave them with nothing left to say. "En Concert" is recorded in October, during the Belgian leg of the tour, in Brussels, and is released on the eve of the two Bercy shows that will mark the culmination of Mylène's first-ever series of concerts.

The first of three singles to be taken from the album, "A quoi je sers..." is released on 17th July, its text (and that of its B-side, "La veuve noire") having been written barely a month before by Mylène in a villa in Nice, in between two tour dates. The self-questioning song was born as a direct result of the singer's first encounter with her public, and the strong emotions this invoked within her. Faced with an already extraordinary level of affection on the public's part, unusual in its intensity and undoubtedly impossible for one human being alone to rationalize, it is no surprise that the singer should have felt the need to stop and ponder on the meaning of it all. The photograph chosen as cover for the single, a Marianne Rosenstiehl shot of Mylène in her dressing-room immediately after a concert (and taken without her knowledge at the time), perfectly illustrates Mylène's probable state of mind in what must have been an overwhelmingly powerful and intense moment: seemingly alone, the singer, a towel held to her face as if to mop up the tears, is sitting in a chair with her back slightly bent, head down, reflecting on what has just come to pass, as if struggling to take it all in. Behind her, a lamp casts a bright light, while in front of her all is dark: already, perhaps, an intimation of the "great void" she will confess to experiencing after these astonishingly intense moments in time, these electrifying concerts that some won't hesitate to call by other names: a communion, or even Mass…and why deny it? It doesn't even take a religious outlook on life to experience this for yourself, just a concert ticket! It is undeniable that attending a Mylène Farmer concert has something of the spiritual about it: the love of the crowd for the petite red-haired woman up on the stage is unlike anything else, and it is no wonder if this initial contact led Mylène to ask herself "What am I for?"

The "A quoi je sers…" lyrics will be strongly influenced by the writer Luc Dietrich, whose "L'apprentissage de la ville" has made a marked impact on Mylène, after she read him on Bertrand Le Page's recommendation:

indeed, she will rework his "poussière vivante" into the song's opening line, while other references also pop up later on in the verses, just one of the many manifestations of Mylène's literary tastes to emerge through her songs. Some fans, however, are slightly alarmed by the "A présent je peux me taire (now I can shut up)" lyric, seeing in it the possible announcement of an early retirement; thankfully, we now know this was not the case, but it is easy to see how imaginations ran wild, especially in view of what the video had in store for us.

By Boutonnat standards, the "A quoi je sers..." video was a fairly modest endeavour. Filmed over a period of two days at the Lac de Grand-Lieu, in the Loire-Atlantique region, with a budget of a mere 30,000 Euros and a surprisingly sober running time of just under five minutes, it is a far cry from the "Pourvu qu'elles soient douces" levels of expense and grandeur. Nevertheless, the clip, shot entirely in stylish black and white, is another gem in the Farmer videography. While it is beautifully shot and edited as usual, it is really the content of the images themselves that make this clip so special: to the fans already worried by Mylène's ambiguous lyrics, what to make, indeed, of what Laurent is now showing us on screen? A soberly-dressed, almost prim Mylène waits by the banks of a river for the boat that will take her to some unspecified destination: as the boat comes into view, however, and as the features of the man wielding the oars are more clearly glimpsed, the viewer is reminded of the mythical river Styx, and of Charon, charged with ferrying the newly-departed's souls over to the other side, into the depths of Hell. With the pensive-looking woman on board, the boat sets off, making its slow way through the reeds and high grasses, until suddenly a presence makes itself felt. Mylène turns around, squinting through the fog: could it be...? And indeed, it shortly becomes apparent that some old friends -and foes- have come to greet her and see her on her way. The "Sans Logique" matador, the "Sans Contrefaçon" puppeteer, the "Tristana" lover, the English captain from "Pourvu qu'elles soient douces", and of course the Rivale from the same clip as well as the earlier "Libertine". Leaving Charon to go on his way, Mylène joins the not-so-merry group, and they slowly head off into the waters...Only Mylène and Laurent could have made such a video: only they had the backstory needed in order to pull off such a conceptually ambitious scene. In another example of the performer blurring into the character they have created, Mylène finds herself surrounded by characters from her previous videos, most of whom, apart from the English captain and the Rivale, had no previously assumed connections: all were supposed to exist within their own enclosed universe. And yet here they are, side by side as they escort...well, who, exactly? If not Mylène, then their own personal version of her: a possessed, lethal lover crowned with horns of metal; an inanimate wooden puppet, flitting in and out of life; an innocent, pure beloved pursued by evil forces; another conquest, hard-won on the battlefield; and of course, a deadly rival, the arch-enemy to surpass all arch-enemies. Once again, Laurent Boutonnat delivers a masterpiece in visual magic, at once further mythologising Mylène while at the same time blurring even further the thin line that separates fiction from reality in the viewer's mind. The unlikely scenario is also a neat device with which to turn a page on what has gone before, a quick recap before moving on to the next: although, as previously mentioned, some fans will fear this to be some kind of a covert farewell from Mylène. And in a way, they were right too: with the singer by now so inextricably linked with her persona, this can perhaps be said to be, indeed, a farewell to the Mylène of old, the "early-phase" Mylène. Sadly, not all of the actors will be able to reprise their previous roles: the parts of Rasoukine, the English captain and La Rivale will be played by other actors for the occasion. Sophie Tellier was prevented from taking part in the shoot by existing professional obligations (Mylène's own tour being one of them), although she did personally select her replacement. Shortly after shooting on the clip wraps up, Mylène jets off to India for a well-deserved few days' holiday.

Mylène will only perform "A quoi je sers..." on TV on three occasions, all in the first half of September: though this may seem like a rather measly amount of promotion, she can be forgiven as she is slap bang in the middle of her tour at the time. With around 140,000 copies sold, the single reaches its peak position of number 16. On stage, the song is performed for the first time, naturally, during the '89 Tour. Although initially selected for the Mylènium Tour setlist, "A quoi je sers..." will eventually be replaced by "Rêver", meaning fans will have to wait as long as until 2009 to hear the song performed live again, when it is included in the setlist for the indoor '09 Tour concerts. For the 2009 Russian concerts, in Moscow and St Petersburgh, the song, less well known to the local public, is replaced by "L'amour n'est rien...", by then a huge hit in Russia.

"A quoi je sers..." will be released in three formats: a 7", 12" and Maxi CD single, the latter two formats featuring the Extended Club remix, with a mysterious male voice at the very end that appears to be asking "quoi?" himself. On the promo side, a custom-sleeve 12" with black titles on a grey background is sent out to the media, featuring once again a mix totally unavailable anywhere else, the "Orchestral version", on the B-side. Essentially an instrumental, this version nevertheless has some alternate vocals by Mylène as she breathes some sweet "ya-ya-ya's" over the chorus section. With the item's price accordingly high, this was another version that remained unheard by many fans for a long time, at least until the internet came around.

With the tour in full swing, and such a success, it was only natural to expect that more singles would emerge as a result: another two, in fact, before another triumphant era could start getting under way.

12/ Allan Live - 13/ Plus Grandir Live

It is on 4th December 1989 that the second "En Concert" single is released: it is "Allan" that will be chosen to do the honours. An ode to Edgar Allan Poe, one of the singer's favourite authors, her bedside read, even, according to her declarations of the time, the song was one of the many "gothic" gems from the "Ainsi soit je..." album. Dark and melancholy, as befits the subject matter, the music and lyrics are classic Farmer. Indeed, it would have been easy to imagine it getting proper single status, given how much it reflects the album and Mylène's universe at the time. And who knows, maybe it was even considered for single release at some point: the existence of a quality "Extended mix" certainly seems to suggest some work went into it. But, of course, time waits for no-one, especially not Mylène Farmer, who happens to be very busy in this end of the year '89: with a successful tour underway so soon after the album's exploitation period has barely come to an end, there isn't much choice. To remain coherent, any singles issued from now on must be presented as coming from the album currently being promoted. And so, "Allan (live)" is born, with a little something special on the B-side, a little glimpse of the future, although of course this won't become apparent until April 1991, and the release of the following studio album: the brand new track "Psychiatric" is offered here in two different versions, the "New Beat remix" on the CD single and 12" and a shorter, four-minute mix on the 45 Tours. ("New Beat", at the time, is a popular stark, sparse sound, seemingly originating from Belgium, although its popularity will be short-lived.) Punctuated by a beat seemingly constructed around a sampled horse's hooves sound, these versions can be seen as an early rough mix when compared to the polished, slickly-produced edit that will eventually appear on the "L'Autre..." album.

Laurent Boutonnat comes up with yet another arresting concept for the "Allan (live)" video: the stage set, headstones, cemetary-style iron gates and all, is rebuilt in a field and then set on fire by a man wielding a flame-thrower, another neat way to make a clean break with what has come before. Mylène stands in front of the burning wreck, looking thoughtful as the flames lick at the setting for her previous triumph. The resulting filmed images are interspersed with live footage of Mylène's performance, as well as a few shots of horses in distress and a brief glimpse of a photo of Edgar Allan Poe, also going up in flames. Much later, an interesting clip will emerge on the internet: the film, which appears to be genuine, shows Mylène (easily identified by her hair) and others standing near the burning wreckage when a sudden explosion occurs, clearly not planned, and much too close for comfort. Although it is hard to make out what is being said, there is much shouting going on, and a sense that something that could have been potentially catastrophic has just happened. Clearly, no-one came to harm at the time, thankfully, but the short clip remains eerily disturbing nonetheless.

Not surprisingly for what is a live single, there will be no TV promotion to mark the release of "Allan". The single will go on to sell around 80,000 copies, a more than respectable figure for a live release, a format traditionally generating less popular interest than single releases proper. "Allan (live)" will reach number 32 in the Top 50. There will be a strict minimum of formats for "Allan": a 45 Tours, Maxi 45 Tours and CD single. For what is the first time in Mylène's career, the CD single is presented inside a "cristal" box, also known as "jewel box", the new standard, plastic packaging for singles, although cardboard and paper sleeves will make a comeback before too long. There were no promos issued for this single.

The final single to be taken from Mylène's first live album -also bringing to an end the glorious early phase of her career- is "Plus Grandir", which gets a second lease of life when it is released on 23rd April 1990, a little under five years since its original 1985 release. It also has the distinction of being Mylène's first single of the new decade! For its re-release, "Plus Grandir" gets two brand new remixes, on top of the single live mix: an extended, "Mother's live remix", unusual in the sense that it is a remixed, extended version of what is a live track to start with, not a very common practice. Mylène also shows a keen eye for future trends with the second remix, the "Mum's rap", a bass-heavy track on which she and Carole Fredericks engage in a verbal battle in which Carole tries to convince Mylène that she is her mother, with little success. The track, bizarrely, ends on a "bonsoir!" from Mylène and a brief cheer from the crowd.

The "Plus Grandir live" video opens on images of the famous cemetary gates being solemnly opened by a cloaked monk-type figure, in what constitutes a recreation of the original opening to the show. The rest of the video itself consists of excerpts of Mylène's performance, not only of "Plus Grandir" but also of several other songs, with Sophie Tellier being spotted in the background on several occasions, at one stage clad in her full "Rivale" get-up. Just before the end of the track, the music fades out, replaced by ominous, melancholy notes as a shot of a clearly emotional Mylène comes into view: it is clear to see, from the audience shots, that the magic was operating even back then! Just as with its predecessor, there will be no TV promotion for "Plus Grandir live", naturally enough. The single will sell in the region of 70,000 copies, climbing to number 35 before heading out of the Top 50.

Though a slightly smaller success than "Allan", "Plus Grandir live" will nevertheless be accorded a couple of extra formats: in addition to the regular 7", 12" and Maxi CD single, fans can also purchase the very first picture disc of Mylène's career. With a close-up shot of the singer wearing a black outfit on side A and a longer shot where she is dressed in white on side B, not to forget the "Édition limitée" mention on the vinyl, this is a beautiful piece, now very scarce and worth around 100 Euros amongst collectors. On top of an extra and new format, "Plus Grandir live" was also graced with a promo 12" single, featuring the short live mix on both sides and coming in a different sleeve to the commercial release, with "vente interdite" mentions on both sides.

Curiously, both "Allan" and "Plus Grandir" will be omitted from the VHS version of "En Concert", even if they do feature on the CD. A running time issue? Or perhaps the performances were deemed unsatisfactory by Laurent, and not fit for inclusion in the film? This isn't beyond the realm of the possible, when we know of Boutonnat's exigence on visual quality, to the point where the entire concert was performed in front of a non-existent audience on at least one occasion, in order to allow him to get the best possible shots of Mylène. But the vinyl and cassette editions of the album also found themselves bereft of a couple of tracks: no doubt, this time, because of running times limitations, both "Déshabillez-moi" and "Mouvements de lune (partie I)" have disappeared. In the end, the "En concert" double album will go on to achieve sales of 250,000, with a highest chart placing of number 9: a more than good showing for this type of release. The "En Concert" film will itself sell around 100,000, mostly on VHS, the prevalent format of the era: indeed, it is so successful that it will be reissued a total of four times. A VHS of the concert was also made available in Russia. For format completists, there also exist Laserdisc and CDI versions, although those have become increasingly difficult to track down. To the despair of many fans, of course, as the original VHS is often perilously close to disintegrating, and each further play is tantamount to a game of russian roulette! And in spite of persistent rumours of, at last, a DVD re-edition, no such thing has yet come to pass, and it is unfortunately easy to think that it might never do so: in view of Laurent Boutonnat's insistence on quality, it is doubtful whether he would allow this pre-digital recording to be viewed in the harsh

DVD light. (Blu-ray, even less so.) Of course, there is always hope!

With "En Concert" having marked the end of an era, and Mylène having categorically proved herself on the stage, the time has come for a new chapter to be written in the Farmer story. It will be less than a year from the release date of "Plus Grandir live" until Mylène makes her comeback with a brand new single. And what a comeback it will be...

Part 3: L'Autre... / Dance Remixes

14/ Désenchantée

"Désenchantée" almost never happened. After coming up with the melody, although Laurent Boutonnat very quickly senses he has a potentially massive hit on his hands, finalising the song's arrangements is proving to be very tricky: initially, the composer wants to give the track a dancy, techno flavour, but the end result just doesn't sound right. The song is recorded once, twice, three times, but somehow he just can't get it to work. Fed up, he threatens to "bin" the song altogether. This is when sound mixer Thierry Rogen -immensely excited by the song from the very first time Laurent played it for him on the piano- comes to the rescue. Overnight, he works on the track, building a whole new rhythm section, discarding the techno overtones in favor of a more traditional, almost brassy feel. The next day, he shares the fruits of his labour with Laurent, who falls in love with the new arrangements on the spot: at last, a fourth and final version of "Désenchantée" can be recorded: from then on, no more question of discarding the track. The whole team know they're on to something huge.

When "Désenchantée" is released on 18th March 1991, the fans have been waiting just under a year to hear something new from the singer. And while this may have seemed like a long wait at the time, they don't yet know that there will be far lengthier periods of inactivity to be endured in future...not that Mylène has been twiddling her thumbs, however: the last few months have been spent taking care of some promotion abroad, as well as working on the new album, written in around five months. In any case, when "Désenchantée" makes its radio début, its impact is immediate, and strong: apart from the obviously catchy melody, the song seems to capture the zeitgeist of the times perfectly. In the early '90's, France as a whole is as if in the grip of a collective depression, with a sense of morosity that pervades on every level: the economy, social problems, disillusionment with its leaders...Mylène has her finger on the pulse far more than she could have predicted when she sings "tout est chaos". And the "Génération désenchantée" she evokes in the chorus quite naturally gives the song a collective dimension, one that enables the listener to identify with it, and, perhaps, find some kind of solace within...Mylène, however, is quick to play down the song's possible political overtones: though she was, of course, no doubt very much aware of the possibility of such a scenario, she has no intention of being anybody's flag-bearer, even less of being saddled with the role of spokesperson for this disenchanted generation: very quickly, the singer makes it abundantly clear that the song is nothing more than a narcissistic portrait, in which she can only claim to be speaking for herself. A wise move that allows her to neatly sidestep any potentially unstable political ground and retain her independent artistic status.

But politics and the socio-cultural problems of the day were not, of course, the main reason why "Désenchantée" became such a monster hit: it is, of course, quite simply, a great tune, and its chart success will attest to the fact: entering the Top 50 at number 12, "Désenchantée" takes only three weeks to reach pole position, where it will remain for an astounding nine consecutive weeks, selling around 800,000 copies, which will earn it a gold certification. The single becomes the hit, not only of this early part of the year, but also of the summer of '91. Reluctant to leave, the song will hang around in the Top 50 for close to six months; to date, it remains Mylène's biggest hit single by quite a margin. In fact, "Désenchantée" will be a success in every possible way: on the radio, in the charts, in the clubs, where, once again, the dancefloors heave to the Boutonnat/Rogen Club remix, and on TV via the video, the song is omnipresent. But that's not all: on top of an entry in the Guiness book of world records for best-selling single by a French artist, the song will go on to enjoy extraordinary longevity and will be covered by over ten different artists in the following years. The most notable of these, Kate Ryan's 2002 version, will earn "Désenchantée" seventh place in the top 10 of most played Francophone songs in the world in that same year. Yet another cover, by Liloo, remixed by the in-trend Mad'House, will once again turn the track into a club hit, more than ten years after its original release.

Surprisingly given its considerable success, there will only be four TV prestations of "Désenchantée": but of course,

Mylène is by now a pop phenomenon whose appearances are already becoming scarcer by the minute, and the new single is a huge hit without the singer having to drag herself from one TV set to another anyway. Even amongst those four appearances, only three take place on French networks: the fourth being on an Italian TV show. There will be some efforts to promote "Désenchantée" abroad, but it seems the language barrier was too much for the world: apart from other Francophone countries such as Belgium and Switzerland, the song will not manage to repeat its success on an international scale.

"Désenchantée" has, of course, become absolutely unavoidable on the stage. Who could imagine a Mylène concert without what is now considered to be the "ultimate Farmer hymn"? It is not impossible to conceive of crowd riots, should the song ever be omitted from the setlist! Unfailingly presented in a crowd-pleasing, long version with plenty of opportunities for acapella joining-in, and always with a new arrangement (although the beloved choreography, known by heart by countless fans, remains the same), "Désenchantée" is always a highlight of any Mylène Farmer concert: in '96, '99 and 2006, the song never fails to send the crowd wild. During the "Avant que l'ombre…a Bercy" concerts, Mylène, standing on a suspended bridge over the adoring audience below, peeks over the railing as her fans sing her own words back to her, in what is a spine-tingling moment of pure show(wo)manship. Obviously present for the 2009 Tour, the song finds itself left as closer for the Stade de France concerts: 80,000 voices sing in unison as Mylène gradually eclipses herself, handing over to her audience as she prepares to leave the stage in what is a deeply moving, unforgettable and euphoric finale. It is no exaggeration to say that "Désenchantée" has become, more than a song, a veritable anthem: as Mylène herself tells us, "this song is yours", and it is only fitting that we should sing it for her, to her.

No-one knows it yet, but "Désenchantée" will turn out to be the last of the "epic" videos to be directed by Laurent Boutonnat. (So far, at least!) Work on the shoot begins as early as January '91, when scouting for suitable filming locations takes place around Budapest. Concurrently, locations are determined for the "Regrets" video: shooting is scheduled to start as soon as work on "Désenchantée" is complete, and Jean-Louis Murat, Mylène's first-ever duet partner, will be joining the team later on in February, on the 23rd. A casting also takes place as the video requires around a hundred extras, mainly children. They will be recruited from the École Française de Budapest, Laurent having specifically requested that all extras should be able to understand French. At the time, Mylène says a few words on the team's choice of location, explaining that, in addition to a desire for new scenery, Laurent was also intent on finding actors whose faces conveyed a sense of gravity, of hardship, and Eastern Europe, "unfortunately for them" as she goes on to say, seemed like the best place in which to find actors with the most fitting physiognomy. With these preparatory tasks out of the way, shooting on the clip can begin. On the 16th of February, Mylène arrives in Hungary, accompanied by Thierry Suc, Thierry Rogen and Marianne Rosenstiehl, come along to act as official set photographer. Filming starts shortly afterwards, on the 18th, ending on the 23rd and taking in two locations: an old abandoned factory a few miles out of Budapest, and the Puszta Plain for the video's final scenes. (The factory now no longer stands, having been pulled down a few years later.) It's almost a brand new team this time, as most of the technicians have been recruited locally and are, for the most part, Hungarian.

The video, not date-specific but apparently placed somewhere in the earlier part of the 20th century, sees an androgynous-looking Mylène being forcibly made to become part of an ill-treated workforce that consists mostly of young men and children, in what can only be described as the workplace from hell: beatings, confused old men tied to posts and slap-happy wardens are all part of the job description. The fare available in the staff canteen is also less than stellar, with the most reliable source of protein coming from the odd cockroach drowned in the disgusting-looking thin gruel offered as sustenance. Luckily, smoking in the dormitory is allowed, and Mylène finds some comfort bonding with one of the younger inmates, who finds his own fun by hacking great gobs of spit onto his unsuspecting sleeping comrades. Soon, however, their inhumane treatment at the hands of their heartless jailers gets too much for Mylène. Gamely forgetting about the less than warm welcome she originally received from them, she goes on to incite her fellow prisoners to rebel, starting her own revolution after one slap too many. Chaos ensues as the prisoners violently revolt against their captors: the sadistic warden gets what was coming to her, the place is trashed, the tied-up old man liberated. After a final assault on the security guards patrolling the outside, Mylène and her friends can at last escape to freedom...but their hopes are quickly and cruelly extinguished: what greets them as they make their way outside is nothing but empty, desolate plains as far as the eye can see. Freedom gained, but for what? Stopped in their tracks, the escaped prisoners are momentarily helpless, hesitant as to what to do next. But Mylène quickly regains her determination: eyes straight ahead, she takes the first few steps into the unknown, the others soon following her lead, even if the path ahead is unclear: better an uncertain freedom than guaranteed oppression. There will be two versions of "Désenchantée" to be screened on French TV music shows: the shortened version, ending right after the prisoners have overpowered their captors, is somewhat different in feel, as it ends on a euphoric note, free of the doubt and uncertainty inherent to the final scenes contained in the full-length, 10 minutes 12 seconds version. Some scenes featuring skeletons were also allegedly filmed, but eventually left out of the final edit.

For the first time in Mylène's career, a TV crew is allowed on the set of one of her videos: an interview is granted, and a small documentary about the video shoot is filmed. This will form the basis of a show broadcast on the music channel M6 on 7th April, just a few days after the video premiere on Antenne 2 on the 3rd. On the show, Mylène is seen answering host Laurent Boyer's questions on her career and the shoot, sporting her newly short hair, perfect for giving her the androgynous, almost Dickens-like look necessary for the video. A new hairdo is not the only change to occur lately in Mylène's universe: recently, a new name has got on board, a certain Henry Neu, a talented graphic artist and designer who will now be taking charge of the visual aspect of Mylène's musical output and merchandising, from promo items to album covers to T-shirts, through the Com' N.B design company. He is not the only new name on the team: Mylène now also has a new manager, Thierry Suc, a concert promoter who had already been involved with the production of the '89 Tour. Thierry Suc assumes the role of manager from the tail-end of 1989 onwards, after working relations with her former manager Bertrand Le Page had reached the point of no return. Dealing with health and substance abuse issues, Le Page's already volatile character reached boiling point one night in December '89, culminating in events that would forever sever his professional ties with the singer: at a dinner given in her honour at the École des beaux-arts in Paris, with 500 guests in attendance, and where she is due to receive a diamond-disc award for a million sales of the "Ainsi soit je..." album, Bertrand loses his cool and makes a huge scene after judging the night to have gone off without the magic and sparkle he deems worthy of his artist: he is particularly offended by the fact that Mylène was handed her award in a discreet, almost unnoticed manner, at the same time as the guests were being served their food. While he initially keeps his anger in check, Bertrand turns to alcohol for solace, and around 1am, as the function is winding down, his anger finally explodes: loudly deploring the proceeding's lack of glitz and glamour, he grabs a chair and sends it flying into the ones already piled up. The pile collapses to the floor with an almighty noise and Mylène quickly has words. Years later, Le Page will readily admit that his behaviour at the time was out of control, partly because of a heavy cocaine habit.

In view of its incredible success, it will come as no surprise that "Désenchantée" turned out to be the one Mylène Farmer single to benefit from the most supports. At least 22 if including all variations, although only the most interesting of those, and promos, are listed here. Within France, as usual, a 45 Tours, Maxi 45 Tours and CD single are made available. Also, for the first time, a "2-track" cassette single is put on the market, a format that will survive for two or three years before being progressively phased out. In a much plainer packaging than the elaborate "Tristana" release a few years previously, the item is nevertheless an interesting piece, and a nostalgic reminder of times gone by. As well as France, the single also gets a release in various European countries, in all formats bar the cassette single. For the European pressings, the "remix club" is renamed "club remix", logically enough as all other sleeve and label mentions are also now in English. Outside of Europe, "Désenchantée" also gets a release in Japan, as another "pop-up" 3" CD single, which will also be available as a promo. Curiously, there also exists an Australian format, and only one: a 3-track cassette single that is the only known official Australian Mylène Farmer release. It is probable that this was an aborted project, that never actually made it into Australian record stores: nevertheless, a few very rare copies do exist, now fetching relatively high prices, naturally. In Canada, the single also gets a release, albeit a limited one: there only appears to be a 12", in a plain black sleeve with English mentions, including the song title which has been changed to "Disenchanted". (The song itself remains sung in French, however.) On the promo side, "Désenchantée" is equally well served: no less than 2 promo 12"s for France, almost identical save for the fact that one version is one-sided only. Canada also does well on the promo front, as five different versions are released (four more than the actual commercial release itself): to start with, two 12"s: the first, in a white sleeve and intended for French Canada, goes by the name of "Désenchantée", while the second, in a black sleeve and meant for English-speaking parts of the country, has again been renamed "Disenchanted", although once again the actual song remains the same. French Canada also gets a promo CD and cassette single: this last item is a beauty, with its black packaging with white crow silhouette. Finally, a promo CD is also produced for English-speaking Canada. In the UK, a promo 7" in a plain black paper sleeve is sent out to the media, sometimes accompanied by a short paper bio. In Italy, a different promo 7" is produced, featuring a track by Zucchero and Paul Young on the B-side. A couple of amusing typos on this one, as the song is credited as "Desanchantee" and the artist as "Mylene & Farmer". One final item to be added to this long list, and a real rarity too: a European early pressing of the CD single, featuring totally different artwork, and a picture of Mylène with her hair still long, eventually abandoned in favour of the short-haired, more visually coherent French release artwork. Having most probably never reached the shops, and only ever produced in very small quantities, this has become an extremely hard to find piece.

At this point I must make a confession, a shameful one for a so-called Mylène Farmer fan. Although "Désenchantée" was released in March of 1991, I myself wasn't even aware of its existence until the summer. Not only that, but my knowledge of Mylène's career was non-existent after the release of "Sans Logique", way back in February 1989. Though I was aware of the '89 Tour, I had no idea that a brand new song and two further live singles had come from it: I won't even know about "A quoi je sers..." until the "Dance Remixes" album is released towards the end of '92. How come? In early '89, at some stage after the "Sans Logique" single release, I leave home and France, my country of birth, and settle in the UK, in London. Preoccupied with putting down some bases, I somehow "forget" about Mylène. There is no internet in those days, and keeping in touch with a foreign music scene is complicated, especially when there is a great UK music scene right on your doorstep to distract your mind. But in the summer of '91, I invite an old schoolfriend on a two-day trip to London to swing by my place, and the first thing she does after walking in is whip out a CD single and say "listen to this!" Thus I get my first listen to "Désenchantée": in no time at all, me and Mylène have renewed our acquaintance, and before I know it I am spending all the money that can be spared on all things Mylène-related: within just over a year, I will have succumbed to Farmeritis, and become a hard-core collector. So, Catherine P., wherever you are now, for re-establishing the link, thank you!

Back in Hungary, Mylène and Laurent aren't yet finished with the hard work: with "Désenchantée" in the can, they now turn their attentions to the follow-up.

15/ Regrets

1989: Mylène is a guest on the French radio show "Secrets de stars" on France Inter. Questioned about her taste in music, the singer namechecks a young artist, Jean-Louis Murat, still not very well known at the time. Not only does she like his music, she also goes on to say that she wishes she could tell him that she does. But for the reserved person she is, such things do not come easy, unfortunately. Still, the singer vows to let him know, someday, perhaps under different circumstances.

July 1991: Mylène releases the first-ever duet of her career, the haunting ballad "Regrets": her vocal partner for the occasion is none other than the very same Jean-Louis Murat, by now a successful singer/songwriter. Clearly, Mylène has managed to make good on her earlier vow of somehow establishing a line of contact. Since that '89 radio interview, she has gotten to know Jean-Louis' "Cheyenne Autumn" album: after falling in love with it, she makes up her mind to suggest to him the possibility of an artistic collaboration. Of course, Mylène being Mylène, her approach will be markedly different to what one might expect of an artist on the lookout for a musical pairing: there will be no impersonal messages relayed through agents, and her people won't be calling his people. No phone call from her either, at least not initially: too forward, too direct, and as Mylène says herself, she is "not good with long speeches". Instead, the singer opts for a decidedly old-fashioned method, one that is resolutely unusual for someone in her line of business, and yet fits her like a glove: she writes Jean-Louis Murat a letter. Clearly, this was a wise decision: the two artists thus begin a year-long correspondence, an exchange of words that will culminate in friendship as well as song. Jean-Louis Murat will later evoke his surprise and delight at coming home one day to find a letter from Mylène Farmer in his mailbox, speaking of the star's beautiful handwriting, free of any spelling mistakes. Indeed, who wouldn't dream of getting such a letter in their own mailbox, one unsuspecting day?

That these two particular artists should have come together on record is, in the end, not so surprising: just like Mylène, Jean-Louis Murat has been able, through his words and music, to create his own particular universe, one whose sensibilities and colours are not without echoes of those of a certain Ms. Farmer, though within his own specific style. But beyond mere musical affinities, both singers also experience a strange, troubling bond with the other: while recording "Regrets", Mylène tells of how she came to wonder whether Jean-Louis was, in some strange way, her double, her male equivalent, going as far as telling of her feelings that she and he were of the same blood. Jean-Louis, for his part, will also linger on this impression that he and Mylène were somehow twins, talking of a brother and sister relationship. Clearly, "Regrets" was always meant to be...

Being the follow-up to a monster hit such as "Désenchantée" was never going to be an easy proposition, but "Regrets" will rise to the challenge in a more than honorable manner. Released on 29th July, the single goes in at number 20 in its first week, quickly climbing up to its peak number 3 position. Altogether, the song will remain in the Top 50 for 16 weeks, eleven of those inside the top 10, garnering sales of 250,000: yet another sizeable hit. TV promotion for the single is even more restricted than in the case of "Désenchantée": alongside Jean-Louis, Mylène performs the song on "Stars 90", on 7th October. This will be the one and only TV prestation to be accorded for "Regrets". Later on, the single will almost get another outing: it was at one time supposed to be the second live single to be taken from the Mylènium Tour album, and would have been issued following the release of "Dessine-moi un mouton", probably in the early part of 2001. (The Mylènium Tour is, to date, the only instance "Regrets" has been performed in concert.) But alleged disagreements between Mylène, who wanted to release her live version of "Pas le temps de vivre", and her record company, who were pushing for "Regrets", put a spanner in the works, ending in no second single release at all for the live album. All that remains of the abandoned project is a promo VHS of Mylène's solo rendition of the song during the Mylènium concerts: a tantalizing glimpse of what almost came to pass.

Also shot in Budapest in February '91, work on the "Regrets" video kicks off as soon as the "Désenchantée" shoot is over, Jean-Louis Murat having joined the team towards the later part of the month. Filmed on location at the old Budapest Jewish cemetary, in around 48 hours, the clip, entirely in black and white, is easily one of

Laurent Boutonnat's most moving. A slow-moving train gradually emerges through the fog as the two singers' voices ring out, ethereal and ghost-like, no words clearly discernible as the recording is being played backwards. As the train comes to a halt, Jean-Louis Murat steps off, a bouquet of flowers clutched in his hand, and slowly heads for the cemetary gates. Once inside, he quickly runs across a frightened deer that swiftly flees into the surrounding snow and white before another presence makes itself felt. Out of nowhere, Mylène's ghostly figure suddenly appears: the deceased beloved's spirit summoned by the man's sad presence and everlasting love. For a few precious moments, the lovers reminisce and share precious laughter as they wander through the cemetary's cold paths, whispering silent words in each other's ears as the snow falls around them. Quiet and contemplative, the man rests his head in the woman's lap, words now superfluous. But already, all too soon, an unspoken sadness falls on the couple as their time runs shorter and shorter: until, with a final ambiguous look, the female figure turns away, running off once more into the nothingness, back to the other side. Her lover, alone once more, exits the cemetary and once again boards the train, which slowly departs: six minutes seventeen seconds of pure melancholia and unadulterated sadness. Speaking about the shoot some time later on, Jean-Louis Murat will relate how struck he was by the intensity of the Farmer/Boutonnat working relationship and the levels of rigorous reciprocal expectations between the duo, going as far as talking of "submission" on the part of one towards the other in the cause of their art. An observation consistent with what is known of the symbiotic relationship between singer and composer, forever feeding and bouncing off each other, with compelling results. The video will get its first TV showing on Michel Drucker's "Stars 90" show on 9th September: Mylène is on the set, evoking amongst other things her trip to the Arctic with film director Luc Besson. She will be seen on the same show barely a month later, when her and Jean-Louis Murat's ampexed performance of "Regrets" is eventually broadcast.

Unlike some of the previous singles, "Regrets" will be released strictly within France only. A 45 Tours and Maxi 45 Tours are joined by another cassette single and two different CD single editions: both are similar in their artwork and tracklisting, but the "édition limitée" also comes with a "pin's", a small metal brooch in the shape of a small bunch of roses, as featured on the sleeve artwork. Aside from the Extended club remix, Laurent Boutonnat and Thierry Rogen come up with an interesting version of the song, the "Sterger dub mix", which, as its name hints at, is entirely constructed around the singers' voices being played backwards, to beautiful, haunting effect. The track is by far the fastest, danciest version of "Regrets" to be made officially available, with a background of acid-style synths providing a steady, energizing beat that is hard not to want to move to. Only one promo format will be produced for the single, but it is a beautiful one: a 12" with cut-out sleeve and the word "Regrets" printed in large font beneath the artists' names, with gorgeous "roses" picture labels for the vinyl.

By the time "Regrets" is released in July 1991, I have managed to get hold of a CD copy of "L'Autre..." in one of the larger London record stores (significantly marked up, as an import), and I waste no time in trying to convert unsuspecting listeners, something of a commonly-displayed behavioural trait amongst Mylène Farmer fans. At the time, I work in the backroom of a huge Oxford Street bookshop, unpacking crates of books and checking invoices all day. Luckily, a CD player is provided and I play "L'Autre..." for hours on end, always getting a thrill when English colleagues come up and ask "who is this? I really like it!" Because there is no internet in 1991, and thus no international websites to the glory of the singer, I am yet unaware that Mylène will, in time, gain fans from all over the world, regardless of whether or not they speak or understand French. But something is already very clear: given a chance and some exposure to her music, language is no barrier to people falling under her spell, and her magic goes beyond words: her voice, her sound alone are enough to intrigue and hold the attention.

With her first-ever duet out of the way, it is now time for Mylène to move on to bigger and better things: another big hit is just around the corner.

16/ Je T'Aime Mélancolie

The release of "Je t'aime mélancolie", on 19th November 1991, by which time the "L'Autre..." album is already a huge success, with close to a million sales to its name, brings another first in Mylène's career: for the first time, the singer turns away from the usual darkness and melancholia (in spite of the song's title!) to deliver a lyric rich in irony and second-degree humour. Aimed squarely at the media, in particular the press that is always looking to bring her down, "Je t'aime mélancolie" takes a gentle sarcastic swipe at the singer's many detractors: Mylène doesn't hesitate to make use of metaphors, comparing herself to "la mauvaise herbe", weeds, annoying because they keep on coming back no matter how many times you try to eradicate them: indeed, try as they might to ignore and pour scorn upon her, the singer's wild popular success is a right thorn in the media's side, a success made even more irritating by her persistent refusal to play by anything but her own rules! As she goes on to say, the only way to please the jealous is to be ignored...Unfortunately for those who don't like her, being ignored is a fate which is unlikely to befall Mylène anytime soon, and her latest single is yet another reminder of the fact: entering the charts at number 15, the song will climb up to third place, hanging around the top 5 for four consecutive weeks and selling close to 300,000 copies. Once again, Mylène has the last word, whether the media like it or not: even better, she makes her point without ever actually engaging in any kind of argument or sterile rhetoric, letting her music do the talking instead.

For this third single, the team have decided to go for an uptempo, energetic sound: indeed, the version sent out to radio, remixed by Laurent Boutonnat and Thierry Rogen, is markedly different from that of the original album mix: punchier, more concise, straight to the point. Though previous singles have been edited for radio before, the changes then were more subtle: here, the song can be said to benefit from a proper brand new mix. In addition to a new single mix, "Je t'aime mélancolie" will also be reworked for the clubs via two remixes, the Extended Club remix and Insane Dance remix, with yet another club mix being proposed twelve years later in 2003, when the track is included on the "Remixes" compilation: with Laurent Boutonnat having long given up on remix duties, it is then Felix Da Housecat who reworks the track, transforming it into a stark, fast-paced number that will reach number 24 in the club charts. Back in 1991, another version of the song, the "Smooth mix", is also available on some of the supports: despite its intriguing name, however, it is almost identical to the album version, being only slightly edited. More exciting for the fans is the brand new track

"Mylène is calling", two minutes of telephonic weirdness allegedly built around a message left by Mylène on Laurent's answerphone. The track will be "performed" live during the Mylènium Tour, although the "Mylène" present on stage at the time will turn out to be a fake, the real thing having taken the opportunity to go change into something more (or, arguably, less)comfortable for the next track on the setlist, "Optimistique-Moi".

Mylène will promote her new single with a total of four TV appearances: on "Sacrée soirée" on 11th December, on "Tous à la Une" on the 27th, and on "Stars 90" on 13th January: during this last prestation, Mylène is actually sick and has a fever, but she puts on a brave face and performs the song regardless. It has been said that one of the backing dancers during this promotion period was actually one of Mylène's cousins. The fourth and final TV showing for "Je t'aime mélancolie" takes place not in France but on the set of a German TV show, "Ein kessel buntes", on the MDR channel. Indeed, the single is amongst those, alongside "Désenchantée", who will benefit from the widest foreign distribution: sadly, it will fail to make much of an impact anywhere, including Germany, in spite of Mylène's promotional efforts. On the stage, "Je t'aime mélancolie" will get its first live outing in 1996, during the Live a Bercy concerts, with a choreography almost similar to that of the above four TV prestations. The song will be present again for the Mylènium Tour, although only during the Russian dates: the performance then will be almost identical to the one given in '96. It will be performed once more during the "Avant que l'ombre...a Bercy" concerts, with next to no choreography this time around, and Mylène singing half-hidden from behind huge white drapes. There will be no memorable covers of "Je t'aime mélancolie", apart from a half-hearted attempt by Biba Binoche, a former reality TV show contestant: this particular version will slip under the radar and promptly be forgotten about.

In order to shoot the video, Mylène and Laurent return to the scene of previous gems like "Plus Grandir" and "Ainsi soit je...", the Sets studios in Stains. With a budget of around 45,000 Euros, and shot over a total of four days in November '91 (two days for the fight scenes, two for the scenes with the dancers), the clip's scenario mirrors the song's message quite closely: Mylène takes a few knocks from her opponent (symbolising the media), but always gets up again, and moreover, becomes even stronger as the fight goes on, even after the other side throws the rulebook out of the window by knocking out the referee (possibly symbolising the public). The gloves literally come off, and the match gets personal: forget about sport, this is now a matter of honour. With her opponent now seriously angry, Mylène raises her game and eventually knocks him clear out of the ring: once again, she has won...not that she is the type to wallow in victory, however: the last shot, of the singer dropping to her knees as if exhausted, seems to send out a message in the same way the final "Désenchantée" scenes did: why rejoice, when, ultimately, all is in vain...For the first time in a Mylène video, a full choreography is proposed, the singer's own. She is for the occasion dressed by Jean-Paul Gaultier, creator of Madonna's iconic conical bra. The designer will go on to create the costumes for the 2009 shows including the two Stade de France concerts: there will be a minor sartorial difference between the indoor and stadium concerts, as the blue dress worn during the ballads section will morph into a white version for the 11th and 12th September shows. As for the "Je t'aime mélancolie" fight scenes, Mylène, the ultimate professional as ever, didn't do things by halves: in order to make the scenes believable, she undertook six days of gruelling preparatory training with a professional boxing coach. Just as well really, as her opponent was also genuinely from the world of boxing, a fighter on the Yugoslavian circuit. Her fitness levels no doubt helped her cope with the shoot's punishing schedule as well: the working day begins at 7.30, to finish more than twelve hours later at 8.30pm. But as ever, the hard work soon pays off, and the clip gets its first TV showing on 15th December, garnering rave reviews and a hugely enthusiastic response from fans.

As mentioned earlier, "Je t'aime mélancolie" will be released abroad quite extensively, including in Austria, Germany, Italy, the Netherlands and Scandinavia: the song will, alas, fail to do much business in any of those territories. Nevertheless, this does act as a windfall for collectors, as several formats are made available. In France, a 7", 12", cassette single (featuring the Smooth mix) and CD single are released: a little bonus for French fans there, as the Maxi CD features a brand new track, the somewhat strange yet wonderful "Mylène is calling", that will be absent from the European pressings. The French Maxi CD also features the "radio remix 2" single version: the difference with the original radio remix is rather difficult to tell, however. While Europe may not get a brand new track, they at least get something original: in addition to the 45 Tours and Maxi CD, a 12" is also issued, in a slightly different sleeve for some countries: whereas the French, Dutch and Scandinavian issues have a cut-out sleeve with picture labels, the German, Austrian and Italian copies come in a regular, non-cut sleeve. The promos bring with them an interesting first: the very first of the "Édition Luxe" promos sees the light of day. The very much sought-after item consists of a two-track CD inside a gatefold sleeve, in the style of a gatefold vinyl LP but in CD dimensions. The CD rests inside a white cardboard base, the four sides of which bear the inscription "Mylène Farmer - Je t'aime mélancolie" (17cm to a side). On top of all this rests a cardboard pyramid, 16cm high, with the single sleeve picture printed on each side. Clearly, a collector's dream...Another, more basic promo is also produced, consisting of the gatefold-sleeve CD on its own. And while Canada may not have been graced with any commercial releases, they get one promo item nevertheless, a 3-track digipack CD in a black sleeve with no artwork but a large titles sticker: very scarce, and very expensive.

While "Je t'aime mélancolie" was a huge success, it was, sadly, set to the background of a terrible tragedy. On 13th November -a mere 6 days before the single's release- a mentally unstable fan, angry at the star's failure to respond to his numerous letters, decides to drive all the way to Paris from his hometown of Nancy, in eastern France. He has decided to take revenge on the star's record company, having convinced himself that they must have failed to pass on his letters, since he never got a reply from the singer. He has come armed with a gun and several rounds of ammunition. Upon reaching the Polydor offices, he demands to see Mylène immediately: when told that she isn't actually in the building, he opens fire on the receptionist, a young man in his twenties who will die of his injuries within the next few hours. The deranged man then rushes upstairs, looking for more victims, and it is only the miraculous jamming of his weapon that will prevent further bloodshed. Mylène will, of course, be terribly affected by the incident, and although it will be suggested to her that she be protected around the clock from then on, she will refuse, as a mark of respect for the young deceased receptionist and his grieving family, stating simply that at such times one shouldn't dwell on what could have happened to you, but think instead of the dead and their loved ones.

Although the next single was widely predicted to be "Pas de doute", a fast-paced, upbeat song about an over-impulsive man, the tragedy means the team will rethink their plans. Instead, the role of fourth and final single will fall to a far more somber track.

17/ Beyond My Control

By the time "Beyond my control" is released as the fourth and final single from "L'Autre...", the album has earned a diamond certification for over a million copies sold, a triumphant success. As for Mylène herself, she is on the cusp of making the transition from mere pop superstar to something far rarer, far more elusive: it is around this time that she gains the status of living legend, her myth grown strong on her ever-increasing absences and the aura of secret and mystery that surrounds everything to do with her. And now, with the presumed next single "Pas de doute" out of the picture (taking with it persistent rumours of a "Libertine III" video), her newest release is going to feed the myth even further, thanks to the whiff of scandal.

"Beyond my control", possibly one of the darkest songs from what is, on the whole, a fairly dark album, is a lyrical evocation of the singer's complicated relationship with the masculine half of the human race. Mylène speaks freely on the subject at the time, admitting to her difficulties in dealing with men as romantic objects: back then, her idealistic, impossibly high expectations are at odds with the possibility of any durable real-life harmony with another. A true romantic in the purest sense of the word, she is bound to be disappointed by the daily reality of a life that can never hope to match up to her ideals. A self-confessed hater of all that is tepid and half-hearted, she goes as far as summing up the problem in a way that is almost hopeless in its finality: we only love passion, and we so want it to last, but it never does. Where to go from here? "Beyond my control" explores the theme without hesitation, allowing the singer to take her fantasy to the limit by coming up with a rather extreme solution. In the face of a man who, through his weaknesses and indiscretions, has inevitably let her down, the song's protagonist hits upon a surefire way, perhaps the only way, of keeping their love safe from the constant perils of a cruel reality: death. Or at least, *his*. Unable to explain her actions fully, unaware even of how her hands came to be covered in his blood, she nevertheless makes him a promise: he can rest in peace now, for she will be keeping watch over his grave: their love is safe. A bleak, chilling expression of the existential doubt that is and will remain one of the major constants in the singer's musical and lyrical output.

Released on 13th April 1992, the song is built around a John Malkovitch sample, taken from Stephen Frears' film "Dangerous Liaisons", itself based on the classic book by Choderlos de Laclos. The single enters the charts at number 10 and reaches its peak position of number 8 the following week, before dropping down a few places over the next two, only to climb back up to number 8 the next: quite possibly as a result of the extra interest the song will attract as the "scandalous" video is first broadcast. Shot once again in the Sets studios in Stains, over two days and with a minimal team, the "Beyond my control" clip is a relatively technically simple affair, with no proper scenario as such, only a succession of images that serve to illustrate the song. Laurent's focus, at the time, is of course already heavily turned towards his long-gestating film project "Giorgino", and now is definitely not the time for an elaborate, extravagant music video. Which is not to say that the clip is a half-baked affair, quite the opposite: what it may lack in duration and special effects is certainly more than made up for by the images' extremely strong content. Right from the opening scenes, an oppressive, disquieting mood is set thanks to close-up shots of wolves, their menacing low growls heavy in the foreground: clearly, what follows is not going to be all kittens and roses. Mylène is seen being cheated on by her lover (a rather familiar face, as the role is played by Frédéric Lagache, the puppeteer from "Sans Contrefaçon") with a sulfurous blonde, in steamy scenes that flirt with pornography. (The blonde actress, allegedly, is Laurent Boutonnat's niece. In the more "daring" shots, it is Christophe Danchaud, the star's dancer, co-choreographer and personal friend, who will stand in for Lagache.) After Mylène stumbles on her lover's treason, he is swiftly punished with a kiss that quickly degenerates into a vampiric assault, the lovers' faces soon becoming smeared in blood as shots of wolves tearing into a bloody carcass flash up on the screen. Mylène got her revenge, but of course there is a price to pay, and soon she is left to burn at the stake, to pay for her actions, and his, as further shots of torrid love-making pop up. But the man's demise will be her salvation: after he lets out a final, agonizing cry, the flames at her feet have been extinguished, and she is left to ponder the meaning of her blood-covered hands, before a final shot of a wolf glaring disturbingly into the camera comes and puts an end to the proceedings. Not too surprisingly, the video immediately attracts much attention, and some fairly heavy censorship. In all fairness, it was only to be expected: strong sexual content heavily linked to death, plentiful gore, wild animals in the midst of a feeding frenzy...naturally, some sections of French society go into moral convulsions: M6, one of the major music channels of the time, refuses to play the video before midnight: only Canal+ and MCM will be brave enough to do so. And Michel Drucker, who gave Mylène her very first prime-time break on his "Champs-Élysées" show back in 1984, flatly says no to the idea of an avant-première on his current TF1 broadcast "Stars 90" after viewing the images. The word "scandalous" is worked to death in countless press articles, although of course, in the end, it's all good for Mylène: people may be scandalized, but they certainly want to talk about it -and her. "Beyond my control" will be Laurent's last clip for Mylène for quite some time: he will not be putting images to any of the singer's songs until 2001, when he will once again take his place behind the camera to direct the "Les mots" clip.

Unimpeded by the controversy -Mylène's first real brush with censorship since "Plus Grandir", and certainly not the last- the single will go on to sell around 200,000 copies, yet another sizeable hit with which to bring the album's promotion period to an end. And this time, Mylène achieves those sales figures without any TV promotion whatsoever! "Beyond my control" won't be getting much more representation on the stage either: so far, it has only ever been performed during the Mylènium Tour, in a simple prestation with no choreography: one was originally planned but the concept never made it past rehearsals.

Henry Neu's sleeve design for "Beyond my control" is amongst his most striking: a Marianne Rosenstiehl shot of Mylène holding a stilletto's sharp heel against her temple, set against a vivid red background, brings to mind an image of the singer holding a gun to her own head. Within France, commercial releases consist of a 7", 12", cassette single and Maxi CD, and also, for the first time in Mylène's career, a new format, a "CD 2 Titres": this format, as well as the cassette single, contain the otherwise unavailable "ya ya version", essentially an instrumental with added ya-ya's from Mylène, not too dissimilar from those of the "A quoi je sers..." orchestral version. The usual European countries also get a release of the 7", 12" and Maxi CD, although once again success abroad is limited. Promotional items are few, but mostly hugely desirable: Canada gets a 5-track CD, sadly without a sleeve. The other two promos, however, take pride of place in any Farmer collection. The two-track promo CD is set inside an LP-sized gatefold sleeve with stunning artwork: on the front cover, embossed titles in red on a pure white background; on the inside left cover, an embossed blood-red crow silhouette sits across from the CD: an absolutely stunning item. The third and last promo is one of the rarest, and possibly one of the most counterfeited of Mylène's career. In May '92, NRJ radio runs a competition that gives listeners the opportunity to win one of only 50 copies of a "Beyond my control" promo 12" picture disc. (Only the second picture disc in the singer's discography at the time.) The ultra-rare item can sell for in excess of a thousand Euros, but close inspection is recommended before parting with your cash: while some of the numerous fakes on the market are easy to spot as such, some are of such high quality that telling them apart can be problematic...

The success and scandal around "Beyond my control" mark the end of the "L'Autre..." album exploitation period. With close to an eventual 2 million sales, the album is nothing less than a huge artistic and commercial triumph for Mylène Farmer and Laurent Boutonnat: incredibly, it will squat the top of the French charts for four and a half months, an unequalled record. The album also reaches number 1 in Belgium, while Canada, Switzerland and Germany grant it a highest chart position of 9, 27 and 55 respectively. Consequently, there are myriad editions across the world, not only in the previously mentioned countries but also in Japan, Taiwan, Russia, Greece, Israel, Korea, Argentina, Thailand, Turkey...A short-lived format, the DCC (Digital Compact Cassette) will also represent the album at the time, only to quickly fade into oblivion shortly afterwards. Some beautiful and very hard to find promos are associated with the album: in Canada, a 5-track CD in gatefold sleeve features an edited version of the "Désenchantée" club remix: this version, seemingly, was never to be made available anywhere else. In Canada still, a 4-track cassette in cardboard sleeve, cassette single style, is sent out to the media. An even rarer promo is the Japanese box-set: inside the black 24 x 24 cm box, a promo CD album and 5-track VHS are joined by a twelve-page booklet featuring fifteen photographs. Finally, one more box-set, totally glorious, has become a collector must-have: issued both as a promo and as a commercial release limited to 5,000 copies, the numbered "L'Autre..." 34 x 25cm box includes the following: the CD album, the "Désenchantée" Maxi CD, a numbered "crow" wristwatch, three photographs from the "Désenchantée" clip, and, finally, an actual film cell from the "Désenchantée" film reel...the very same box-set I once had to swallow my pride for, in order to purchase it from an insulting vendor: clearly, the contents made it all worthwhile. There are also tantalizing rumours to the effect that "L'Autre..." also exists in an English version, at least partially, and that the ultra-rare and never released recordings circulate among some "top tier" collectors: sadly, they have never seen fit to share them with the world...

It will be four and a half years between the "L'Autre..." original release date and Mylène's next studio album: something the fans will have to get used to...In any case, Mylène and Laurent have a good excuse, as a considerable portion of that time will be taken up with the laborious and not at all easy-going filming of the trial that was "Giorgino". With the team musically out of action for a while, now is the perfect time for Mylène's first-ever compilation...

18/ Que Mon Coeur Lâche -
19/ My Soul Is Slashed

In spite of its huge success (to this day, it remains Mylène's best-selling album by a comfortable margin), the opus "L'Autre..." will never get its own series of concerts. Of course, this should not really come as a surprise: in her spoken interviews, and in the press, Mylène has made no secret of the fact that she and Laurent will soon be turning their attentions to the world of cinema, in order to fulfill Laurent's life-long ambition to bring his "Giorgino" project to life. Still, this end of year '92 will not be without some activity on the Mylène Farmer front. In November, the "Dance Remixes" album is released, the singer's first-ever compilation. Not a best-of as such, the album instead brings together the extended club versions of the singer's biggest hits, with a couple of brand new remixes and an entirely new track thrown in for good measure: in addition to new versions of "Libertine" and "We'll never die", fans can also discover the new single "Que mon coeur lâche", released on 16th November, just a week before the album itself. Putting out a "remix" album is at the time a fairly new concept in France, certainly as far as French artists are concerned, and by doing so the singer is the first in her field to follow a template previously adopted only by international stars, for whom the remix album concept has nothing strange

MYLENE FARMER — THE SINGLE FILE

about it. Of course, Mylène can afford to do this *precisely* because her success has played out on a level that is in a different league to that of most of her French contemporaries: in a way, the singer has transcended the French model of pop success. A remix compilation is an unashamedly innovative move on her part, and also, one that avoids a premature "best-of" release. With this many huge hits under their belt, a lesser artist might have been tempted to go down the greatest hits road already...

Unusually for a Mylène song, the lyrics to "Que mon coeur lâche" tackle a real-world, topical social issue: love in the time of AIDS. Some will wrongly read the song as an enticement by Mylène to boycott condoms: this was, of course, totally off the mark. While Mylène does, through her song, lament the changes brought upon our love-making practices by this insidious illness, this does not mean to say she is encouraging people to act recklessly. Commenting on the sudden dreary necessity of prophylactics in our love lives is not the same as saying "don't use them!" In fact, Mylène will be very clear on this point: while acknowledging that the sensible course of action in order to protect yourself from the disease seems obvious to her, she will be at pains to point out that it is not her role to be saying to people to wear or not wear condoms, and that the song is merely an observation. Incredibly, the polemic even crosses the channel: one day in early 1993, I very nearly fall off my chair when the London newspaper The Evening Standard carries a small article on the affair, although their version of the facts is totally unlike anything else to be found in French papers at the time: according to the Standard, Mylène is a "sulfurous bondage-loving pop queen", who answered the accusations by saying that "it is of a different kind of rubber that I sing"...As no French press reports of the era mention anything of the kind, and as Mylène is clearly not singing about PVC outfits, it is tempting to think that the London paper was more or less making its facts up on the spot, in the interests of mere titillation...

"Que mon coeur lâche" gets its very first airplay exclusively on Radio M40, usually a dance-centric station, on 1st November, with national airplay rolled out from the 5th onwards. After its release on the 16th, the single climbs up to 9th place in the Top 50, selling 110,000 copies, a respectable but moderate success by Mylène standards. Mylène will perform the song on TV on two occasions: first on "Stars 90" on 11th January, showing she's not holding a grudge against Michel Drucker for refusing to screen the "Beyond my control" video a few months previously, and a little while later on the 12th of May '93 at the World Music Awards, where she performs in front of, amongst others, Michael Jackson. (who is, of course, gently made fun of in the video.) While at the Awards, Mylène also receives a trophy for best-selling French singer abroad. On stage, "Que mon coeur lâche" is performed during the '96 Tour, a chance for Mylène to show off her pole-dancing skills while her scantily-clad dancers writhe suggestively by her side, encased in clear plastic bubbles. The song is also included in the Mylènium Tour setlist, although only exclusively for the Russian dates: on 5th March 2000, in Moscow, Mylène loses her balance and almost falls over at the very end of the song, when she and her dancers adopt a frozen pose on the last note...

For the first time in one of her videos, Mylène is filmed by someone other than Laurent Boutonnat: the new LB behind the camera is Luc Besson, the "Big Blue" director who will later go on to direct the classic "The Fifth Element", starring Bruce Willis and Milla Jojovich. His work is much appreciated by the singer. Far from going behind Laurent's back for this new adventure, it is at his suggestion and with his full endorsement that Mylène turns to Besson for her new clip: in any case, Laurent himself is unavailable, being by then already fully taken up with "Giorgino". It is an entirely new kind of video that Luc Besson will concoct for Mylène: for the first time in her career, a large place is given over to humour, to a levity not found in any of her previous works, much to the singer's delight: the lighter, humorous images enable her to show another side to her personality, one in stark contrast to the perpetually tortured heroines of clips past. Thus we are introduced to an angelic Mylène, listening to the "Extended dance remix" of the single on her walkman as a very business-like God waits for her to kindly remove her headphones. After a brisk telling-off, Mylène is sent down to earth to observe and report on the state of human love affairs, at the expense of Jesus who suggests to his Father that he should send him instead: but, as God replies, "last time was a disaster". Barely landed on earth, the still-angelic Mylène is immediately slapped across the face by an angry human male as she examines the world through the man's female companion's eyes. Compelled to step in in order to put things right, she gives as good as she gets, knocking the man clear across the room and leaving the human woman wondering at her own strength. The angel then goes on to experience other things for herself, enjoying a much-deserved cigarette break afterwards. Along the way, a Michael Jackson lookalike struts his stuff only to be brought down by a falling cross, carelessly dropped from the heavens by an inattentive Jesus: though slightly controversial, the clip was spared any moral indignation, mostly thanks to the touch of humour that runs through it. As the angel continues on her fact-finding mission, her attention is suddenly turned towards the intriguing "Q" club, seemingly so attractive to humans. And of course it is, as "Q", or rather its phonetic equivalent "Cul", signifies "ass", or, in the broader sense, sex: clearly a major human preoccupation. But the door policy is exclusive, and the angel must look into the heart of the hulking figure of a man guarding the entrance in order to gain access: knowing what needs to be done, she morphs into a not-so-angelic-anymore version of herself, a newly-seductive femme fatale all clad in black. Thus effortlessly securing entrance into the club, she is confronted by other various manifestations of love and desire in its human form: amidst a strongly sensual atmosphere, same-sex couples, transvestites and various nightlife creatures jostle for her attention. A beautiful, scantily-clad woman approaches, holding in her hand the same kind of respirator observed outside: as the woman clamps the mask to her face, the angel is overcome and greedily breathes in the mysterious love gas, until she is overcome and her heart apparently explodes in a burst of ecstasy. A sudden cut back to heaven sees a confident, sassy, sensually-awakened angel making her way over to God before blowing a huge chewing-gum bubble in his face, the cheeky look on her face suggesting she may not be quite as angelic as before...

The video is filmed entirely in the Arpajon studios, scene of the earlier "Sans Logique" and the future "Les mots", nine years later in 2001. Shot over four days on three different sets, the clip will involve the talents of not one, but two prominent fashion designers: for her white "angelic" outfit, Mylène is dressed by Azzedine Alaia, while Jean-Paul Gaultier takes care of the black, "fallen angel" ensemble. With a running time of close to seven minutes, this will be the last of the "long" Mylène videos for a while, at least until "L'Âme-Stram-Gram", almost seven years later. "Que mon coeur lâche" premieres on Match Music on the M6 channel on 12th December '92. As for Luc Besson, it isn't the last time the director will collaborate with Mylène: in 2006, they meet up again when the singer lends her voice to the Princess Sélénia character, from his computer-animation film "Arthur et les Minimoys", a movie that will meet with great success and eventually give rise to a trilogy. The same role will be played by Madonna for the English-language version.

"Que mon coeur lâche" will be released in four different formats, within France only. This is the last-ever showing for a Mylène Farmer 45 Tours single: the 7" format is largely abandoned from this period onwards. Also available are a Maxi 45 Tours, a 2-track CD single (curiously, there is no Maxi CD for this particular release), and another doomed format, the cassette single: the last in the Farmer discography. The one solitary promo item for the single is unusual in its presentation: a 1-track CD affixed to a cruciform carboard support bearing four identical kneeling Mylène silhouettes, slipped inside a 12" sleeve similar in design to the commercial Maxi 45 Tours.

While "Que mon coeur lâche" was only ever released as a single in France, Mylène will offer an English version of the song in May '93: released in the usual European territories, "My soul is slashed" is Mylène's second English-language single to get an official release. Initially, the singer hands translation duties over to Ira Israel, but after hating the first draft, she joins in and the English lyrics are worked on by both of them, line by line, word by word. Ira Israel will talk of a great exigence on the part of the singer, of a meticulous attention to detail and to the sonorities of each and every word: a demanding experience that the translator will nevertheless remember as being "great fun". There will be no TV prestations of "My soul is slashed", and the video will remain the same bar the French subtitles. The single will appear on the 1-disc, European edition of "Dance Remixes", with the brand new "Rubber remix" for the occasion. The only formats to be released commercially will consist of a 2-track CD as well as a Maxi CD single. There was also a promo 12": strangely though, this was only sent out to French DJ's. The single will sadly fail to meet with much success abroad, most of the sales coming from French fans! The single version will make a reappearance in 2001, when it is included as one of three bonus track on the collectors' edition of the best-of "Les Mots".

Around the time "Dance Remixes" is released, I get another opportunity to "convert" people to Mylène: in 1992, I get a job working in a then-thriving major UK record store chain, in London's Trocadero Centre in Piccadilly Circus. As I am based in the "world music" section of the store, this is an unmissable opportunity to play both "L'Autre..." and "Dance Remixes" to an unsuspecting audience, several times a day, and the result is frequently the same: customers stop, listen, and then approach the staff counter. "Who is this you're playing?" On average, each week sees 3 to 4 copies of each album being sold in this devious way: once again, people who wouldn't usually give the time of day to anything sung in a foreign language fall under Mylène's charm purely on the strength of her voice alone. I get a thrill each time, happy to play my however-small part in the Farmerisation of the world.

"Dance Remixes" will go on to achieve sales of approximately 200,000, a respectable figure for this kind of release and enough to earn it a double gold certification. The "L'Autre..." era is now well and truly over, and the fans will now have to wait until September 1995 for anything new on the musical front from the singer: Mylène and Laurent have some trials to endure in the meantime...

Part 4: Anamorphosée / Live à Bercy

20/ XXL

Shooting on Laurent Boutonnat's long-dreamed of "Giorgino" movie finally begins in January 1993, in Slovakia. Five gruelling months will ensue, five months of tense, difficult working conditions that will pile great stress upon the whole team and test the Farmer/Boutonnat relationship to its very limits. "Giorgino", more than a film, has become a veritable obsession for Laurent, a life-long ambition that blinds him to anything else, including his relationship with Mylène, which inevitably suffers as a result. And when "Giorgino" is finally released in October '94, it's as if the nightmare has only just begun: universally panned, the film is a huge critical and commercial flop. Pulled from cinemas within weeks, the unequivocal failure is a huge blow to Laurent: years of work reduced to nothing overnight, a scathing press that leaves him absolutely no chance of appeal. A huge blow to the Farmer/Boutonnat tandem, too: accustomed to nothing but overwhelming success, the fiasco comes as a huge shock to the duo, who now have some serious soul-searching to do. Laurent deals with it by barricading himself inside his Parisian residence, and forbidding his film from ever being seen again by anyone. (At least until 2007, when the film finally gets a DVD release and, eventually, some recognition.) As for Mylène, for whom living in Paris has by now become unbearable, she looks West and flies off to the States, where she will exile herself for a whole nine months, time enough to be reborn.

Mylène's American odyssey will be a chance for her to resource herself, to explore new horizons, to open herself up to a new outlook on life. In the USA, mostly ununcumbered by her for now too-heavy celebrity, she revels in her new-found anonymity, going as far as dyeing her famous red hair platinum blonde: virtually unrecognizable, the star can -at least temporarily- enjoy a life that is as close to mundane as she has known in years. Of course, she is still a huge star elsewhere even if not here, and it would have been unrealistic to expect to be left completely alone: in early '95, pictures emerge in the French tabloid press of a blonde Mylène hanging out in Los Angeles with Jeff Dahlgren, sparking rumours of a possible rift with Laurent Boutonnat. Of course, after the film's failure, and after so many years of unrivalled success, an envious press can't wait to spell out the beginning of the end for Mylène and Laurent...

Unfortunately for them, their grave-dancing will turn out to be a tad premature: in spring 1995, exciting rumours begin to surface, reporting that Laurent Boutonnat is in L.A. with Mylène, working on a new album with a rockier sound...and for once, the rumours are correct. Indeed, Laurent has flown out to rejoin Mylène and start work on the singer's next album. Initial recording sessions take place at the A&M studios before relocating to the Record One studios on Ocean Way, with Jeff Dahlgren and Thierry Rogen on board. Thierry, however, will only last a few weeks before throwing in the towel, uncomfortable with the still somewhat tense working atmosphere among the team: he will be quickly replaced by Bertrand Châtenet. Of course, Jeff's presence is a sore reminder of recent events for Laurent: they will barely speak to one another the whole time, according to some reports. (Concerning Thierry Rogen, a rumour will emerge in later years that he was killed in the 2006 Boxing Day tsunami: he was not.) The first track to be recorded during these early sessions is "Laisse le vent emporter tout": in itself, a clear indication of Mylène's new musical direction: more live instruments, and, lyrically also, a radical shift. The dark, tortured Mylène of years past appears to have turned towards the light, to have adopted a more serene outlook on life: as the singer herself will go on to reveal later, the change is brought on, amongst other things, by her reading Sogyal Rinpoche's "Tibetan book of living and dying". The book's influence, indeed, will be felt right across the album, giving a Zen, almost mystical flavour to lyrics that evoke themes such as impermanence, a fundamental tenet of Buddhism. The album's lighter, airier feel will be commented on later by L'Express magazine, who will call it "a farewell to tears". The bulk of "Anamorphosée" is recorded towards the end of August, with François Hanss and his camera in hand in the studio as he shoots a "making-of" of the recording sessions that will end up in the bonus section of the Music Videos II&III DVD. An interesting anecdote has emerged from the "Anamorphosée" recording sessions: for some of the duration, Mylène and co. share the studio space with Bon Jovi. And rather curiously, one of the tracks recorded by the rock band at this time, "Hey God", uses the exact same guitar riff as the one heard in "XXL": the similarity is too great for it to be mere coincidence. So, who "inspired" who? The mystery was never cleared up...Around the same time, Mylène works on a photoshoot with the late, great Herb Ritts for the album cover and artwork: the resulting images show a transformed woman: radiant, sexy and more feminine than ever, Mylène is miles away from her former tortured, gothic image, almost unrecognizable. Even more so on the cover itself, where her head is lopped off entirely...

The track picked to spearhead Mylène's long-awaited comeback is "XXL". Released on 19th September '95, with an exclusive, much-publicized first showing of the video on M6 the night before, the single goes straight in at number 1 in its first week, making it a total of three chart-topping singles for Mylène so far. It is also the singer's twentieth single release! It will remain in pole position for one week only, eventually reaching sales of 120,000. A fairly modest figure for Mylène it would seem, though it must be said that by 1995, already, record sales generally aren't what they used to be: times are changing. Also a success in Belgium and Switzerland, "XXL" is remixed by Laurent Boutonnat and Bertrand Châtenet...for the most part, anyway: the song has the distinction of being the first of Mylène's singles to be remixed by someone other than Laurent, although the version in question, the "UK Remix" by Richard Dekkard, will not see the light of day until over a year later, when it is included on the "Rêver" Maxi CD single. While "XXL" reaching number 1 is obviously good news for the singer after her lengthy absence from the music scene, it also marks a point in her career when some of her fans go off her somewhat. To some of those who have been following Mylène from the start, the change is just too great: where is the dark, gothic

Mylène, and who is this smiling woman come to take her place? The song, and its accompanying video (once again directed by someone who is not Laurent Boutonnat) afford them few points of reference either. Thus Mylène loses a few fans, although many will come back over time, as the true colour of the album is revealed over the course of the following singles. But equally, Mylène's new image also makes an impression on a new wave of enthusiasts, a new generation perhaps slightly too young to enjoy her first time round, or put off by her earlier, darker image. Things are made worse for hesitant fans by Mylène's complete promotional invisibility at the time of the single's release: it is only after a few weeks have gone by, once it is clear the song is a success, that she will grant a few radio and press interviews; and it will be December before she is seen on TV again. By this time, the singer is already promoting the next single: "XXL" will not get even one solitary TV prestation. One can almost feel Mylène's anxiety around the time of her comeback, through what she did not do: no promotion, obviously, but more tellingly, Mylène, for the very first time in her career, fails to appear on the cover of her new single. Understandably cautious after the disastrous reception accorded to "Giorgino", the singer must inevitably have wondered at some point whether her career, too, would be affected.

Of course, we now know that on the contrary, it went from strength to strength. "XXL" will also become more and more of a success as time goes on: initially performed live during the '96 Tour as closer for the show, it will be overlooked for the Mylènium concerts but then make a brilliant return to form during both the

2006 and 2009 concerts: now a crowd favourite, "XXL" was the track that really got the party started in 2009. It has now become one of the classics of Mylène's répertoire, one of those songs that seem unavoidable on the stage, and was also granted a brand new remix in 2003, when JXL rearranged it for the "Remixes" compilation. But "XXL" is also the soundtrack to a probably rather painful memory for the singer: on 15th June '96, an over-enthusiastic fan in the front row pulls a little bit too hard on the train-like prop behind which Mylène is performing: the structure comes loose, Mylène falls off the stage, along with one of her dancers, who lands on top of her. Result: an open wrist fracture, and a cancelled tour, with all dates having to be rescheduled. A slightly traumatised audience as well, no doubt, what with an unconscious Mylène being stretchered out and urgently taken to the nearest hospital: still, the incident will soon allow the singer to show us all that she does not lack a sense of humour...

Shot in August '95 in an orange grove in Fillmore in southern California, the "XXL" video is the second of Mylène's "infidelities" to Laurent Boutonnat and his camera, a pattern that will endure from now on: it would seem the "Giorgino" shoot really *was* tough. In the first of what will be several clips under his helm, Marcus Niespel sticks Mylène to the front of a speeding locomotive, a figurehead declaiming the collective need for love as black and white shots of train passengers of all colours and creeds flash by. (Although the "stuck to a train" concept is said to have come from Thierry Mugler, who designed the azure blue dress Mylène wears in the video.) Once again, Mylène suffers for her art, spending close to five hours stuck to the front of several tons of speeding, hot metal. (She will suffer a couple of superficial burns as a result.) Not only that, but filming takes place under a burning hot sun, with temperatures close to 40 degrees celsius...nevertheless, the star refuses to use a stand-in, preferring to perform all her own stunts instead. As if that wasn't perilous enough, in order to get the necessary shots, another train is travelling just in front, with cameras recording Mylène from various angles. The train to which the singer is attached is an authentic 1906 locomotive, which was previously used in the Richard Attenborough "Charlie Chaplin" movie. All in all, the filming of the video will take three days, working on an estimated budget of around 230,000 Euros. The finished result is another indication of the singer's clear desire to break her image: as it is shot entirely in black and white, an uninitiated viewer wouldn't even know Mylène is a redhead. Once again, some of the fans deplore the lack of scenario, the short running time (4 minutes 22 seconds), and the absence of the usual Farmer references, even if, aesthetically, the clip is beyond reproach.

There will be less formats than usual for "XXL", and indeed for all further singles to come, but of course by now that is only to be expected, what with the 7" and cassette single editions having gone the way of the dinosaurs. CDs are still around though, and the single is issued on no less than three different editions in France: a 2-track version as well as a Maxi CD either in a regular "cristal" box, or a gold digipack sleeve slipped inside a die-cut "XXL" outer sleeve, if you were quick enough to get one of the precious "Édition limitée" copies. A 12" is also released, thus rounding up all the French commercial releases. Abroad, the single is only released as a regular edition CD, apart from Japan, which gets another 3" pop-up CD with extra photo art. Collectors will have four promos to choose from: while the first three are pretty much run of the mill items, the fourth is a superb object. The first three include a simple, 1-track CD for France, with a cover fairly similar to that of the single; a 2-track CD for Germany (featuring the German radio edit), in a sleeve identical to the commercial Maxi CD; and finally, Japan gets a promo CD that is identical to the commercial Japanese version, save for legal mentions. But it is really the deluxe promo that Farmer aficionados lust over: a cast-iron, stand-up "XXL", 30cm long and 18cm high, on which is affixed the 1-track CD. The fairly heavy item is presented inside a large black cardboard box in a matt finish: the song name is printed out in large letters on the lid in a contrasting glossy varnish, just above the singer's name. A beautiful, luxury item that I will be lucky enough, at one point, to add to my collection: sadly, it will be gone again just a year and a half later.

Mylène and Laurent had an awful lot riding on the singer's comeback: thankfully, it has turned out to be a success, and the brand new, luminous Mylène can now take a renewed step into the spotlight, and show us what's in store next...

21/ L'Instant X

In this late part of the year 1995, "Anamorphosée" is off to a fairly sluggish start: with "XXL" an adequate yet not overwhelming success, leaving many fans dubious as to the singer's new musical direction, public and media interest is not as high as it could be. Mylène's continued lack of promotional activity is not helping, especially when coming after a silence of almost four years that was broken only by the debacle that was "Giorgino". Seemingly running out of steam, the album leaves the Top 10 a mere four weeks after its release. Luckily, the release of "L'Instant X" will be just the tonic needed to wake things up. The song (almost) borrows a couple of lines from the holiday classic: "Petit Papa Noel, quand tu descendras du ciel...", making it a topical choice and the perfect Christmas release. Out on 12th December, the song at first looks like it's off to a shaky start: in at number 9, it swiftly drops down the charts, almost leaving the top 20 altogether. But then, no doubt thanks to Mylène, who has finally agreed to do some TV promotion, it steadily works its way back up, reaching its highest position of number 6 and remaining in the top 10 for seven consecutive weeks: at the same time, the album also gets a new lease of life: during the "L'Instant X" exploitation period, "Anamorphosée" occupies the 2nd place spot for several weeks running. With sales of almost 200,000, and hanging around the Top 50 for close to five months, the single will become the album's biggest hit, and the one that brought it back from the brink of disaster.

With "L'Instant X", Mylène explores a theme that is very much in vogue towards this latter part of the 20th century: the coming new millenium and all the associated fears that come with it. With a light lyric full of dry humour, the singer pokes gentle fun at our millenial obsessions: 2000 will be spiritual, it's written in "Elle", she says, a witty reference to the countless magazine articles that abound on the subject at the time, including in the above publication. Of course, this being a Mylène Farmer song, the somewhat random lyrics, more than ever, incite the fans to come up with possible interpretations: when the singer evokes her "bloody lundi", some see in it a possible wink to the "sunday, bloody sunday" of her friend Bono. The "Zoprack" of which she sings is of course the barely disguised name of a well-known anti-depressant: once again, the singer plays around with words as she sees fit, freely making up her own, leaving fans to wonder at any possible meanings behind the rejigging of the word: a way to convey a confused, altered state of mind? A possible legal issue? Mylène only knows... Aside from possible interpretations, the fans are also busy digging up potential influences on the single, specifically in regards to its name and sleeve artwork: and all credit to them, they do come up with something rather amusing: a movie poster for a 1966 film, by Ross Hunter and starring Lana Turner, that features a "head tilted back" black silhouette, eerily similar to the one found on the single's cover artwork. And the name of the film?

"Madame X"... Other peculiar images thrown up by the lyrics include a suicidal cat, Mylène informing us that she has the "complexion of a dustbin", or even a dry, sardonic commentary on her star status: in a blasé tone of voice, she sings that the time has come for her to strike the pose, and think of something else... With this dry, tongue-in-cheek lyric, Mylène moves even further away from her previous incarnations: after the resolutely positive affirmation of "XXL", so at odds with the hopeless melancholia of the early days, the singer now shows us that not only can she be hopeful, she can laugh at the world and herself too! "L'Instant X" marks a change in other ways, too: chronologically, this is the first of Mylène's issued singles where the remixes are produced, at least in part, by someone other than Laurent Boutonnat or one of his associates Thierry Rogen and Bertrand Châtenet. For the very first time, an outsider is invited to offer their interpretation of a Mylène Farmer song. The honour falls to Ramon Zenker, who delivers two of the four remixes. At the time, Ramon Zenker is an internationally renowned musician and remix artist, who has already worked with several international stars, including...Moby. Small world...

To the great joy of the fans, who have by now been waiting a long time to see her once more on their TV screens, Mylène finally gets round to doing some promotion for the new single. On the 17th of December, she is guest of honour on "Déja le retour", a show hosted by Jean-Luc Delarue, where she invites the author Marie de Hennezel, who has recently published "La mort intime", one of the most successful books of the year, to talk about her work. The book, which deals with death and our human approach to it, found an echo with Mylène: when it is her turn to speak, she also evokes the theme of death, though perhaps in a more serene fashion than usual as she also says a few words on the subject of Buddhism. While she doesn't perform on this show, a short sequence of images from the clip, all featuring the singer, are shown towards the end. Actual TV prestations of "L'Instant X" will have to wait until January 13th, when she appears on "Le betisier du samedi soir", on TF1. The second, and more widely remembered performance will take place as late as the 9th of March, (only two weeks before "California" is released) when Mylène shows up on "Top...aux Carpentiers", again on TF1: on the night, she spices up her performance by kissing both her female dancers on the mouth, another nice little nod to her gay fans, and no doubt a little delight for fans of other persuasions too... On the stage, "L'Instant X" has had a relatively modest presence: performed for the first time during the Tour '96 concerts (with a long instrumental section at the end while Mylène is getting changed), it will then be another thirteen years before the song is pulled out of retirement, in 2009, and even then only for the two Stade de France dates: it goes down a storm, with plenty of audience sing-along. The song is also revived in 2003, when a brand new remix is commissioned for the "Remixes" album: indeed, One-T's version, out of the three remixes released as 12"s only from the album, will be the one that gets the most radio plays.

For the video, Mylène once again turns to Marcus Niespel. Shot over three days in New York city towards the end of '95, the clip alternates shots of a more-glamorous-than-ever Mylène as she frolics in some weird foam-like substance, and images of various New Yorkers struggling as the same foam goes on to overwhelm and submerge them (and the Empire State building, too). No real scenario, but a possible evocation of some kind of end of the world storyline, or a huge purifying soapy wash, depending on your viewpoint. Clearly the video does not take itself too seriously, with Mylène as some kind of heavenly creature rolling around in the foam with gay abandon, cheerily drowning countless people at the same time. Indeed, it is surprising to see Mylène so relaxed and smiling, as she must have been absolutely freezing at the time: not only is she wearing little and moving about in a wet environment, but temperatures were said to be as low as -10 degrees celsius during filming. With a relatively small budget of around 80,000 Euros, the "L'Instant X" video, although aesthetically pleasing, has never been a huge fan favourite, even if it is true that the single itself was the most successful of that particular era. Nevertheless, the video will make an impression on the band The Third Eye Foundation, who in 2000 use stills from it (slightly doctored close-ups of Mylène) for the cover of their snappily-titled album "I poo-poo on your juju".

Very few formats exist for "L'Instant X", be it commercial releases or promos: in shops, fans could get hold of a 2-track CD (featuring the alternate "arachnostring" version of "Alice"), a 5-track Maxi CD and a die-cut sleeve 12". No European pressings were issued, the single receiving a French release only. The only promotional item available came in the shape of a

1-track CD mounted on a stiff cardboard sheet slipped inside a 12" sleeve with a design similar to that of the commercial 12".

With two successful singles off the album, which is now doing much better as a result, Mylène has managed to re-ignite the fans' enthusiasm, and her comeback is a success: yet, for many, the next single and its daring, stylish accompanying video will be an even better chance to renew their love affair with the Mylène of old.

22/ California

After the rock stylings of the preceding two singles, it is the jazz/funk-tinged "California" that is chosen to further promote the album by acting as third release. More representative of "Anamorphosée" as a whole, more indicative of its overall colour and sound, the track has a semi-autobiographical dimension, having been directly inspired by the singer's extended stay in the USA, and California specifically. The lyrics themselves reveal the strong influence the country has had on Mylène: more than any other song, "California" positively bursts with anglicisms: jet lag, freeway, on the road, L.A.P.D., pretty much every other line has something on offer as Mylène, deftly playing with words in that unique way of hers, playfully mixes French with English like it was the most natural thing in the world. These random excursions into English will indeed become something of a regular occurence in future, sometimes with just the odd few words thrown in (the "shut up, shut the fuck up" in "Peut-être toi"), entire lines slipped into songs (the "blood and tears/blood and soul" of "Fuck them all"), or even songs sung in both languages ("Les mots", "Looking for my name"). The singer's imaginative creativity does not stop at weaving languages, however: creating entirely new words is not a problem either! Thus, in the "California" chorus, Mylène comes up with another one of her neologisms, by turning into a previously unheard-of verb the scientific noun, "anamorphose", that will give the album its name (and there, once again, in yet another non-existent adjective form). And why not, after all? The laid-back, sun-drenched groove of "California" is indeed a hymn to change, renewal, and it is only fitting that the singer should switch between languages, as if exploring different facets of herself: it is this thirst for new horizons that gives the song its more luminous, almost optimistic feel. Having said that, the singer still finds a way, amidst all the word games, to pay homage to one of the big names in French literature: her "vienne la nuit et sonne l'heure" is almost word for word a quotation from Guillaume Apollinaire: Mylène may have experienced a rebirth of sorts, but she is still down with the classics. The singer will also make use of her US stay in other ways: on top of working on her own album, she will find the time to compose, all by herself, the music for a rap mini-album for her English tutor, Henry Biggs: the project goes by the name of Shade/Underbelly, and one of its six tracks, "Madeleine", features a melody that will be "recycled" on the self-penned song "Et si vieillir m'était conté", from the 1999 "Innamoramento" album.

Released on 26th March '96, "California" enters the singles charts at number 7: this will be its highest position, although the track will do well overall, remaining in the top 50 for close to four months. On the radio, especially, the song is quite the hit: in May, it even reaches first place in the palmares of most-played track on French radio networks, not an easy accomplishment. While it does less well than "L'Instant X" on sales alone, selling "only" 110,000 copies, the track will nevertheless establish itself as a Farmer classic over the long run, something its predecessor won't achieve quite as successfully. "California" will only be performed once on TV, in "Les années tube" on TF1 on 18th May, in a prestation that sees Mylène paired up with a handsome male dancer, with plenty of suggestive gyrating going on. But if just one TV appearance seems a bit stingy, Mylène at least has a good excuse: the '96 Tour is by then only one week away, scheduled to kick off in the southern town of Toulon on the 25th. There will be plenty of opportunities for "California" to be performed then. Indeed, the song's enduring appeal, and its status as a classic, are probably due in no small part to its quasi-omnipresence on the stage: in 1996, the singer, aided by her backing dancers, presents a finely choreographed and extremely sensual version: who can forget Mylène's tantalizing upper-body moves (at times, almost Egyptian in their styling), or the sight of her dancer offering herself up as a seat? During the Mylènium Tour, the song gets a new, laid-back, jazzy arrangement, Mylène delivering a languorous performance under warm blue-tinged lighting while flanked by vocalists Esther Dobong'Na Essienne and Joanna Manchec-Ferdinand. At the Bercy concerts in 2006, the police-style introduction, complete with "Do not cross - Crime scene" tape projections, brings to mind the spirit of the video as Mylène slowly makes her way forward on a moving conveyor belt, with the faithful Esther and Joanna still on background vocal duties. Mylène, looking resplendent in gold thigh-high boots and heavily-bejewelled two-piece matching number, brings the track to a torrid conclusion with a few unashamedly erotic "C'est sex" exclamations, making it one the most sensual versions of the song to be brought to the stage. The track is back again in 2009, although only for the two Stade de France dates, where it replaces "A quoi je sers...". Another great version, with Mylène supported by no less than four backing dancers this time around.

For those fans slightly thrown off-balance by the optimistic, smiling Mylène of the two previous clips, the video for "California" will be a chance to reassure themselves that the singer has lost none of her taste for the darker side of life, when it is premiered on French TV on the 20th of March. There was little chance of the video being a bundle of laughs in the first place, the director being none other than the legendary American screenwriter and independent film-maker Abel Ferrara, responsible for such classics as 1979's "The Driller Killer", or 1992's "Bad Lieutenant". Having noticed his work after watching "Snake Eyes", his Madonna-starring 1993 movie, Mylène sets her sights on the wildcard film director: he will, however, prove to be one hell of a slippery fish to catch. It is only after endless negotiations on the part of Anouk Nora (video producer) and Mylène herself, involving several late-night/very early morning calls, that the apparently unimpressed Ferrara will finally agree to the gig. Indeed, he has made no secret of the fact that his initial reasons for accepting were mostly financial: in his typical blunt style, he will go on to say that to begin with, he didn't give a damn what that "Frenchwoman and her song" were like: instead, he just heard that the shooting budget would be roughly equivalent to what he would usually require for an entire full-length movie! And it is true that, with a budget estimated at 610,000 Euros, "California" is one of the singer's most expensive videos ever, coming second only to "L'Âme-Stram-Gram" and its budget of €900,000. It is easily the most expensive French video of 1996. Abel Ferrara's initial reluctance and indifference towards the singer will soon change, however: encouraged by the fact that she writes her own lyrics, he quickly enters into long conversations with Mylène in order to find out exactly what it is that she wants to put across in her music video, a format to which he is a newcomer himself. Mylène explains that she has long wanted to play the role of a prostitute: from there, Ferrara proposes some of his ideas, to which the singer adds her own. There is no denying that the end result is compelling, a real little gem in Mylène's videography.

For the first time, the concept of "twins" is introduced, with Mylène playing two roles, at once a well-heeled, high society woman and a ballsy prostitute working Sunset Boulevard. Also playing two different characters is Giancarlo Esposito, famous for his roles in films such as "Cotton Club", "Desperately Seeking Susan" or also "Malcom X": on the one hand, Mylène's equally well-heeled husband, on the other, her violent and abusive pimp. As the well-heeled couple get ready for a glitzy reception in the husband's honour, with a clearly frustrated Mylène being dictated what to wear, their "trash" twins are playing attitude games in a cheap motel room, with a far more confident Mylène unafraid to show how she feels. On both sides, the domination games end up in a spot of sexual activity of varying degrees of intensity, before both couples head out to their respective destinations. On their way to the function, chic-Mylène is spooked by the sight of a somewhat familiar-looking prostitute being maltreated by her pimp: for just a moment, the two women lock eyes, the shock of recognition written on the prostitute's face. Although she wants to help, the classy Mylène is held back by her husband, who gets slapped in the face for his trouble; as for her prostitute double, she is quickly put back to work by her knife-wielding pimp. Once they have arrived at the glittery do, Mylène quickly loses her companion as he revels in congratulations and accepts a cigarette from an interested stranger, the stress plain to see on her face. The husband looks for her in the crowd, but it's too late: she's already nipped into the loo to give herself a radical makeover, earning a slightly disapproving look on her way out from the woman standing by the sinks. Not that she cares: stripping even further, chic-Mylène swiftly transforms her look from classy to trashy, as stark flashbacks of prostitutes flaunting their wares race through her mind: the quick edits seem to convey a sense of urgency, as if the classy woman is feeling a hunger to become someone else. And soon, she gets her chance: now appropriately dressed for the occasion, she returns to the Sunset Boulevard scene of her weird earlier encounter, only to make a grim discovery: the body of her murdered twin is being covered by a sheet before being taken away. Taking the slain prostitute's place on the sidewalk, the scantily-dressed newcomer soon catches the eye of the murderous pimp, and lets herself be led away to what the man probably thinks is going to be a good time. Things won't work out so great for him though: enacting revenge on behalf of her murdered doppelganger, Mylène takes a leaf out of Sharon Stone's book and gets busy with the icepick, in scenes of extreme violence, in spite of the stabbing not actually being shown on screen.

Shooting takes place over five days, with Marianne Rosenstiehl on hand as set photographer: to date, this is her last professional collaboration with Mylène. All of the extras on the Sunset Boulevard scenes were actual working girls (and, possibly, one "girl"): a self-evident casting decision, in view of the gritty realism the director was after. But before the finished clip has even had a chance to air, stolen pictures of Mylène on the set are published in the magazine Voici: amazingly, the moment the photos were snatched is seen happening in real time on the "California making-of" video. A sudden commotion is heard outside as the paparazzi snap away, and Ferrara is heard to say "What was that flash? That was great, whatever it was, that was great!" From the moment the clip is finally shown on 20th March, fans are unanimous in their praise, and to this day, the consensus is that it remains one of Mylène's best, certainly among her most stylish. In October '96, Mylène will describe the "California" video as being "a 90's version of Libertine, a possible evolution". As for Abel Ferrara, he will be won over in the end by the singer's commitment and professional dedication: Anouk Nora will go on to state that the director was rather "seduced" by Mylène.

Giancarlo Esposito can also be added to the "seduced" list: "I like that girl...", he can be heard saying in the making-of. And who can blame them?

"California" will be released on a fair few number of formats: in France, fans get a choice of three different editions of the CD: a 2-track single, which is also made available in a limited edition tri-fold digipack sleeve. The Maxi CD, which also comes, for the first time in Mylène's career, in a digipack sleeve, contains no less than six versions and over 30 minutes of music: because of this lengthy duration and high number of tracks, it will actually be classified as an album, resulting in this item still being widely available in stores, years after its original release: to this day, copies can still be fairly easily found. Another first for Mylène: the vinyl 12" contains not just one but two records inside its "Mylène on railroad tracks" sleeve, with picture by Claude Gassian. Once again, Laurent Boutonnat shares remixing duties with Ramon Zenker, as well as Gaspar inc. (actually Ramon Zenker under another alias.) Europe also gets a release, with a 2-track CD and 4-track Maxi CD: less music, but a totally different sleeve with an alternate picture taken from the "Anamorphosée" photoshoot with Herb Ritts. On the promo side, it's all about CDs this time: for Europe, a 1-track edition inside a plastic case, with artwork almost similar to that of the commercial release. In France, two different promos see the light of day: the first, the "promo simple", is a 1-track CD inside a cardboard sleeve. The second, much more imposing, "promo luxe" is one of the pieces of which graphic designer Henry Neu is the proudest: an LP-style gatefold sleeve with unique artwork that opens to reveal a pop-up Mylène cut-out, under which the CD is placed. A beautiful and rare item, and priced accordingly, especially if the pop-up Mylène is still in an excellent condition!

"California" will have only just barely left the Top 50, on 2nd August, before the next single comes along just a few days later: and Mylène's choice of track for the next release will be painfully appropriate.

23/ Comme J'Ai Mal

After an initially slow start, the "Anamorphosée" album is at last doing proper business and nearing the million mark, thanks to three successive hit singles, a new sound and image that have finally won over her early fans and even attracted new ones, and a newly launched tour that enables Mylène to reconnect with her public. But, not even a month after the first date in Toulon on the 25th of May, disaster strikes: on 15th June, in Lyon, Mylène dramatically falls off stage, fracturing her wrist in the process. The tour is immediately brought to a halt. The album exploitation, on the other hand, must carry on, especially now that sales are finally picking up. And so, after "California", it is "Comme j'ai mal" that is chosen as fourth single: the timing of its release is, of course, not without a hint of irony, and brings a smile to the face of many a fan. Clearly, Mylène, who is convalescing at the time, is not above laughing at herself and her misfortunes. The track is sent out to radio as early as July, and while airplay is reasonable, it will not achieve quite the same levels of success that "California" did. Released on 6th August, the single is one of the rare Mylène releases to miss out on a Top 10 placing, although only by a whisker: it will have to do with a highest showing at number 11. With sales of 80,000 in total, "Comme j'ai mal" will in fact turn out to be the album's poorest-selling single: nevertheless, in spite of its relatively low sales figures, it has always been a strong fan favorite, and, for many, one of their favourite songs off the album.

"Comme j'ai mal" will benefit from only one TV prestation, broadcast shortly before the interrupted tour is due to resume. On 24th October '96, Mylène appears on the TF1 show "Tip Top", where she performs not one but two songs: in addition to a rendition of her new single, the singer also performs, for the very first time, "La poupée qui fait non", together with the Rai singer Khaled who is enjoying huge commercial success in France around this time. Their cover of the Michel Polnareff classic (apparently, one of the first songs Mylène ever learned), re-arranged with a slight Arabic twist, will in fact itself become a single just a few months later. On stage, "Comme j'ai mal" will only be performed during the '96 Tour, and has not been revived to date, further contributing to its relatively "forgotten" status: strange, considering that the song was probably one of the "Anamorphosée" album's strongest links with the Mylène Farmer of the early days, in terms of mood and thematics. Or perhaps not so strange, if we accept that Mylène had by then successfully completed the transition from dark, tortured heroine to exalted, luminous icon...

While "Comme j'ai mal" may not have enjoyed the same level of chart success as its predecessors, its release as a single was nevertheless the occasion for yet another gem in the Farmer videography. Shot in Los Angeles towards the tail-end of August '96, it is Marcus Niespel's third clip for Mylène, and arguably one of his best. (The singer will call on him once more, in 1999, for "Souviens-toi du jour".) The aesthetically-superb clip revolves around images of a young girl who finds refuge from an abusive father in a most unusual way: hidden inside her closet, the little girl forms a friendship with various insects she keeps inside a cardboard box, allowing them to run freely over her body as she feeds them on sugar cubes, while Mylène pops up at random intervals in white undergarments, singing and emoting from what appears to be one of the closet's darkest corners. Seeking further refuge, the child then takes things to the extreme: in the face of her father's constant violence, she retreats even deeper into the insect world, feeding herself on sugar cubes in preparation for what will turn out to be a period of hibernation, a complete shutdown as the little girl is progressively enveloped within an insect-like cocoon. Speeding clocks and abandoned toys indicate the passing of time, until signs of life can be glimpsed again from within the now gluey and sticky cocoon: and as the creature inside struggles to break free of its bonds, it becomes apparent that the young girl has completed her metamorphosis, and transformed into a strangely insectoid Mylène: wings, sharp talons, pointy hair, everything about the newborn creature is designed for defence. The terrorized young girl has emerged from her long protective sleep as a new creature, stronger, now equipped with the weapons she needs in order to defend herself from life's harsh realities: the father, left alone, can only ponder on his mistakes. A complex, highly symbolic scenario that is strangely compelling. And yet, it would seem that the original concept for the video was something altogether different: according to persistent rumours, shooting on an alternate version of the clip had begun in June, this one also involving animals but on a slightly bigger scale: black panthers that unfortunately went on to totally wreck the set, thereby missing out on their chance to star in a Mylène Farmer video. Not surprisingly, producers then decided to work with more compliant, and more easily manageable animals (not to mention less dangerous.) It appears that Jeff Dahlgren took on the role of set photographer for this particular video: only one of his shots, however, was eventually approved by Mylène; it is featured in the "Music Videos II&III" booklet. The first images from the clip will be shown on the "Plus vite que la musique" broadcast, quickly followed by the first exclusive showing on the music channel M6.

Because of their relatively low sales at the time, the "Comme j'ai mal" supports are now slightly more difficult to track down than those of other, more successful singles. A shame, as the remixes are particularly good, and practically the last to come from Laurent Boutonnat: the "Pain Killer" mix is a hypnotic, deep laid-back groove while the "Upside Down" remix is a frenetic, pulsating, almost trance-like number, the vocals of which consist almost solely of Mylène's sampled "Je bascule" repeated over and over to great effect. In France, there were almost as many promo releases as there were commercial ones. On the commercial front, two versions of the 2-track CD single were edited, one of these a limited edition in tri-fold digipack packaging. A Maxi CD was also available, featuring both remixes plus an instrumental version (unusually, not available on the 2-track CD), as well as a

12" single. Surprisingly, "Comme j'ai mal" also saw a European release, although extremely limited: the only format available was a 3-track CD, with a completely different tracklisting from the French issue, as well as a different sleeve design. Promotionally, the single saw the light of day as two different CDs: a 1-track CD featured the radio edit and a totally unique sleeve, while the 2-track version, featuring both the radio edit and the "Aches remix", came in a sleeve almost identical to that of the limited edition commercial release. The most enticing of the "Comme j'ai mal" promos is probably the final one: a 12" featuring both remixes and a totally gorgeous die-cut "Mylène x 4" sleeve.

Already, the "Anamorphosée" exploitation period is nearing the end...With a new image and new sound, Mylène has managed to make a hugely successful comeback, in spite of a shaky start. But the era is not quite over just yet: one fifth and final single to go, and another classic in the making.

24/ Rêver

Initially, "Anamorphosée" was supposed to give birth to no more than four singles. But Mylène's unfortunate off-stage fall will change all that: once she is fully recovered and the tour can resume, kicking off again on 29th November in Toulon, releasing a further single to mark the occasion seems like the obvious thing to do. And so, just ten days before the first date of the second half of the abruptly interrupted '96 Tour, on the 19th to be precise, "Rêver" becomes the album's fifth and final single. As it acts as precursor to the forthcoming live album, the concert version is included on the various formats: the accompanying live video constitutes the first opportunity for fans and the general public to see quality images from Mylène's latest show. Entering the charts at number 8, the song will go on to sell over 100,000 copies, with a highest showing of seventh place. While these sales figures do not technically make the song one of the singer's overall greatest hits, or even the best-selling single to be issued from the "Anamorphosée" album, "Rêver" will nevertheless go on to occupy a very special place in the

Farmer universe: a radio favourite, the track will go on to benefit from some serious and sustained airplay, to the extent that it is still frequently played on French radio today. One of Mylène's numerous literary efforts, "Rêver" is strong on nods to the singer's love of books: "J'irai cracher sur vos tombes", Boris Vian's legendary work, which created a scandal when it was first released in 1947 because of its violent, sexual content, earning the author a 100,000 Francs fine for "outraging public morals", is fairly obviously name-checked. Another literary reference is even more blatant: in his poem "Toujours là", the poet Pierre Reverdy, whose surname even manages to incorporate the song's title, wrote the following words: "Le monde comme une pendule s'est arrêté, les gens sont suspendus pour l'éternité." A clear homage, and just one of the singer's many throughout her career. It is also thanks to "Rêver" that its parent album finally reaches number 1, over a year and a half after it was released: by this stage, the album has already hit the million sales mark, and its success is undeniable. Still, reaching pole position at last, after such a long time, is the icing on the cake. Today, "Rêver" has become one of the undisputed classics of the Farmer répertoire, its inclusion in concert setlists having become something of an inevitability, even if some fans do feel that, perhaps, on the stage at least, the song is starting to wear out its welcome.

But after so long, it is somewhat difficult to picture a "Rêver"-free Mylène Farmer concert, its appearance at shows having taken on no less than ritualistic proportions: in terms of combining emotion with audience participation, it is hard to beat. In 1996, a very emotional Mylène, clad in a stunning silver dress, is so overcome that she occasionally struggles to finish her lines: to the audience's great delight, of course, as it means they can finish them for her. The slightly shorter Mylènium Tour version is punctuated by a final acapella chorus from the public, in a moment of osmosis that is breath-taking in its emotional intensity. In 2006, for the thirteen Bercy concerts, Mylène delivers a stunning rendition, accompanied by Yvan Cassar on a piano that magically popped up on to the stage; and in 2009, the song's performance was of course a golden opportunity for fans to wish Mylène a happy birthday in person, on the 12th of September at the Stade de France, in what must be one of the most emotional and euphoric audience participation instances ever. Will it be back for the next series of concerts? Who can say, but the thought isn't an unlikely one.

"Rêver" will be performed on television twice, with an interval of just over six years between both prestations. The first appearance, around the time of the single's release, takes place on 27th November '96, on "Les enfants de la guerre": no doubt a painfully difficult performance for Mylène to give, as she had only just heard of the death of her brother in a traffic-related accident the night before. It is during filming for this show that Mylène's and Luciano Pavarotti's paths almost crossed, although the legendary tenor's behaviour towards Mylène on that day may perhaps be described as somewhat cavalier, though no doubt not intentionally so. To begin with, Mylène is performing wearing the same silver dress as worn during her live shows: the dress is quite heavy, and her dressing-room is quite a way from the stage. Producers offer her the use of a golf-cart-type vehicle to ferry her to the set, which she gratefully accepts: but the vehicle is then requisitioned by Pavarotti, who by then was already suffering from reduced mobility: Mylène must then make her way to the set on foot. This in itself was no big deal, but the second incident must have grated somewhat: after recording is over, Mylène is told that Pavarotti loved her performance ("eyes popping out of his head" was one of the more irreverent descriptions of the singer as he watched Mylène on stage) and has invited her to come meet him in his dressing-room. Mylène duly turns up, waits outside for a fair amount of time, but in vain: the tenor's door will, inexplicably, remain tightly closed. (Perhaps Luciano's notoriously over-protective girlfriend had something to say about it?) The second TV performance for "Rêver" takes place on 18th January 2003 at the NRJ Music Awards, where Mylène also receives the trophy for best female francophone artist of the year, for the fourth year in a row. On the night, and for the very first time in 17 years, Mylène sings live on TV, accompanied by Yvan Cassar on the piano as she delivers a brand new version of the song. The lengthy gap between live televised performances can no doubt be explained by the previous instance, when a rendition of "Tristana" was beset by numerous technical problems that meant Mylène could hear neither herself nor the music, resulting in a performance that was fairly described as "shaky". No such problems at the NRJ Awards, however: the performance is world-class. On top of prestations from Mylène herself, "Rêver" was also the official 2002 theme song for Les Enfoirés, the yearly charity French supergroup: on this occasion, it is a young singer by the name of Alizée who gets to sing solo on the first verse.

"Rêver" is among the few Mylène Farmer singles never to be released in vinyl form. In addition to a 2-track CD featuring the radio edit and live version, a Maxi CD, also available as a limited edition digipack, featured the "Stripped Dream remix": as the name suggests, an even more stripped-down version of the song, even more laid-back than the original, and the only official remix to date. But the Maxi CD also carries another little gem, the Richard Dekkard "UK Remix" of "XXL". The remixer, however, is listed as "Robert Dekkard" on the sleeve, an error he will later go on to describe as having left a bitter taste in his mouth, in spite of an apology from Mylène herself. Released only within France, "Rêver" will also occasion two promotional items: a "promo simple", in the shape of a monotrack CD in exclusive titles sleeve, and a "promo luxe", much sought after by collectors, consisting of the 4-track CD on a 12" cardboard support slipped inside the legendary "nude kneeling Mylène" sleeve.

And so the "Anamorphosée" era comes to an end. A real change of musical direction, as well as a dramatic overall change of image, meant that the album initially struggled, no doubt giving Mylène's detractors a temporary thrill at the idea that her career may have run out of steam. And yet, after five successive hit singles and a hugely popular tour, the album will eventually go on to become 1996's sixth best-selling album, as well as earning a Victoires de la Musique award for most exported album of the year, with sales of more than 100,000 across Europe. (An award begrudgingly given by the Victoires organisers, famously at odds with the singer: her accomplishment will hardly be mentioned at all during the ceremony that year.) Released in several countries, there exist numerous editions of the album: one specimen of note is the Japanese CD issue, that contains two bonus tracks, "Alice (new mix)" and "XXL (Extra Large remix)". A collector's edition of the album was made available in December '96: a numbered, limited edition LP-sized box with oversize booklet and CD on the last page: a great format to appreciate the beauty of Herb Ritt's photographs in detail. The only French promotional issue for France was the very same item, although not numbered and with "limited edition-not for sale" mentions.

With the '96 Tour such a resounding success (in spite of a lengthy, enforced break right in the middle), fans are now waiting for the live CD and DVD: released in May '97, these will enable Mylène to break yet more records.

25/ La Poupée Qui Fait Non (live) - 26/ Ainsi Soit Je...(live)

Preceding the album's release by a month, "La poupée qui fait non" is the first single to be taken from "Live à Bercy". Initially performed six months earlier on the TF1 broadcast "Tip Top", in a Rai-styled version that will finally never see the light of day, the song is, according to Mylène herself, amongst the first she ever became familiar with. By the time the single is released on 29th April '97, Khaled is himself enjoying huge success within France with a Jean-Jacques Goldman-composed album: the single "Aicha", in particular, being a huge popular success. The release of "La poupée qui fait non" as lead single from the forthcoming live album is nonetheless a little surprising, as the track is not really representative of the tour *per se*: indeed, it was only ever performed on stage twice, towards the end of the tour, when Khaled joined Mylène on stage during the Bercy and Geneva concerts. Some fans will think the single is a way for Mylène to put some further distance between herself and the 1995 Le Pen affair: indeed, rumours went around at the time to the effect that the Farmer/Khaled collaboration had come about as a result of a direct request from Polydor, anxious to erase any lingering unpleasant associations in the wake of the whole sordid business by asking Mylène to publicly collaborate with a foreign (and, more specifically, Arab) artist. But whether the collaboration was artistically or politically motivated is, in any case, irrelevant: it is an undeniable fact that the National Front's devious actions at the time -employing a Mylène Farmer lookalike to perform at one of their high-profile political functions- were potentially hugely embarrassing for the singer: while most people would have seen the situation for what it was, there still existed a risk, no matter how small, that some members of the public would not be able to make the distinction, and end up believing that the singer actually condoned the party's abhorrent policies. Something that would be totally unfair, when we know of Mylène's liberal and enlightened outlook in all areas of life, including politics.

The "La poupée qui fait non" recording sessions take place at the Mega studios, under the supervision of Thierry Rogen, in what is a very relaxed atmosphere: of his working relationship with Mylène, Khaled will remember mostly the laughter, as well as the singer's seemingly ravenous hunger for bananas. All in all, the sessions take just over four hours. For the first time, something very rare occurs: Laurent Boutonnat is not implicated in any way. His services won't even be required for the remixes, as for the occasion it is Mylène herself who takes care of things, with Thierry Rogen's help. (This will be the first and last time -to date- that Mylène works on remixing her own tracks.) When the single is released on 29th April, however, the reception is lukewarm: though it debuts at a respectable number 6, the song -Mylène's second-ever duet- quickly heads down and out of the charts, not helped by almost non-existent radio play. It will have a better fate in Belgium, where it will eventually become the 41st best-selling single of the year 1997. Total sales for the single will remain relatively modest, with around 90,000 copies sold. Independently of this single, a collaboration between Mylène and the song's composer, the legendary Michel Polnareff, was once briefly considered: a meeting was even arranged at the Sunset Marquis hotel in Los Angeles, although nothing came of it. Asked some years later whether she could say a few words on that particular episode in her life, the singer will reply with a simple "no!"

Released only within France, "La poupée qui fait non" is available as a 2-track CD single on which also features the live version of "L'autre...". The Maxi CD, available as a regular or limited digipack edition, also includes the "Say it like you used to" and "I want a man" remixes of the title track, both co-produced by Mylène herself: sadly, the remixes will fail to find much favour amongst fans. Rather surprisingly, "La poupée qui fait non" is issued on as many promotional formats as commercial ones: not only do we get two versions of the CD, one "promo simple" 1-track CD as well as a "luxe" edition consisting of a CD inside a 12" cut-out "Mylène & Khaled" silhouettes sleeve, itself slipped inside an outer tracing paper sleeve, (quite the elaborate package) but a promo vinyl featuring the remixes is also issued, a format completely bypassed in the shops! Given their relatively low "must-have" factor, these particular promos are now amongst some of the more affordable in the Farmer discography, although the deluxe edition has been known to fetch sums around the €100 mark on occasion.

The second, final single to be taken from the "Live à Bercy" album is an old favourite: close to ten years after its original release, "Ainsi soit je..." gets another single outing. Released on 20th August, the live single flies in at number...35, before climbing to its best position of number 27 the following week. It must be said that airplay for the song is particularly poor, with radio stations hardly playing the game in the first place: preferring to go with an uptempo track, Europe 2 begins to broadcast the live version of "Que mon coeur lâche", while NRJ goes for "Désenchantée"...After spending just over a month in the Top 50, "Ainsi soit je..." makes a discreet exit with sales of around 50,000, a low score for Mylène. This, in spite of a promotional TV appearance to defend the single, on 6th September on "Les enfants de la Une", where Mylène performs a brand new studio version of the song, close in flavour to the stage version. The low sales figures can perhaps be explained in part by the extremely limited supports made available in the shops, a grand total of one, a 2-track CD single that also includes the live version of "Et tournoie...". A solitary promo is also issued, a digipack 1-track CD in an alternate sleeve: while nice enough, it is not one of the most sought-after items around.

Around the time of the release of "La poupée qui fait non", I make a huge mistake: something about the single, and particularly the accompanying remixes, really doesn't do it for me, and I suddenly, inexplicably decide to sell off my Mylène Farmer collection. Not that I've gone off the singer, I plan to keep on following her, but all of a sudden my obsessive collecting seems like a pointless and ruinous thing to do. At the time, my collection is still relatively small, with around 60 items from the singer's discography. In a decision I will come to bitterly regret, I foolishly sell the whole thing to a UK-based mail order firm, accepting their pitifully low prices for items that took me untold time and money to acquire: I will shortly be learning the true meaning of the saying "act in haste, repent in leisure". For as soon as the "Innamoramento" album is released, I will be bitten by the collecting bug again, and start the whole thing over from scratch, going on to build a collection of almost 250 items from Mylène's discography alone. (Not including books, clothes, and other various items.) And while I will somehow manage to reacquire most of my hastily sold items, there are two I will never be able to come across again: the "L'Autre..." collectors' box-set, and, even more crushingly, the "XXL" cast-iron promo...although, ironically enough, it will be no trouble getting hold of the various formats for "Regrets"...

With two singles off the album, the exploitation period for "Live à Bercy" now comes to an end. Whatever the singles' performances, the album itself has been a huge success, selling around 900,000 copies, unheard-of sales figures for a live recording. It is the 11th best-selling album of the year, and the biggest-selling live album ever released in France. There was a collectors' edition made available, although it pales when compared to subsequent live collector releases: in a box hardly bigger and similar in design to the regular edition CD, the only extra is a small tour poster. Much, much more interesting is the fantastic and ultra-rare promo, extremely limited in number: inside a large stamped black box, a silver-coloured spider, quite scary, houses the two live CDs within its abdomen, with a VHS of the concert also included in the packaging. This is one of the most sought-after items in the whole discography: prices, naturally, are through the roof. The film of the concert will also go on to sell in record numbers: all formats included (VHS, DVD and even Laser Disc), sales figures come close to nudging the 300,000 mark.

The "Anamorphosée" album, and its sister live release, have both been huge successes: Mylène can fall silent again for a while. Waiting time comes around again...It will be a fairly long wait (from the release date of the final live single, almost two years), but when it finally arrives, the next single will announce the dawn of a glorious new chapter in the Mylène Farmer story.

Part 5: Innamoramento / Mylènium Tour / Les Mots / Remixes

27/ L'Âme-Stram-Gram

Mylène Farmer has been totally absent from the media, unseen and silent, for about a year and a half when the first rumours about a possible return to the spotlight begin to emerge towards the end of 1998. According to various whispers, the singer's comeback is imminent, with a new single, "The small world", due any minute, soon to be followed by the brand new album called "Mes Moires". The rumours are only partially wrong: while there is no single or album going by those names, Mylène's comeback is indeed not very far away. The new single's genuine title finally leaks in late January: a few weeks later, "L'Âme-stram-gram" gets its first exclusive play on NRJ radio. For countless impatient fans, the long wait is over at last: Mylène is back with a new sound. At first, the techno vibe of "L'Âme-stram-gram" leads some to speculate that the singer has effected yet another radical change in style and moved over into the world of dance music; the track, however, will turn out to be not very representative, as a whole, of the album yet to come: if anything, "Innamoramento" will be a nod to the Mylène of old, a return to the musical source. But for the time being, in any case, the only thing to go on is the new single, and fans waste no time in dissecting the lyrics in an attempt to decrypt the singer's message this time around. Most obvious is the profusion of puns, of a steamy nature mostly: clearly, for this comeback, Mylène has gone for a theme that is dear to her: sex. With much mention of orifices, combined with the singer's knack for suggestive sonorities, it was difficult, on first listen, not to feel that the notion of penetration had somehow come to mind. Of course, while sex may be all over this particular song, it is not the only theme that's on offer: psychoanalysis also gets a look-in, as well as childhood, inevitably brought up by the song's title: "Am-stram-gram" is collectively known to most people of French origin as the song recited by children to pick a person out of a group at random when playing games. Of course, the games now conjured up by Mylène's lyrics are of a somewhat more explicit nature...

Very quickly, the track begins to receive some heavy rotation, with NRJ and Fun Radio in particular giving it some seriously frequent airplay, clearly a good sign for the singer. And yet, when "L'Âme-stram-gram" is finally released on 9th March 1999, it is not quite the hit that may have been hoped for. While it does manage to go straight in at number 2 in its first week, the song then immediately begins its slow but inexorable descent down the charts, leaving the countdown altogether in less than sixteen weeks: while four months may seem like a respectfully long time for a single to hang around, it must be noted that the Top 50 has by now become the Top 100, and therefore releases are charting for longer periods of time. (Mylène only just misses out on another potential record at that time: had "L'Âme-stram-gram" hit the top spot, she would have had four number 1's from four consecutive studio albums. Sadly, there will be no chart-toppers from the "Innamoramento" era, and the album itself will peak at number 2.) Nevertheless, the single's sales figures remain honourable, especially in a fast-crumbling record market, with around 160,000 copies sold, enough to earn it a silver certification. Fans getting their hands on a copy of the single are greeted by a Marino Parisotto Vay photograph of Mylène half-hidden behind a translucent veil, a somewhat grave expression on her face. And when the CD is turned over, time for another surprise, and another first: for the very first time in the singer's career, Laurent Boutonnat leaves all remixing duties to others, calling, in this instance, on the hip DJ's Perky Park and Lady B. (Rumour has it the legendary DJ Laurent Garnier was also approached, but turned Mylène down: no doubt the idea of working with such a popular singer was too much of a threat to his cool underground credentials.) This shift towards outsiders is not in itself a commentary on Laurent Boutonnat's remixing skills, but merely a sign of the times: in recent years, dance has gone massive, with DJ's attaining almost God-like status at times; any remix worth its salt, nowadays, must be signed by a DJ, preferably a big name: that is just the way things are done now, you just don't remix your own material anymore. The good old days of the "extended versions" are well and truly over...

Not only does he not deliver any remixes, but Laurent Boutonnat is also once more absent from the video-making process. For "L'Âme-stram-gram", Mylène will this time call on the services of Ching Siu Tung, the legendary Hong Kong-based director. Issued from a cinematic family, the director began his career as an actor and martial arts instructor in the Hong Kong movie industry in the 60's, before going on to direct "A Chinese Ghost Story" in 1987, more recently acting as action director/choreographer on huge blockbuster movies such as 2002's "Hero" and 2004's "House of Flying Daggers". His unique style will inevitably be stamped all over the singer's new video: indeed, "L'Âme-stram-gram" heavily draws from "A Chinese Ghost Story" for its looks and inspiration. Shot in early '99 in Peking, China, the clip, at almost eight minutes long, is a welcome return to the grandiose video days of the early years. The estimated budget is correspondingly large, at €900,000, a fair amount of it on the screen for all to see: for the first time in Mylène's career, a video makes use of extensive digital special effects. But even more impressive is the reconstruction of an entire section of the Great Wall of China, in what must be the single most ambitious prop ever conceived for the needs of the singer's videography. But an epic video does not only rely on its looks and sets, no matter how extravagant: in order to meet the high expectations of both fans and an ever-more sophisticated public, a suitably dramatic and compelling story must also be present. On this count, Ching Siu Tung -and Mylène herself, equally involved with the scenario- do not disappoint: drama, explosive action, tragedy, the clip has got it all. Revisiting, for the second time since "California", the theme of twins so dear to Mylène (a theme that will be back in 2005 with "Fuck them all"), the video introduces a pair of blissfully happy sisters who spend their time frolicking joyfully amongst brightly-coloured drapes, until a group of evil bandits on horseback rudely intrudes upon their harmony. The frightened sisters defend themselves at first, using a uber-cool killer tongue power that brings down the horses and their riders in a blinding flash of blue lightning, but are eventually overcome when one of them is knocked out with a blow to the back of the head from a passing horseman; with her twin barely conscious and unable to help, the other sister is carried off on horseback to the bandits' hideout, where she is mercilessly terrorized by the maniacally laughing brutes as various unfortunates are tortured in imaginative ways all around her. The fallen sister valiantly gets up and follows after her kidnapped twin, but her forces are draining fast and she struggles painfully on her way, as her other half is being cruelly tossed into the air by the evil bandits. Finally, when she is half-way up the steps that lead to the rogues' hideout, almost within reach of her captive sister, her strength gives out completely and she collapses, falling backwards and rolling all the way down until she lands at the bottom, quite dead. Sensing her sudden departure, the other sister is overcome; but presently, the ghost of the fallen twin, clad in white, rises out of the body lying prone at the bottom of the stairs. Moments later, the doors to the hideout are blown open by an otherworldly blizzard that sweeps the men off their feet as a whirling shape heads for the rafters: reunited, the sisters overcome their enemies with a few well-placed tongue lashes, eventually blowing up the whole place before flying off to freedom. But their reunion will be short-lived: as the sun rises, the ghostly twin is wrenched from her still-living sister, who falls back to earth with a thud, left to watch helplessly as her dead half stylishly vanishes into the ether. As images of their past times together flash in front of her eyes, the remaining sister knows what she must do: running to the edge, she throws herself off the Great Wall, her death the only way to be reunited with her missing half once more. Now, at last, the sisters can fly off together...

Right from its first TV broadcast in late March, the clip immediately becomes a strong fan favourite, and also earns Mylène numerous new fans in the process! Shortly after its premiere, the video is the subject for a special broadcast in "Mister bizz" on the music channel M6, where excerpts from the clip are shown along with an interview of the director. Ching Siu Tung praises Mylène's interest and level of involvement in his work, and it is true that the singer has strongly implicated herself: in addition to collaborating on the scenario, Mylène is also responsible for some of the financing via her production companies. And while the video shoot itself took only five days, the singer spent two weeks in China overseeing the production side of things: a rare level of commitment for any artist. A couple of familiar names shared the journey with her: Claude Gassian was the set photographer, and her friend and co-choreographer Christophe Danchaud doubled up for the occasion as make-up artist. The video's twin and stand-in for Mylène is also a face from the past: Valérie Bony, dancer on the '96 Tour. With the superb "L'Âme-stram-gram" video, deservedly described as one of her best, Mylène renews the links with the visual glories of the past years, reminding us exactly of what it is that makes her so special; and once again, we watch, enchanted and thrilled as she expertly weaves her magic.

On the stage, the song has so far seen two outings: first during the Mylènium Tour, when it is accompanied by a performance that is somewhat slightly hispanic in feel; forgotten for the 2006 Bercy shows (when not a single track from "Innamoramento" makes it onto the final setlist), it comes back in 2009, for the indoor shows as well as the two Stade de France dates, with Mylène and her dancers presenting a choreography that, while similar to the original, seems somehow more...suggestive. The tight "muscles" outfits, perhaps? On television, Mylène will perform "L'Âme-stram-gram" on three different occasions, all in April 1999: first, on "Les années tube" on TF1, then "Hit Machine" on M6 and finally "Tapis Rouge" on France 2: each time, she performs accompanied by several backing dancers, delivering a finely choreographed prestation that is orchestrated to the millimetre: by now, Mylène Farmer is much more than a singer, she is an absolute superstar, and everyone of her public appearances must be star-like. Recently she has even gained a new nickname, and it is not the old "Vilaine Fermière" that some bright spark had coined during the "Ainsi soit je..." era anymore: no, the new monicker, strongly suggested by the amazing, ambitious '96 Tour, is instead "the French Madonna". A lazy and obvious comparison, some may say, but not totally inaccurate either: while drawing comparisons between the two singers' work is pointless, the Madonna analogy helps to accentuate and more precisely express the level of fame and cultural impact that Mylène has built for herself: and if a comparison is drawn with an American artist, it is only because no comparisons could be made on home turf: Mylène's success, her career trajectory and the devotion of which she is the object have no other genuine equivalent within France...

When the single is released on 9th March 1999, French fans and collectors can add to their Mylène Farmer collection with one, or more often all, of three separate formats: a 2-track CD single, exclusively featuring the splendid "L.A. instrumental", surely one of Laurent Boutonnat's best upbeat numbers; a Maxi CD and 12" both feature the single version as well as three pretty good remixes. (A new remix of the track, by Full Intention, will be commissioned in 2003 for the "Remixes" album.) There is also a European release, although somewhat limited, with just a Maxi CD for the usual foreign territories. Some fairly interesting promo items will emerge from the "Innamoramento" period, and "L'Âme-stram-gram" starts the ball rolling with a beautiful "luxe" piece: a 1-track CD inside a gold-stamped title sleeve that is itself slipped inside a black envelope, also stamped with the song's title in gold letters. Some, but not all, copies of the envelope carried an "MF" red wax seal on the back. And also inside is a facsimile letter from Mylène herself, under the guise of the lyrics with the singer's signature at the bottom. Two other promos were also issued: the monotrack CD in its gold-stamped sleeve but without any of the above extras, and a 12" with unique sleeve design.

Mylène's new video has delighted existing fans and newcomers in equal measure, and has been much commented upon for its overall look and style: with the next single release, the following clip will attract an even greater amount of attention, but for quite different reasons...

28/ Je Te Rends Ton Amour

Which track to choose as follow-up to the lead single? As early as April, speculations begin to abound. After the adequate but not exactly overwhelming success of "L'Âme-stram-gram", many are hoping for an obviously commercial release, something that will keep the album (off to a great start, this time around) in the upper reaches of the charts for a long while yet. Initial rumours point to the track "Dessine-moi un mouton": some even go as far as saying that a clip has already been filmed, based on Antoine de Saint Exupéry's classic "Le Petit Prince", the song's obvious reference point. But this time, the rumours have got it completely wrong: there never was any such clip, and the second single will instead be "Je te rends ton amour", a choice apparently imposed by Mylène herself. The singer makes no secret of how she feels towards the song: in an interview with NRJ on 6th April '99, her response to the hypothetical (and idiotic, according to her) question "which song would you take on a desert island with you?" is quite unequivocal: in all her years in the business, "Je te r⟨

ton amour" is her favourite yet. Easily one of the singer's most complex and cryptic lyrical efforts, the song has encouraged wild speculation and endlessly diverse interpretation amongst fans: while some see in it a simple, straightforward end-of-a-love-affair story, others have suggested that the song was actually about Laurent Boutonnat, with Mylène comparing herself to a work of art, prisoner of its creator. Interestingly, one of the painters namechecked by the singer is Egon Schiele, the legendary Austrian artist, born in 1890 and dead at 28 from the Spanish flu, extremely well known for his somewhat disquieting but achingly beautiful paintings of angular, tortured-looking red-haired women: Mylène will later go on to say that she could totally see herself in these "écorchées" pieces, that looking at them was like looking into a mirror. So, who can say exactly *what* the song is about? Well, Mylène could, but she's certainly not about to do so: in a later interview in October of the same year, she admits that its precise meaning is indeed very well known to her. She adds that she does not, however, have any intention of imposing one specific meaning upon it, and would rather leave it open to individual interpretation. So it is left to the listener to try and read between the lines, and come up with their own version, make their own choice. In the end, this ambiguity only adds to the song's mystique and enduring appeal: just as she has done on numerous occasions throughout her career, the singer would rather avoid the risk of confining our imaginations by setting too-obvious markers; unsure as to the song's precise meaning, we can invent our own. Thus, apart from the clear references to Schiele and Gauguin, nothing in the song is spelled out for us, and we are free to each envision our own story, as enigmatic and uncertain as it may be.

What is more certain, however, is that "Je te rends ton amour" has a past, a surprisingly long past stretching way back before the "Innamoramento" era: as a demo, the still lyric-free composition was originally briefly considered for inclusion on the "Anamorphosée" album, before being put back in a drawer and temporarily forgotten about. In 1997, Laurent Boutonnat digs it out again and proposes the melody to the actress/singer Nathalie Cardone, who has just enjoyed a huge summer hit thanks to Laurent's reworking of the Cuban revolutionary song "Hasta Siempre": but Cardone passes on it, her own singing career burning out shortly afterwards. Finally, the composition comes Mylène's way again, and she eventually puts words to it: at last, "Je te rends ton amour" is born into its definitive incarnation. Upon its release on 8th June '99, the single enters the charts at number 10, its highest placing, before slowly but steadily heading out of the Top 100. With sales of around 100,000, the song is a modest hit for Mylène, and the second-worst selling single from the album: nevertheless, the track is generally appreciated, by fans and the greater public alike, and also enables "Innamoramento" to maintain itself in the upper regions of the charts. In the end, while it is true that a more commercial single could have been chosen as follow-up, it is undeniable that Mylène's choice was the right one: although "Je te rends ton amour" may not have been an obvious smash, its single release allowed the general public to get a taste the album's broad palette of colours and styles, thereby increasing interest and boosting sales.

And of course, while the song itself may have created but mere ripples on the radio and in the clubs, its impact on the small screen was about to make a much bigger splash...

A blind Mylène, resplendent in a long red dress and clutching her braille Bible, makes her way to confession in a nearby church. As she enters the confessional box, however, the fingers of the "priest", smoking as they come into contact with the holy water, presage nothing good: further weird goings-on inside the church only serve to reinforce the unsettling mood, with statues crashing to the ground, chairs tilting back in an eerie, unnatural fashion and the dancing light casting menacing shadows over a crucified Christ. Some evil presence appears to have taken over this holy place...And indeed, the priest, far from being a pious man of the cloth, is in fact the Devil himself: as she begins to bleed inexplicably, the blind woman is suddenly attacked from the other side of the wooden partition, and then promptly violated by the Dark Lord and submitted to some unholy, bloody ritual that culminates in her own gruesome crucifixion. Yet her eventual demeanour seems to indicate that she has now become a willing servant of darkness, or has been seduced in some way, as the naked woman abandons herself to the man's lustful touch and then goes on to swim around in a pool of her own blood, before leaving the church newly dressed all in black. A final shot of a gold wedding ring -a sign of eternal alliance before God- being abandoned to the pooling blood further reinforces the idea of a pact with God being broken, as if the woman had switched sides in the wake of her fateful encounter. The "Je te rends ton amour" video, shot in May '99 over two days at the Abbaye du Val in Mériel, in the Oise region near Paris, has become one of the ultimate classics of the singer's videography, for obvious gory reasons. Any fans worried that the singer may have lost her taste for provocation are quickly reassured by the graphic images on display! Directed by François Hanss from a scenario written by Mylène herself, the clip immediately becomes a huge fan favourite after its first TV showing. Although actually getting to see the video on television, of course, quickly becomes a little complicated: sex, blood, and especially religion...playing with those is still taboo. Mixing them up is even worse! What happens next doesn't really come as a huge surprise: as well as inspiring dozens of breathless "le clip scandale!" articles in the press, the video immediately attracts the full attention of the CSA, the French regulatory organisation concerned with the promotion of moral values and good standards on TV and in the media: while they stop short of imposing an outright ban, the CSA, after consulting with a mothers' committee, do issue strong reservations about the clip's content to the various TV channels. M6, the leading music channel at the time, decides to simply amputate the last two minutes of the video: other stations follow suit, and the clip is shown in its entirety only late at night, if at all. Effectively censored, Mylène, who of course does not take such things lying down, responds by promptly putting out on the market a VHS tape proudly bearing the legend "Le clip censuré", in a package that also includes a picture booklet featuring exclusive images from the video shoot. Available mostly at newsagents' kiosks, the 70,000 copies that are manufactured swiftly sell out, with all profits being donated to the HIV/AIDS organisation Sidaction. A neat gesture that allows Mylène to do something substantial for a good cause while at the same time making the censors look slightly ridiculous, without her having to say a single word or justify herself in any way on the subject of that so-called "scandalous" video. Later on, however, she will briefly comment on the matter during an interview, although not in any kind of an apologetic way: rather, she will simply state that she does indeed have a predilection for thorny, even taboo subjects, and go on to conclude that the levels of censorship in France may be a little excessive...

Mylène makes two TV appearances (she is of course still welcome on the small screen, even if her video is not so much) in order to promote the single, on both occasions wearing the same red dress as worn in the clip. On 19th July, in "La Fureur du Parc des Princes" on TF1, she performs "live", or at least under live conditions as playback is used for her appearance: nothing surprising about that, this way of doing things being the inflexible rule by now for Mylène. It is her second TV prestation, on "50 ans de tubes" on the 30th of July, also on TF1, that is really noteworthy: looking like more of a clip than a simple performance on a TV set, the scenarised prestation is hugely reminiscent of the video, with artful edits, lingering close-up shots and ominous lighting effects: although she will forego the naked bloody bath on this occasion, this is easily one of the singer's most sophisticated television appearances. On stage, "Je te rends ton amour" is first performed during the Mylènium Tour concerts: Mylène often ends the song on an acapella chorus from the audience, but sadly this will not be kept for the CD or DVD versions of the live release. Initially included in the 2006 Bercy concerts setlist, the song makes it as far as rehearsals before being abandoned altogether, giving the "Innamoramento" album no representation at all that year. Three years later, the song is back for the 2009 Tour, although only for the indoor concerts: it will disappear for the Stadium dates, the addition of "L'Instant X" and "Fuck them all" creating a need for some setlist re-jigging.

The release of the single "Je te rends ton amour" will be an opportunity for Henry Neu to come up with some of the most striking pieces he has yet created for the needs of the singer's discography. On the commercial side, a 2-track CD and Maxi CD in digipack sleeve are issued: to the fans' delight, both contain the brand new song "Effets Secondaires", a dreamy, hallucinatory composition that alludes to pornography and an altered state of mind (amongst other things), and also somehow manages to namecheck Nightmare on Elm Street's Freddy Krueger before abruptly ending on a rather startling wake-up alarm. On the Maxi CD and vinyl versions, Laurent Boutonnat has once again handed remixing duties over to Perky Park, who deliver fairly solid club and dub versions. A 12" is also available, as well as a limited edition picture disc, still only the third such format to be edited in the course of Mylène's career, after "Plus Grandir live" and the astronomically-priced, frankly impossible to find "Beyond my control" NRJ-competition prize only edition promotional 12". Showing a beautiful Marino Parisotto Vay shot of Mylène in a crucifixion pose on both sides, with a different-coloured dress on each, the item is now a favourite amongst collectors. Three promotional items, including a much sought-after rarity, can also be searched for by Farmer completists: in addition to the standard monotrack CD (in a unique titles sleeve) and 3-track 12" (quasi-identical to the commercial issue, save for the limited edition/not for sale mentions), Henry Neu and his society COM'N.B deliver one of the most unique promos ever manufactured for Mylène: a cruciform 1-track CD that rests inside a stamped red velvet sleeve, itself slipped inside a tracing-paper envelope adorned with red titles and held shut by a red wax "MF" seal. Extremely rare and very hard to come by, the item has been known to sell for several hundred Euros in specialist shops catering to collectors, and is one of the most coveted pieces around.

"Je te rends ton amour" may not have been as huge a hit as some of the singer's previous singles, but the song has nevertheless made a strong impression, thanks in no small part to its visually arresting video and the accompanying scandal around it (clearly, nothing less than great publicity for the singer and her album, and at no cost or extra promotional effort to her): as a result, "Innamoramento" is flying high, and Mylène's star is brighter than ever: time to bring on the third single.

29/ Souviens-Toi Du Jour

By the time August comes around, the rumour mill has gone into overdrive once more as fans try to guess what the third single to be taken from the "Innamoramento" album will be. Some are still backing "Dessine-moi un mouton", a bit of a fan favourite, and one hoped for with every new single release: they will still have to wait a few months for that one, however. Another rumour, strangely persistent and yet demonstrably without any foundation, says that the next chosen single release is "Et si vieillir m'était conté". Not only that, but according to whispers the promos for this one have already been manufactured! Yet this was clearly not the case: in the bonus section of the Mylènium Tour DVD, Mylène can be seen working on the "Souviens-toi du jour" supports, as early as July...Radios finally receive the promo CD at the very end of August; off to a good start from the word go, the song will go on to benefit from sustained frequent airplay, and over quite a lengthy period of time too: in fact, "Souviens-toi du jour" doesn't achieve its top airplay placing until the end of December, four months after its initial radio début. Some radio stations, NRJ amongst them, have by then ditched the radio edit in favour of the more laid-back "Sweet guitar mix", thereby giving the track a new lease of life. The single itself, when it is released on 28th September 1999 (making it Mylène's final single of the 90's, of the 20th century, and of the millenium!), goes straight in at number 4. This will remain its highest position (and its one solitary week in the Top 10), as thereafter it begins its inexorable slide down the charts, but overall the single will do quite well, selling somewhere in the region of 150,000 copies, enough for another silver certification. Another hit for Mylène, and a good way also to mark the beginning of the Mylènium Tour, which was launched just a week earlier in the southern city of Marseille, on the 21st.

Like "Désenchantée" before it, "Souviens-toi du jour" is one of those Mylène songs whose upbeat rhythm and catchy melody contrast with its serious, even dark, lyrical subject matter. Strongly referencing Primo Levi's book "Si c'est un homme", the song is an evocation of the Holocaust, although with a sense of hope and optimism that is most definitely not present within Levi's book: this in itself should come as no surprise, given that the tome is a harrowing account of life, and mostly death, in the hell on earth that were concentration camps. One of Mylène's bedside reads, she decides to pay her own homage to Levi's work, asking us to remember days past while still keeping an optimistic eye on the future, believing in the redemptive powers of the human race. (At the same time, sending a quick nod to one of her earlier songs, when she asks the listener to remember the "jours désenchantés".) On the back of the single, printed in the Hebrew alphabet, are the words uttered by the singer towards the latter part of the song: "Zokher Eth Ayom", or "Souviens-toi du jour". The song's somber subject matter will, indeed, cause a few eyebrows to be raised when the accompanying video makes its debut, with some premature and somewhat knee-jerk criticism being levelled at the singer.

Shot in '99 in Los Angeles, "Souviens-toi du jour" is Marcus Niespel's fourth video for the singer, and also, to date, his last. The clip is first shown on French TV from 25th September onwards, initially getting a mixed reception from fans: while the images are undeniably aesthetically superb, Mylène's ultra-glam look is, in the first place, a bit too much for some, who feel that they struggle to recognize their favourite singer from under such heavy make-up. But more seriously, others even go on to say that Mylène's appearance, and the somewhat lascivious poses she goes on to strike at various points in the video, have nothing in common with, and even make light of, the song's subject matter. It is true that on first look, the "Souviens-toi du jour" video comes across as little more than Mylène at her sexiest, parading around a hotel as it is being consumed by flames; and yet, as is the case with so many others in her videography, there is much more to the clip than meets the eye. The most obvious theme, running through the entire film, is the destruction of symbols of human endeavours, such as letters (some, we can see, addressed to Mylène herself) and books through fire: fire, in this instance, symbolizing the ultimate evil, an all-consuming force whose aim is to eradicate all traces of a persecuted section of humanity. A hotel, an archetypal place of human habitation, its rooms being cleansed of all traces of its former inhabitants through an all-engulfing, raging fire. This allegorical approach to illustrating the song is consistent with the singer's legendary discretion and sensitivity: those complaining that the video had nothing to do with the track could surely not be expecting anything as crass and inappropriate as a clip set in an actual concentration camp to illustrate a Holocaust-referencing song. As for Mylène's appearance and demeanour, also at times condemned as being slightly inappropriate, it is worth remembering the overall feeling of hope and optimism that pervades through the song itself: the ultra-sexy Mylène walking from room to burning room, occasionally lying back suggestively in a chair, stands for more than just one woman, representing instead the whole of humanity, defiantly vibrant, beautiful, and sexual too, even in the face of the overpowering forces that would seek to destroy it. The final shot brings the point home quite strongly: the flames have finally burnt themselves out, leaving behind nothing but totally ravaged surroundings. And yet, in the centre of it all, crouched in the foetal position as if ready to be reborn, life endures...

The white, almost see-through dress that Mylène wears in the video was designed by Thierry Mugler, and had made an earlier appearance in September 1997, when it was worn by the singer for a prestation on the show "Les enfants de la Une". Almost crystal-like in appearance, the garment was actually made out of plastic, causing some unexpected problems on set: amidst the rising temperatures brought on by the fire, the singer sees her outfit slowly beginning to melt right off her back...luckily, a back-up is at hand, saving Mylène from unnecessary embarrassment. The firemen present on the set as a precautionary measure will not have to jump into action after all (to their possible disappointment.) Also present on set is the photographer Claude Gassian, who takes a number of pictures of the star: unfortunately, none of these appear to have been approved by Mylène in the end, as they have never surfaced anywhere as of yet.

Mylène will appear on TV twice in order to promote the single: first on "Tapis Rouge" on France 2, on 11th September '99; then almost exactly two months later, on 12th November, in the "100% Johnny" special on TF1. (Speaking of Johnny, yet another rumour stated that an early demo of the song, composed years before its actual release, had originally been intended to become a duet between Mylène and a French male singer, supposedly Johnny Halliday himself.) On the stage, "Souviens-toi du jour" has so far only ever been performed during the Mylènium Tour: most nights, before Mylène walks off stage right before coming back for the two encores, she ends the song with a simple "Je vous aime, bonsoir...". But on the very last French date of the tour at the Zénith d'Orléans, however, she gives everyone present a bit of a fright: instead of the usual words, she takes her farewell with a chilling "Au revoir...ou adieu." Understandably, fans in the audience can't help but wonder what was meant by this: is the singer saying goodbye for good? Is she retiring? We clearly know now that this wasn't the case: rather, it is now plain to see that the disquieting farewell was nothing more (and nothing less) than a touching expression of Mylène's own sense of uncertainty. Just as fans inevitably wonder, when the curtain falls on the last date of a tour, whether Mylène will ever come back to the stage, so must she...

The remixes for "Souviens-toi du jour" come courtesy of Stray Dog and Royal Garden Sound, ranging from laidback grooves (the "Sweet Guitar" mix, favoured by radios) to more dance-floor orientated arrangements

("Remember mix"). A 2-track single featuring the Royal G radio mix is available, as well as a digipack Maxi CD featuring the remixes. A slight printing error with the vinyl release will mean that some very few copies will inadvertently become even more of a collectors' item: the very first few copies released for sale were stamped with the mention "limited edition/not for sale", when they were clearly destined for the shops, and not promotional items in any way. These will be fairly quickly withdrawn, even after a black sticker has been plastered over the offending mentions, and have thus become unintentional rarities: so, if you own a copy of the 12" single, and notice a black sticker on the back of the sleeve, in the bottom right-hand corner, you're in luck...The promo editions of the single are all fairly attractive items, thanks to their ingenious and unique sleeve design: broadly similar to the commercial release artwork, apart from the fact that Mylène has magically morphed into a candle, with her flowing red hair representing the flame. As well as a monotrack CD and 12", collectors can also hunt after the deluxe edition, a great package and one of the nicest promos of the era: a copy of the 1-track CD inside a larger envelope with "flames" design, stamped with the song's title and sealed with a black "MF" wax seal. Inside of the flame-coloured envelope is also a smaller, grey envelope, also stamped with the words "Souviens-toi du jour": inside are seven translucent pebbles made of plastic. The seven "stones" are a reference to the Jewish faith: in Judaism, it is a custom to leave seven stones on the coffin or grave of the deceased, the stones being seen as a symbol of the strong, eternal link with the departed. There are no foreign editions of this particular single, its release having been limited to France only.

"Souviens-toi du jour" has been yet another hit for the singer, and her final offering of the last century: for her first Millenial (or should that be "Mylènial"?) release, in the early part of the year 2000, she is going to treat herself to a little something extra special: for the first time ever, a single that is 100% pure Farmer is going to see the light of day.

30/ Optimistique-Moi

When it is finally announced that "Optimistique-Moi" will become the album's fourth single, fans are generally pleased: it may still not be "Dessine-moi un mouton", but the song is nevertheless a fan favourite, and potentially one of the strongest tracks off the album; some had even been hoping to see it released immediately after the lead single "L'Âme-stram-gram". One of the main reasons for the fans' enthusiasm, of course, is the fact that "Optimistique-Moi" is one of five songs on the album to be not only written but also composed by Mylène herself: after a tentative first effort on "Anamorphosée", with the rock-flavoured number "Tomber 7 Fois", the singer has outdone herself and taken on Laurent Boutonnat's role as composer for more than a third of her latest album, with surprisingly solid results. This is also the very first time that a 100% Farmer composition is being put forward as a single: a chance for Mylène to begin the new Millenium in style. And for this, already her thirtieth single, the singer has no intention of doing things by halves: "Optimistique-Moi" is going to benefit from a treatment that could, perhaps, be described as preferential. Of course, in view of her already enormous accomplishments, Mylène, by now, has more than earned the right to indulge herself if she wants to, and no-one is going to begrudge her the few extra perks the new release will enjoy. The single itself is out in shops on the 22nd of February 2000. From the 23rd onwards, 30-second ads featuring images from the clip are shown on M6, the first time in Mylène's career that a single has enjoyed such a privilege and extra promotional push. On the 7th of March, a second Maxi CD hits the shops, featuring new remixes: also a first, and something that will not be repeated for over nine years, not until "C'est dans l'air" comes around in 2009. Also, in a move that has so far remained a totally unique event in her discography, the singer, through her production company Stuffed Monkey, collaborates with the legendary DJ Roger Sanchez in order to produce a promotional 12" specifically intended for American DJ's. Generally speaking, commercial and promotional supports for the song will also be fairly plentiful. Mylène also doesn't stint on her own promotional efforts for "Optimistique-Moi": no less than four TV prestations, a fairly high number at this stage of her career, certainly the most for any of the tracks taken off the album, and also the last time she will make this many television appearances for the needs of a single's promotion. There will be three prestations on various shows in March alone, preceded by the legendary appearance at the NRJ Music Awards on the 22nd of January. During this event (the first-ever edition of the Awards), Mylène picks up no less than three trophies (for best album, best concert and best female artist). She also performs "Optimistique-Moi", now revealed to be the next single, accompanied by six of her dancers, in a prestation that is almost similar to that of her Mylènium Tour performance. In the end, it is really on the stage that the song will receive only minimal representation: Mylène's performance of the track while wearing the famous metal "bum-cage" contraption remains its only live appearance to date.

From the very start, "Optimistique-Moi" puts in a strong performance. Radio play begins from January 11th, which is slightly later than was originally planned: the initial 4th of January radio premiere is delayed after a large batch of promo CDs are stolen, just as they were about to be sent to the various stations. After a new pressing is hurriedly issued, radio rotations can finally begin and are overall pretty good for the song, which goes on to reach 18th place in the airplay chart. Although they usually stick to the single version, some radio stations such as Europe 2 decide to go with the "opti-mystic" radio mix. After its initial release on 22nd February, the single enters the charts at number 7, then drops down to number 18, only to climb back up to 7th place the following week: a classic demonstration of the "Farmer effect", as fans rush to buy the newly-available second Maxi CD, sending the single flying back up the charts. With total sales of over 150,000, "Optimistique-Moi" is yet another silver single certification for Mylène. But not only is the song a success on the radio and in stores, it is also quite the hit on a saturday night, reaching the top 5 of most-played tracks in French clubs around that period. It also helps the album to maintain its position in the charts: and by the time the "Optimistique-Moi" exploitation period comes to an end, "Innamoramento" has reached the million sales mark, making it the singer's fourth consecutive million-selling studio album: another record. The single will get one more taste of the spotlight in 2003, when it is remixed once again by Junior Jack for the "Remixes" compilation.

Of all the Mylène Farmer songs, "Optimistique-Moi" must be one of those whose lyrics have been the most dissected and pored over by fans. Not surprising, given that the text is probably one of the singer's most obscure, and definitely one of the most ambiguous. To begin with, the meaning of the song's title itself is not immediately obvious. Although the word "optimistic" can be found in the English language, it is certainly not found in any French dictionary; once again, Mylène comes up with one of her unique neologisms, creating a brand new word when existing ones just aren't enough. Thus, using her brand new verb, the singer can finally get her message across. And that message is, well, as mentioned earlier, fairly ambiguous. The song is often seen as dealing with the thorny theme of incest: which is fair enough, indeed, as Mylène goes as far as (almost) saying the word, if only phonetically, when she sings "qu'aussitôt tes cal*ins cessent t*outes écchymoses". Not only that, but some of the chorus lyrics are arresting, to say the least, especially for a song that repeatedly mentions a "papa": "petit bouton de rose, aux pétales humides un baiser je dépose", or "little rosebud, on the damp petals a kiss I plant": on first listen, even the most casual of listeners couldn't fail but to think "did I just hear what I think I did?" Of course, in many cases, the first reaction -perhaps a natural one- is to assume that the lyric is autobiographical. Almost tempting, when we have been enthralled for so long by the singer's self-declared almost-forgotten childhood, these "blank pages", that mysterious "trouble" deep inside her of which only she knows. But such an assumption would of course be highly risky, and more likely than not, completely wrong. In the first place, it is important to keep in mind that the incestuous situation as depicted in the song is most probably no more than the expression of an artist's uninhibited imagination: in the past, the singer has made no secret of her taste for the kind of subject matter that is usually swept under the carpet. Her work alone is proof of that. The theory several different sources have put forward on the subject is that the song is a chance for Mylène to symbolically stage her very own "Oedipal complex", the famous subconscious incestuous fantasy as put forward by Freud. What's more, given Mylène's self-confessed predilection for provocation, it is almost tempting to put oneself inside her head and imagine her wicked delight as she wrote her lyrics, gleefully anticipating the eventual reaction: because, of course, she knew exactly what she was doing, and the effect the words would have. But that, of course, is Mylène Farmer in a nutshell, and one of the reasons she is so loved today.

To set images to "Optimistique-Moi", Mylène calls on the services of Michael Haussman, a talented American producer/director and screenwriter who has previously created two clips for Madonna, "Take a bow" in 1994 and "You'll see" in '95. Mylène is dropped into a circus universe, playing the part of a tightrope walker with decidedly unsupportive work colleagues: as she makes her uncertain way along the rope, clowns, fire-swallowers and trapeze artists all attempt to destabilize her. Dodging their assaults from above and from below, Mylène manages to keep from falling, but is soon faced with another trial anyway: she must now balance herself and stay atop a big circus ball, something she manages to do until a knife-thrower literally bursts her bubble, sending her crashing to the ground. Mylène appears to temporarily lose her head over the incident, but a kind-looking young magician then invites her to step inside a cushioned box, which he proceeds to close and then pierce with swords as the gawping clowns theatrically flinch in mock horror. The swords are pulled out again, the box falls open: birds fly out, but Mylène is gone! And suddenly here she is, arms raised up to the sky on the back of a moving truck, smiling and free, before images cut back to the circus, where the young magician is suddenly revealed to actually be a greying old man, with the same kind look on his face: a father figure who protected her from harm and set her free. Shot over three days in early February in Prague, the clip gets its first TV showing on the 21st, immediately enchanting fans with its quirky atmosphere, more-beautiful-than-ever Mylène and superb aesthetic. Later on in the year, on 17th November, the M6 Music Awards acknowledge the clip's quality with a best video trophy for the singer, further cementing the song's success. Unbelievably, and somewhat comically, the clip almost came to be censored, and for the most unexpected of reasons: the scenes where Mylène stands in the back of a moving truck were, apparently, deemed to be a violation of highway code regulations... Luckily, common sense prevailed, and the uncut video was allowed to be shown with no restrictions.

Once again, it is easy to see the extent of the promotional drive behind "Optimistique-Moi" when looking at the variety of supports the single occasioned. While commercial releases totalled four, no less than six different promos were issued altogether! The initial 22nd February release date sees two supports hitting stores: a 2-track CD and the first digipack Maxi CD. On

7th March, two further additions are available: a 12"
and digipack Maxi CD number 2, featuring the Sanchez
remixes: the staggered release allows "Optimistique-
Moi" to shoot straight back up into the Top 10 the
following week, a clever marketing ploy that ensures
prolonged chart longevity. For the promo completists,
the time has come to dig deep, as no less than three
different versions of the promotional CD are issued. First
is a monotrack item in white "lips" sleeve, featuring the
radio edit; another 1-track CD, this time featuring the
"opti-mystic radio mix", is issued in a similar "lips"
sleeve but with a black background; and finally comes
the "deluxe" promo, a not exactly environmentally-
friendly but absolutely gorgeous, must-have item: the 1-
track CD, featuring the radio edit, mounted on a 12"
cardboard support adorned with a picture of a stunning,
extreme close-up of the star, slipped inside a "lips" sleeve
that is itself slipped inside a white envelope, stamped
with the words "Optimistique-Moi", and to the front of
which are attached three (artificial) rose petals. To top it
off, the envelope is sealed with another one of those
ultra-cute red wax "MF" seals. That is all for the CDs,
but three different vinyl promos must also be found for
any self-respecting obsessive collector: vinyl number 1
comes in a die-cut "eyes" sleeve, while the second has the
"lips" sleeve on a white background and features the
Sanchez remixes. As for the third and last item, it is a
unique piece in the Farmer discography: originally
intended as a promo to be sent out to DJ's in the States,
the record ended up being sold in some of the larger
French record store chains, giving it the rare distinction
of being at once a promo and commercial release. While
Mylène's name or picture are not featured anywhere on

the sleeve or label, a large sticker on the sleeve, under the heading "Covert Ops. Vol 1", features the initials M.F. in large red letters above the DJ's name and the "Optimystique" title. The record is distributed not by Polydor, but through a small independent New York label.A great, unusual piece, and (relatively) not too pricey.

"Optimistique-Moi" has been yet another hit for Mylène, and one that was no doubt gratifying on a further, personal level also, as the self-penned tune allowed the singer to display yet another facet to her talents: Mylène Farmer, songwriter. Not only that, but the single has enabled the album to reach the symbolic million mark. Four singles in, there is life yet in the "Innamoramento" opus, and it still has more to give: not least, the title track.

31/ Innamoramento

After four singles and more than a year of hugely successful exploitation, the "Innamoramento" album has easily passed the million sales mark. It is almost time to move on to the next project, but for now there is still time to release one fifth and final single, the title track, the song that gave the album its name and overall theme. The lyrics to "Innamoramento" reference the essay by Francesco Alberoni, "Le choc amoureux", published in 1979. A few words taken from it introduce the album booklet: "The burgeoning love, the Italian "Innamoramento". The spark in the daily grey. Happiness mixed with worry because we don't know whether the feeling is shared. A transitory state that sometimes leads to love. A phenomenon comparable to collective revolutionary movements." As such, the song sounds like nothing less than a call to love: or as expressed by the singer, the hope to, at last, find an echo...The track is sent out to radios on the 25th of May: airplay, however, will be less intensive than for any of the previous singles. After being postponed a couple of times (it had originally been scheduled for a June 27th release), the single finally comes out on 18th July. It enters the charts at number 3, a great performance although it quickly heads south thereafter, selling a relatively low 90,000 copies, which makes it the album's worst-selling single. Nevertheless, "Innamoramento" the single does enable its parent album to make a re-entry in the Top 75 album charts, after a temporary exit at the end of April: indeed, the album even climbs back up as high as 21st place, thanks to both the single and a new TV ad campaign from mid-July onwards.

For the video, Mylène renews with a tradition not seen since the days of "Allan live": a clip that is half live performance, half new footage. Directed by François Hanss, the video contains footage shot in September 1999 (for the live section) and June 2000 for the outdoor scenes. These show a sublime-looking Mylène at her luminous and natural best, dressed all in white as she moves through an idyllic, sun-drenched nature setting. (A forest in the l'Oise region of France, near Paris.) As she lays on the impossibly bright green grass, the sound of many voices calling out her name reaches her ears, causing her to stir and awaken: the clip thus enables a neat transition between the studio album and the forthcoming live Mylènium Tour release. Shown on TV from the 12th of July onwards, the clip is appreciated by fans and the general public alike, although once again it does not generate interest on a level with the singer's recent offerings. It does, however, give the public an opportunity to see the first images from the Mylènium Tour concerts.

The commercial supports are illustrated with a Claude Gassian photograph, part of a series taken in Prague around the time of the "Optimistique-Moi" video shoot. For completist fans, the 2-track CD single that is made available presents something of a headache: two slightly different versions exist, one with a white label disc, the other, slightly rarer, with a picture disc label. However, there is nothing on the outer sleeve to indicate which is which! As CD singles are most usually sold still sealed, getting hold of the picture disc edition is somewhat tantamount to a game of pot luck: unwrap it, and see what you get...the digipack Maxi CD and 12" both contain the single version and three remixes, ranging from the "R&B lite" flavour of the "anamor remix" to the unashamedly europop stylings of the "momento dance remix", not forgetting the slightly darker, aptly-named "darkness remix". On the promotional side, a 1-track CD in unique "hand" sleeve contains the radio edit, although some very rare copies somehow feature 14 tracks of music totally unrelated to Mylène, the whole of CD 2 of a "Buddha Bar" dance compilation! The deluxe version is an unusual and rare item, hard to find in good condition nowadays because of its inherent fragility: an "Innamoramento" cardboard cube, 20cm to a side, each side featuring a different fragment of the word and a picture of Mylène, with the monotrack CD stuck on one side. Not an item to inadvertently sit on. The final promo is a 12" in a die-cut sleeve with totally unique design: an interesting feature of this item is that, unlike any other promos, this one does not have a single feature on it (other than the alternative sleeve art) that can identify it as such: no promotional mentions on the sleeve or label whatsoever. I was lucky enough to once find a copy in a small record shop in northern France, and it was clear from the price tag that the seller believed it to be a regular commercial issue. A more honest man than I would have pointed out the mistake, but...hey, a bargain is a bargain.

And thus the "Innamoramento" era comes to an end. None of the singles, or even the album itself, have made it to number 1, and yet it is impossible to label "Innamoramento" as anything other than a further triumph for Mylène, both in France and abroad, where close to 200,000 copies have also been sold. In France, the album is the year's fourth best-seller, even holding on to 36th place the following year! Mylène's position as the uncontested leader in her field is even further consolidated as a result, and she can also add another diamond certification to her already quite full trophy cabinet. Once again, the album's success has seen a multitude of editions: in addition to the French supports, "Innamoramento" is also issued in Europe, Canada, Taiwan, Russia, and Japan, where buyers also get a bonus track, the "Perky park pique dames club mix" of "L'Âme-stram-gram". And while none of the singles taken from the album can truly be said to have been huge mega-hits at the time of their original release, the passing years will nevertheless go on to confer classic status onto tracks such as "Je te rends ton amour" or "L'Âme-stram-gram". There are no particularly exciting promotional editions of the album, but the collectors' box-set is probably amongst one of the best ever created throughout Mylène's career: the "carnet de voyage de Mylène Farmer" consists of a deluxe, "extended" edition of the booklet, with additional art and photographs (including a cute Laurent Boutonnat picture of E.T., Mylène's pet monkey), inside a hard-back spiral-bound 22x22cm book that is itself kept inside a plastic maroon outer sleeve with picture label. Some of the song lyrics are printed on translucent paper, or even presented on loose sheets inside envelopes stuck to the inner pages, with one envelope holding a totally unique shot of Mylène on top of her cage, in a pose slightly different to that of the album cover. This is quite simply a stunning item, and pretty scarce too as it was limited to just 3,000 copies: now pretty hard to find, especially in good condition, it usually comes with an outrageously inflated price tag.

On a sadder note, the release of "Innamoramento" will also coincide with the end of the road for a legendary name in the Farmer story: on Easter Sunday 1999, a mere few days after the album has come out, Bertrand Le Page, by now very sick and no doubt in a very dark place, commits suicide with a bullet to the brain. According to those who were his friends in his final hours, Bertrand was listening to the new album non-stop in the days leading up to his death. As a mark of respect, the album promotion is suspended for a few days, and an interview with RTL radio planned for the same day is cancelled. Whatever his past failings, Bertrand had undeniably played an instrumental part in the rise of Mylène Farmer from young hopeful to pop icon: as such, his name will forever remain a key part of the Farmer story, which may very well have turned out differently without him on board in those heady 80's days.

Six years: that's how long fans will have to wait between "Innamoramento" and the next studio album. Not an easy wait...but at least other projects will come and help sweeten the pill. First of those will be Mylène's third live release, the majestic, mystical "Mylènium Tour".

32/ Dessine-Moi Un Mouton (live)

At last, the track felt by many fans to be one of the most obvious hits on the "Innamoramento" album is released as a single! A choice that had been hoped for with every successive single release, even inviting crazy rumours to fly around in May '99, before the second single had even been announced: according to the whispers then, a clip had been shot for "Dessine-moi un mouton", featuring a crashed plane and Mylène amongst a herd of sheep...when Mylène was, in fact, shooting the "Je te rends ton amour" video. But never mind, the time for "Dessine-moi un mouton" has come at last, and it is finally being released as a single...well, sort of. As the first track to be taken from the Mylènium Tour album, the live status of the song kind of puts a dampener on things: with no radio edit version, and no proper video to speak of, its potential as a single is inevitably lessened: what's more, live releases don't usually tend to turn into big hits anymore...The promos are sent out to radio around the 27th of October: for a live track, the song gets a relatively good amount of airplay, although some stations, such as NRJ, quickly opt for the "World is mine" remix instead. Released on the same day as the album, on 5th December (with a special late-night launch event at the Champs-Élysées Fnac and Virgin Megastore the night before), "Dessine-moi un mouton" makes an initial good showing, entering the charts at number 6. It doesn't hang around for very long after that, however, and quickly heads out of the Top 100, selling around 80,000 copies in total. It is not quite the hit fans could have hoped for, but at least the song serves as a good introduction for the album: the video, a straightforward excerpt from the concert, is fun and energetic, with Mylène clearly having a good time on her swing as her dancers play hopscotch (known as "saute-mouton", in French) around her. Clearly, given the song's thematics, the live prestation was never going to be anything other than playful and dynamic: "Dessine-moi un mouton" is one of those Mylène songs in which childhood plays a huge part, with the singer urging us to "turn back into the child we once were" in order to deal with a morose adult world. Without mentioning it directly, the song fairly obviously references the classic "Le petit prince" by Antoine de Saint-Exupéry: the book's influence will also be felt on the single's sleeve artwork. For the very first time, Mylène makes use of some of her own drawings on some of the supports, with some of her characters going on to enjoy further later adventures: the bouncing, slightly stoned-looking sheep can be seen again in 2002, in the animated "C'est une belle journée" video.

"Dessine-moi un mouton" is available in stores as a 2-track CD, and as a digipack Maxi CD and 12", both featuring the live version and remixes: the remixes, while not being Mylène's best, are nevertheless fairly interesting, and a tantalizing glimpse of what could have been, had the song enjoyed a bona fide single release. The promos are all quite desirable as they all feature exclusive artwork: the 1-track CD comes in a cartoony black and white "sheep astride the world" sleeve, and the 12", with its die-cut, deep purple sleeve, is markedly different from the commercial release. It is the deluxe promo, however, that is of most interest: the monotrack CD is mounted on a 30x30cm cardboard support that folds open to reveal a small picture of Mylène on her swing. The photograph is hanging from the cardboard support, held up by two metallic chains, and the whole thing is slipped inside a gorgeous gold sleeve stamped with large "MF" initials: this "3D" promo is one of the most sought after by collectors.

With not a single TV prestation, and no further live performances to date beyond the Mylènium Tour, this was pretty much the end of the road for "Dessine-moi un mouton". Uniquely for a live Mylène album so far, this will be its one and only single release, even if the solo version of "Regrets" came very close to acting as second: a promo VHS will even be manufactured, but a slight disagreement between Mylène and her record company over the choice of follow-up (she wants "Pas le temps de vivre", they want "Regrets") will end in a stalemate, with no second live single coming out at all. Boo.

Second single or not, the Mylènium Tour album is a big success regardless: indeed, it is the first of Mylène's live albums to reach the top spot in the charts, even if overall sales are inferior to those of "Live à Bercy" and its almost-million. Still, with over 600,000 copies of the album sold, it earns itself a double platinum certification, on top of the 350,000 copies the DVD and VHS will also manage to shift: hardly a failure. Also taken to Russia, the Mylènium Tour setlist will undergo a couple of minor changes for the occasion, with "Que mon coeur lâche" and "Je t'aime mélancolie" being added exclusively for these foreign dates. The Mylènium Tour is also an opportunity for the singer to make one of her most breath-taking entrances, emerging from the splitting head of the huge statue of the goddess Isis that served as stage set; magically suspended in the air, Mylène slowly descends and lands in the statue's outstretched hand as the adoring crowds look on in stunned amazement. Her exit is similarly themed, as Mylène once more curls up inside the huge hand that slowly rises up as the end music plays on, until only a dim light remains: one of the singer's most astounding stage entrance/exit combos, although she will manage to top even that in future. Collection-wise, the Mylènium Tour album will engender two pieces that can aptly be described as collectors' items: and while one of those is fairly easy to get a hold of, the other is so rare and expensive it will remain no more than a dream for all but the luckiest Farmer enthusiasts. The first, fairly common item is a limited edition of the album, sold in shops and presented inside a silk-imitation box that contains the double CD in a gold-coloured metallic case as well as a booklet with eight extra photographs. As it was limited to "just" 30,000 copies, this item can still be found at fairly reasonable prices. The second item, on the other hand...limited to only 200 and sent out to the star's friends and close associates as well as a few fortunate media recipients, this is one of the ultimate rarities in the Mylène Farmer discography: an exact plaster replica of the Isis statue as seen on stage. The only difference is the scale: Mylène would probably struggle to come out of *this* statue's head as the item is just 27cm high, and 30cm across. Bearing one CD in each hand, the sculpture also comes with a copy of the DVD, inside a plain white box with no identifying markings, and was delivered by a courier wearing an Egyptian costume. This numbered item rarely comes up for sale nowadays, but when it does it is never for less than astronomical sums, especially if it is still in one piece: sometimes, over the years, the statue will weaken and a hand will drop off. A distressing prospect...

As the Mylènium Tour album exploitation period draws to a close, forever turning the page on the legendary "Innamoramento" era, it is almost time for the singer to reflect and take stock. But before that, there is still time for one little gem of a single...

33/ L'Histoire D'Une Fée, C'Est...

It has long been rumoured that "L'Histoire d'une fée, c'est..." came about as a direct request from Madonna herself for Mylène to be one of the artists featured on the 2001 animated movie "Rugrats in Paris" soundtrack. This has never been officially confirmed (or denied, either), but it is easy to see how such a rumour would have come to be, as the soundtrack was produced by none other than Maverick, the American icon's production company. And after all the endless Mylène/Madonna comparisons, who could blame the fans for being easily given to imagining this frankly cool scenario? It is kind of tempting to picture Madonna, dressed in her sharpest businesswoman outfit, hunched over a desk and bellowing "Get me Mylène Farmer!" down the phone. But aside from wildly imaginative speculation, what is more certain is that following an initial meeting with George Acogny, responsible for putting together the soundtrack, Mylène agrees to take part. It is her first foray into the world of animation, a world that is clearly attractive to her: in addition to her own output in the drawing medium, via the "Dessine-moi un mouton" sleeve artwork or the book "Lisa-loup et le conteur" in 2003, there will be more animated dalliances in future, from the "C'est une belle journée" video in 2002, or "Peut-être toi" in 2006, to the Princess Sélénia role in the Luc Besson "Arthur" trilogy. A role seemingly created especially for the singer, as the computer-generated Sélénia bears an unlikely physical resemblance to Mylène herself. (Yet another Madonna connection here, as it is the American superstar herself who lends her voice to the English-language incarnation of the pointy-eared princess.)

For the needs of the "Rugrats" movie, Mylène comes up with a playful lyric, one that is only just a little bit naughty (the song's title barely concealing the word "fessée", or spanking), but that still manages to be appropriate for what is primarily a kid's cartoon: in fact, the song's fairytale feel and references to childhood make it a surprisingly fitting companion to the film, and this without having to reference it in any way. The song can be faintly heard in the background for all of fifteen seconds in the actual movie, but Mylène is in no way offended, and she attends the première on Hollywood Boulevard in early November 2000, looking stunning in a long black leather coat and blue silk trousers. The film and its soundtrack have already been out for several months in the USA when Mylène decides to release the track as a single through her record company Polydor: consequently, many fans are already familiar with the track when "L'Histoire d'une fée, c'est..." eventually lands in French record stores on 27th February 2001. Nevertheless, they duly go out and buy the one and only support to be made available, a digipack 2-track CD single with beautiful sleeve art that also includes the instrumental version: the single goes in at number 9, and eventually manages sales of 75,000. An amazing score, when the following factors are taken into consideration: radio stations hardly play the track, with NRJ in particular almost blanking it completely; it is only

Europe 2 that will play the song with any kind of regularity. The fact that no promotional supports were ever pressed for this particular single (to the dismay of collectors everywhere) may not have helped in this instance. What's more, promotion for the single amounts to precisely zero: with no TV appearances, and in particular no clip (the second of three such "orphan" singles, after "On est tous des imbéciles" and before "Sextonik"), exposure for "L'Histoire d'une fée, c'est..." cannot be anything other than limited. And yet, in spite of all this, and with just one support to choose from, sales figures are still highly respectable: in 2001, few other artists could have managed such a feat.

Of course, Mylène can be forgiven for not finding the time to do a video for her latest song, as early 2001 finds the singer probably fairly busy with an ambitious and time-consuming side project: a few months earlier, in July 2000, the Farmer/Boutonnat composition "Moi, Lolita" has gotten a young Corsican singer by the name of Alizée noticed all over the globe. A huge success in France, the song spends an incredible 31 weeks in the Top 10, selling somewhere in the region of 1,300,000: more than "Désenchantée", and an amazing sales tally for any single at a time when the record market is already in great difficulty. In no time at all, the track crosses the English Channel: the thrill of seeing a Farmer/Boutonnat track in the UK Top 10 is easily recalled, more than ten years later! But it is not only in Great Britain that Alizée is a hit: the song enters the Top 10 (and often goes to number 1) in several countries worldwide, and the young singer is suddenly in demand in places as diverse as Japan and Mexico. So, when the "Gourmandises" album is released in late 2000, it is clear that Mylène is going to be busy in her mentoring role for quite some time yet...And as if the ignominy of having no accompanying video wasn't enough, "L'Histoire d'une fée, c'est..." must also endure a complete absence of remixes, even if a demo version (extremely similar to the version released commercially) will surface online in later years. The song is also one of five Mylène singles never to have made it to the stage, the four others being the ever-forgotten "On est tous des imbéciles", as well as "Pardonne-moi", "Slipping away" and "Sextonik". And yet, there were a few rumours going round to the effect that "L'Histoire d'une fée, c'est..." was originally planned to be part of the setlist for the stadium dates of the 2009 Tour, before being finally cast aside at the last minute...maybe next time.

With the little Rugrats adventure out of the way, the time will soon come for Mylène to take a first look back at almost eighteen years of astonishing success, at a phenomenally successful career whose scintillating trajectory has been unlike any other, arguably, even, on a global level. And in order to do so with some panache, Mylène is going to enlist the help of a familiar-looking British singer friend, scoring herself yet another huge hit along the way.

34/ Les Mots

To the fans' surprise, 2001 will turn out to be a rather busy year for Mylène Farmer. After the huge success of "Innamoramento" and the accompanying Mylènium Tour, as well as the dazzling international success of her protégée Alizée, whom she is busy managing, few dared to hope for much action on the Farmer front for a while. Rumours in the early part of the year hint at a possible "Dance Remixes 2": in retrospect, not a completely inaccurate guess, although perhaps a little early. From September onwards, however, a rumour of a different kind begins to make the rounds: Mylène has recorded a bilingual duet with an international star, a half-French, half-English song, composed, as always, by Laurent Boutonnat. This time, the rumours are spot on. But just *who* is this mysterious "international star"? All becomes clear when it is revealed that Mylène has just completed work on a photoshoot in Los Angeles with the British singer Seal, responsible for worldwide hits such as "Crazy" and "Kiss from a rose" in the 90's. And the time has not yet come for another remix compilation, either:

the new song is to be the first single taken off Mylène's upcoming first-ever best-of. This promises to be something rather special, coming after almost eighteen years of incredible success! Promos are sent out to radio stations from October 10th, and airplay is soon adequate, although not yet at its peak. Released on 13th November, "Les Mots" is off to a good start right away, entering the charts at number 3. But the song's real success is yet to come: it isn't until after Mylène and Seal perform the track at the NRJ Music Awards on 19th January 2002 that things really start to pick up. "Les Mots", by now in the lower rungs of the Top 10, gets a sudden new lease of life and goes shooting straight back up the charts, reaching its best position of number 2 in the week immediately after broadcast. Radio rotation also increases heavily from then on, and the track quickly becomes a genuinely popular hit, reaching far beyond Mylène's fanbase and into the general public. At the time, indeed, it is sometimes said that "Les Mots" is more popular with the public at large than with the long-standing fans, who for their part supposedly find the track slightly bland. This is debatable, and perhaps nothing more than a slightly snobbish response to what is an unashamedly populist track: what is undeniably true, on the other hand, is that the single will go on to spend 17 consecutive weeks in the Top 10, achieving sales of over 400,000 (some sources suggest sales were as high as 500,000, which would put it on a par with "Sans Contrefaçon" in terms of sales), making it Mylène's biggest hit since the days of "Désenchantée": to this day, it remains one of her biggest-sellers, as well as one of the classic ballads in the Farmer discography.

A persistent rumour around the song, never officially confirmed or denied, says that Mylène had originally asked Elton John to perform the duet with her, after promising him that they would do a song together "before we die": the legendary British singer being, of course, a self-confessed Farmer fan. Sadly, Elton only went and turned Mylène down, on the grounds that "Les Mots" was too slow a song: it was to be an upbeat track, or nothing. Nowadays, unfortunately, any idea of a possible collaboration between the two legends seems to have been abandoned, but who knows: perhaps, if that long-rumoured "duets album" ever sees the light of day...In any case, with Elton John's refusal (real or otherwise), Seal gets his chance: and it will do him a lot of good, too, as his career finds itself suddenly revitalized: in France, in particular, the singer encounters renewed success on a par with his early 90's glory days. On "Les Mots", his and Mylène's voices combine beautifully, with Mylène once again venturing into the higher registers, to mesmerizing effect; as for Seal, he sings in his amazingly sensual voice Mylène's own English words, words that at one point appear to reference a much earlier song: the lyric "And to lives that stoop to notice mine, I know I will say goodbye" brings to mind the "Aux vies qui s'abaissent à voir la mienne, Je sais qu'il me faudra prendre congé d'elles" of 1991's "Nous souviendrons-nous", an almost literal translation. Coincidence, or intentional recycling? In any case, this little link with the past hasn't done the song any harm. Not that this is the only look back at earlier times, of course: "Les Mots" needs a video, and for the occasion, it is a very familiar face that can be spotted behind the camera...

MYLENE FARMER — THE SINGLE FILE

Almost ten years after "Beyond my control", his last pop promo for the red-haired icon, Laurent Boutonnat finally gets back behind the camera in order to direct a Mylène Farmer video, allegedly at the singer's personal request. The clip is shot at the studios d'Arpajon, the setting for the "Sans Logique" video shoot, way back in 1989. Filmed over two days, on 8th and 9th October, the video is aesthetically inspired by the 1819 Théodore de Géricault painting "The raft of the Medusa": an inspiration that is immediately evident when looking at the work itself. Inside of a huge water tank, with the help of wave and wind machines, Laurent sets Mylène adrift on a raft out in the middle of the open sea, under a menacing blanket of low-lying, heavy storm-clouds. She is not alone: a muscular man is there to keep her company, but things soon deteriorate as the couple paddle fast against the incoming storm that threatens to tip them over. Suddenly, the man is tossed overboard and into the waters: Mylène tries to help, but it's a hopeless struggle and all she can do is carry on singing regardless, until the storm abates and a few icebergs drift into view: luckily, her matches didn't get wet, and she can strike a light, which she promptly blows out, symbolising, perhaps, the life just lost at sea. One thing that quickly becomes apparent when watching the video for the first time is that Seal, although clearly seen in some of the shots, seems strangely removed from it all: and indeed, the man standing on the raft with Mylène is actually a body double, a fashion model by the name of Imane Ayissi. The video shoot, in early October 2001, comes less than a month after the events of 9/11: totally understandably, US-based Seal did not wish to make an Atlantic crossing by plane at the time: his scenes were therefore shot over one afternoon in the States, with video producer Anouk Nora in attendance, and edited later on into the video. When the clip is first shown on French TV, from 7th November, the initial response is mixed: it's hard to deny the beauty of the images, or the skill of the artful colour composition; and Mylène looks more stunning than ever, in a video that is undeniably pure Boutonnat. Yet, some fans also express a certain disappointment at what they think is a low-key effort from Laurent: yes, the clip is beautiful, and Mylène looks great, but this is not on the same level as previous epic videos such as "Pourvu qu'elles soient douces" or "Désenchantée"...Especially after almost ten years, they had been hoping for more spectacle from Laurent Boutonnat, disappeared from so long from his role as video-maker to his star. An understandable opinion, in view of the ever-present nostalgia for the extravagant videos of the "good old days": in Laurent's defence, however, an epic clip set to a ballad is somewhat difficult to carry off...And perhaps the golden era of videoclips had already come to an end long ago, too, no matter how much we may wish it to be otherwise. In any case, even if the clip is, as some say, a little "plain", and, at under five minutes, short by Boutonnat standards, it is still a visually accomplished piece of work, and a welcome return behind the camera for Mylène's original collaborator.

The one and only TV prestation for "Les Mots" is the one that takes place on 19th January 2002, during the NRJ Music Awards: as well as her ampexed performance with Seal, Mylène is also nominated on the night for "best duet", the title eventually going to Garou and

Céline Dion for their collaboration "Sous le vent". On stage, the song has so far only ever been performed during the series of 13 Bercy concerts in 2006: a long-standing rumour says that original duettist Seal was at first scheduled to take part for at least some of the dates, but was eventually dropped after excessive remuneration demands...But never mind: as Mylène begins to sing the first notes of the song on the first night, fans wonder whether she's about to do another "Regrets" and go solo, but suddenly, surprise surprise, Abraham Laboriel Jr gets up from behind his drum kit, mike in hand, and joins the singer front-stage. Delivering a stunningly soulful performance, the legendary drummer effortlessly proves himself to be multi-talented, even earning himself a quick kiss on the lips from Mylène for his trouble. Despite its relatively discreet presence on TV and on the stage, "Les Mots" has endured well, and is still regularly played on French radio to this day, having become a beloved classic, in much the same way as "Rêver" or "Ainsi soit je..." have before it.

The autumn Los Angeles photoshoot with Seal, where Mylène is photographed for the first time by Isabel Snyder, will give birth to the "embrace" shots that will go on to adorn the cover of the various "Les Mots" single supports. In France, a 2-track CD and vinyl 12" are released, although there will be no Maxi CD this time, and no remixes of the track either. The only other officially available version, the "Strings for souls" mix, is a purer, more stripped down version of the song that puts the singers' voices even more to the fore, rather than a remix proper. A 3-track CD is also issued in Europe, with the song "L'Histoire d'une fée, c'est..." added as a bonus. The promos consist of a 1-track CD with a black and white close-up shot of Seal's arms around Mylène on the sleeve, as well as a deluxe version: the monotrack CD is mounted on a thick cardboard support, 20x30cm, dotted with ten or so small photographs of the couple in various states of embrace. This is slipped inside a black sleeve with holes selectively cut out on the front, revealing some of the images only: a classy item, and fairly pricey when sold in specialist shops...

Inauguring a very good start for the album, Mylène and Laurent have scored another massive hit, one of the singer's biggest, with the first single to be taken from her very first best-of: a fitting result for a compilation representing the accomplishments of the undisputed queen of French pop. Not only that, but they've also gone and created yet another Farmer standard. But the album has more hits to give still, and another future classic is just around the corner...

35/ C'Est Une Belle Journée

When the best-of "Les Mots" is released on 27th November 2001, it encounters an immense and swift success: not only does the first single taken off it become a bona fide popular hit, but the compilation also represents the best of the last two decades in French pop music. It is, in short, the best-of to beat all best-ofs. In less than a month, an impressive 500,000 copies are sold. And very quickly, as fans and casual enthusiasts alike check out the three brand new songs included with the package, one in particular jumps out like an obvious hit: "C'est une belle journée", like "Souviens-toi du jour" or "Désenchantée" before it, is one of those infectiously catchy tunes whose upbeat tempo and cheerful melody actually conceal somewhat dark lyrical themes. Suicide, no less, is the preoccupation that runs through this particular track, and for the very first time in the singer's career, censorship is going to come from a most unexpected source: Mylène herself. In the legendary 2006 "7 à 8" interview on TF1, given shortly before the first of the 13 Bercy concerts, the singer explains that, for once, she had decided to slightly rein in her own words whilst in the process of writing the "C'est une belle journée" lyrics. Not out of a fear of being censored by the networks, or of offending sensibilities, but out of human decency and respect for her public. While the singer's original chorus lyric had been "Je vais me tuer", she quickly felt that such a direct and unambiguous turn of phrase may in fact have been interpreted as an active call to the act of suicide itself by less stable members of her audience. Artistic freedom of expression or not, the singer nevertheless felt that putting those actual words to music would have been "too easy", in view of the safety and security afforded her by her success; the same security not being necessarily available to all those who listen to her. Therefore, in her first-ever (and only) known act of self-censorship, Mylène crossed out her earlier words and replaced them with the somewhat more oblique "Je vais me coucher", a more allegorical expression of her feelings at the time of writing. Yet more proof of the singer's utter decency and profound sense of humanity, if such proof was needed.

In the first few months of 2002, while the Seal duet "Les Mots" is still riding high in the charts, rumours begin to proliferate as to what the next single will be, some right, some wrong. According to whispers, the next single will be "C'est une belle journée", with a video based on Mylène's own drawings...correct. And the single will come out as a limited edition digipack DVD single, featuring an exclusive "making-of" documentary... wrong, sadly. There will be no such edition. As for the "Journée" making-of, also at one point rumoured to be featured on the Music Videos IV compilation, it has unfortunately never emerged, if it ever existed at all in the first place. The name of the next single is finally confirmed in early March, when promos are sent out to radio stations: and right from the start, "C'est une belle journée" becomes an airwaves favourite, so much so that it will end up being one of 2002's most played tunes on French networks. Originally scheduled for a March release, the track is put back by a month as the singles chart success of the duet "Les Mots" is still in full flow, seemingly unstoppable; finally, on 16th April, Mylène's new single can be unleashed at last. Entering the charts at number 5 (which will remain its highest position), Mylène's ode to resigned suicide will remain in the Top 100 for the best part of the year, leaving only in mid-October and selling somewhere in the region of 200,000: another gold certification. A strong showing, and also a good boost for the album, which quickly climbs back up into the compilations Top 3: and by the time the single's exploitation period comes to an end, album sales have already easily exceeded the million mark. "C'est une belle journée" has since then gone on to become one of the singer's most emblematic tracks, one of those songs that is known not only to fans but also to a wide section of the general public: in short, it is yet another Farmer classic.

As the rumours had correctly predicted, the video consists of a short animation film based on Mylène's own drawings. The singer's pure, simple graphic style is immediately recognizable: the spaced-out looking sheep, in particular, being a familiar face from the "Dessine-moi un mouton" supports. This is Mylène's first collaboration with Benoît Di Sabatino, and the start of a working relationship that will in time extend into other areas of the singer's life. With a budget estimated at around €100,000 and built around a scenario written by the singer herself, the clip shows an animated Mylène as she and her sheep companion go through what appears to be a pretty routine, boring and uneventful day (although perhaps not so much for the sheep, who at one point turns blue after getting stuck inside the fridge.) The hands of the clock move on inexorably as the day continues to unfold in the same languid manner until a child-like character, like a younger self, is glimpsed through the mirror: perhaps another reference to Antoine de Saint-Exupéry here, as the child is strongly reminiscent of his "Petit Prince" in both appearance and demeanour. Mylène steps through the looking-glass and emerges on the other side, into a carefree world where a child's play is limited only by their imagination: sheep, child, balloon, all are swept freely on the wind in this magical place, happily ending up at the heart of a whirling tornado. And when the sun eventually sets, returning her to the other side, Mylène appears to have taken on the appearance of a child once more, the temporary detour into childhood and insouciant fun of the day having brought a smile (and a wink) to her face, and to that of the sheep burrowing its way up from under the sheets for a cuddle. Teasingly, the clip ends on the words "A suivre...". While there has been no obvious video continuation so far, it could be argued that this was actually referring to the soon to be released 2003 book "Lisa-loup et le conteur", whose universe is not too dissimilar...Another nod to the past can perhaps be detected in another scene: when the spider pops up out of the sheep's dream bubble, it is hard not to think of Alice, the depressive spider "pendue au bout de son fil", as she swings lazily, hanging from Mylène's upturned palm..."C'est une belle journée" is Mylène's first-ever animated video, and the first time that a French artist has had a clip produced from their own drawings: the singer will go down the animation route again four years later with the "Peut-être toi" video, although this time using the graphic talents of another.

"C'est une belle journée" will benefit from two TV appearances, first on "Hit Machine" on M6 in April and then on "Zidane Ela" on France 2 in May: with a slickly choreographed prestation from Mylène and her backing dancers on both occasions. The same choreography will make a return on the Bercy stage in 2006, in what is the only live showing for "C'est une belle journée" so far, although there are persistent rumours that the song was scheduled to be part of the setlist for all stadium dates of the 2009 tour, and even made it as far as the rehearsal stage: Mylène, however, felt the track didn't quite fit in with the rest in the end, and it was eventually dropped. The song is also part of the 2003 "Remixes" project, where the "Devil Head" remix gives it a brand new re-interpretation.

With sleeve photography courtesy of Ellen Von Unwerth, also responsible for the racy "Les Mots" album booklet pictures, "C'est une belle journée" is made available to French record-buyers in three different formats: on the 2-track CD, exclusively featuring the instrumental version, is a close-up shot of a broadly smiling Mylène. The digipack Maxi CD features the single version and three remixes, including the "What a souci's remix", that can probably be read as a nod to the young heroine of "Lisa-loup et le conteur", who through the course of her adventures can often be heard to proclaim "Quel souci!" Another picture disc 12" is also issued, although this time it is presented slipped inside a full-colour picture sleeve rather than the usual transparent plastic type; the vinyl also includes a mix not found anywhere else, the "Bed & Belle remix". The single is also released in Europe, although non-French countries have to make do with a single format, a non-digipack Maxi CD. Three separate promos are produced for France alone: a monotrack CD, in unique sleeve and with picture label; a black-vinyl 12" (all commercial 12"s were of the picture disc variety for this release); and finally, the deluxe version, a copy of the monotrack CD mounted on a 12"-sized thick cardboard support, adorned with a picture of the singer and a few actual white feathers stuck here and there. The whole thing is slipped inside a bright red sleeve with song title in white, with yet another white feather on top! Quite a pricey item, especially if the feathers haven't come unstuck! Europe also gets their own promotional item, and this one is very interesting as it contains a version of the song that is totally unavailable anywhere else: a 2-track CD that also features the radio edit version of the "Elegie's remix club", an edit that has never been made available on any other format. Consequently, this is a rather hard to find piece, and one much desired by collectors.

When the success and exploitation of "C'est une belle journée" finally wind down in October 2002, Mylène's first best-of compilation has already sold more than a million. Fans have been wondering and hoping, with three new songs on the album, will there be a third single? Towards the end of the month, their questions are finally answered: third new single, coming right up!

36/ Pardonne-Moi

October 2002: almost a year after its release, the album "Les Mots" is still riding high in the compilations Top 10, with over a million copies sold so far: a record for this type of release. As early as the summer, speculation has been rife as to whether a third single will be issued from the album, and if so, which one: while some suggest the last of the new songs, "Pardonne-moi", others bet on a classic single re-release. Others still think: a third single, why bother? It isn't as if the album desperately needs any further promotion. But in the end, it is indeed "Pardonne-moi" that will act as final single from Mylène's first best-of: a logical choice, all things considered, as the trio of releases constitutes a fairly accurate representation of the singer's career so far. First the classic, ethereal ballad, followed by a catchy, upbeat number, and finally this, a mid-tempo, slightly darker, less obvious track. A beautiful, moody composition from Laurent Boutonnat, full of tense and atmospheric strings, over which Mylène lays a lyric in which she appears to be seeking forgiveness for an overwhelming, mad love from a succession of princes of various ethnic backgrounds (as well as a somewhat harder to place, more enigmatic-sounding "Prince aurore"). In what is a neat sound effect, Mylène's reworked voice is transformed into a plaintive, eastern-sounding chant, soaring to beautiful effect over some sections of the track. Released on 21st October, a week later than originally planned, the song enters the charts at number 6 before quickly taking its leave, selling around 85,000 copies all told. A far more confidential kind of release, and a far more confidential kind of success, too: on the radio, as on TV, the song's presence is much more discreet than that of its two predecessors, with no particular promotional drive on Mylène's part either as the track will never be performed on television. A stranger to live performance as well, "Pardonne-moi" has so far never been brought to the stage, and remains purely a studio release, at least to date. Nevertheless, the song and the accompanying TV ads do enable "Les Mots" to remain anchored in the public's consciousness, and album sales keep going strong as a result.

"Pardonne-moi" is also the last time, at least so far, that Laurent Boutonnat directs a Mylène Farmer music video. Shot over two days in the Sets studios in Stains, the scene of previous celluloid classics such as "Plus Grandir" and "Ainsi soit je...", the black and white clip is a fairly sober affair, as reflected by its relatively bargain budget of around €40,000. A scenario-free succession of shots of a radiant, natural-looking Mylène singing to camera, occasionally performing some kind of seemingly possessed dance, interspersed with shots of a slithering snake and a masked horseman apparently galloping on the spot. A simple but beautiful video nevertheless, with heavily symbolic and aesthetically superb images that are not without recalling previous visual glories: it is rather hard not to be reminded of "Sans Logique", for instance, when Mylène once again makes use of the white contact lenses that give her a somewhat demonic appearance (also trying on some black ones for good measure this time); the masked horse-rider, also, can occasionally bring to mind Rasoukine, the lover from "Tristana". Some will see in this an intentional move by Laurent Boutonnat to create a link with what has gone on before, a kind of subtle final farewell to days past through the use of discreet nods in their direction. Others, not for the first time, (the "A quoi je sers..." video springs to mind) will fear that they can read in it the warning signs of Mylène's imminent withdrawal from the spotlight, a departure so many times predicted but not yet come to pass, thankfully.

No Maxi CD will be made available for "Pardonne-moi": instead, a 3-track CD features the instrumental, as well as the "Dark side of the mix" version, a rearranged version close to the original and not strictly speaking a remix. A limited edition of the CD is also available, in a "chevalet" sleeve that can be folded into a display stand, a strange (some will say, somewhat pointless) format. The only official, proper remix of the song is to be found on the 12" single, initally announced as a limited edition but then released as standard: and the "Forgiveness club remix" is indeed quite good, making it even more galling that no "dance remixes"-type CD was ever issued...Strangely, for what is one of the singer's most discreet singles, the release of "Pardonne-moi" will bring about the creation of one of the rarest, and most sought after promos in her discography: as well as the standard monotrack edition of the CD, a deluxe version is produced that makes use of a particular material for the very first time: glass. The 1-track disc is sandwiched between two circular plates of glass separated by soft rubber pads, with artist name and song title laser-etched on one plate, and a negative of Mylène's face etched on the other, the whole thing being presented inside a black 16x16cm cardboard box. Limited to only a hundred copies, this admittedly beautiful item is obviously very scarce, and accordingly expensive...

"Pardonne-moi" marks the end of the exploitation period for the "Les Mots" album, and what a success it has been: 1.5 million copies sold within France alone, nothing less than a consecration for the singer, who deservedly sees her first best-of compilation break all kinds of records. The album is also issued in European territories, in a single-disc edition that features only sixteen tracks: a number still higher than that of many so-called "greatest hits" compilations... Although no promotional editions of the album appear to have ever been manufactured, the collectors' edition is a great, luxurious package: limited to 40,000 copies, the "longbox" issue features 3 CDs (including three bonus, hard to find tracks) as well as a DVD single featuring the "Les Mots" video. An oversize, 52-page booklet is also included, featuring many racy shots of the singer, clearly enjoying herself while brandishing a machine gun or flashing her knickers in front of Ellen Von Unwerth's camera...A suitably lavish package for what is undoubtedly one of the ultimate pop compilations of all time.

More than two years after the original release of "Les Mots", it is yet another compilation that comes to fill the Mylène-shaped void that has been torturing fans for such a long time now. The singer has done a vanishing act and has not been seen or heard from in ages, and some are beginning to despair of ever seeing her again. But they will still have to wait for close to a year and a half for any new music, and the release of a bunch of brand new remixes of classic tracks, even if coming from some of the world's biggest names in dance, is not to everyone's liking: an incensed fan goes as far as spray-painting an angry "Non aux Remixes 2!!" on a bench, known as "*the* bench" to the fans who congregate there, located just outside the singer's then-residence in one of the more affluent areas of Paris. Released on the 3rd of December 2003 with sleeve design courtesy of Mylène's sister Brigitte, "Remixes" is a collection of 11 of Mylène's singles revisited by international big-name DJ's, with Felix da Housecat and Paul Oakenfold amongst others; and while the remixes are of generally good quality, the compilation meets only with limited success: coming after a live album and a best-of, it wasn't necessarily what the fans were waiting for. Still, it cannot be said to be a failure, with 100,000 copies sold and a gold certification to its name, and in the absence of anything else, it will have to do...Three of the remixes will be put forward from the album, although their limited release means they cannot be considered to be single releases as such: the remixed versions of "Sans Contrefaçon", "Je t'aime mélancolie" and "L'Instant X" are successively released in, respectively, August '03, November '03 and January 2004. With a single format each time, a one-sided 12" in a plain titles sleeve intended primarily for DJ's (although sold commercially in some record stores), sales are no more than confidential, even if the first two, in particular, enable the singer to be heard once more on dance-floors across the country. Mylène's name or picture do not feature on the sleeve: her name can only be found, in small lettering, in the credits. There is, of course, no promotion of any kind whatsoever from Mylène herself around this period.

Her last studio album, "Innamoramento", was released in April '99. Although a live album, well-deserved best-of and another dance compilation have appeared at various times in between to keep them waiting, fans will nevertheless have to hold on until April 2005 -six years!- for a brand new studio album. But finally, the long, long, long wait is almost over...

Part 6: Avant Que L'Ombre... / Avant Que L'Ombre...à Bercy

37/ Fuck Them All

Late 2004: fans of the red-haired pop icon are seriously beginning to wonder whether the singer will ever emerge again from wherever it is she's hiding. Her last TV appearance dates back to January 2003, at the NRJ Music Awards, where the singer picked up the trophy for best female French artist of the year, for the fourth year in a row. Oh, and where she also expressed her wish to see her public again "as soon as possible"...Of course, in Farmer-speak, the meaning of the word "soon" can be somewhat elastic, and as December 2004 comes around, fans are still left twiddling their thumbs, killing time with the odd rumour: a collaboration with Benjamin Biolay, with the rapper Diam's...until a different kind of rumour makes its first appearance in the first few days of the month: something about a press conference...There is hardly time to doubt the news before it is confirmed: yes, Mylène is (finally) back! On the 16th, a selection of journalists, mostly from the provinces as well as Belgium and Switzerland, are invited to a chic venue in Paris' 8th Arrondissement. In order to reach the *salon* where the press conference will take place, the gathered reporters make their way up a few flights of stairs smartly adorned with candles. Once inside, they are greeted by Mylène's manager, Thierry Suc, who right off the bat announces the singer's return to the stage in January 2006, as well as the news of the forthcoming new album. As he goes on to explain the unique and untransportable nature of the planned 2006 shows, the reason for most of the journalists present being from the provinces becomes clear: a pre-emptive chance to explain to fans and the public everywhere just why the next shows will take place in the capital exclusively, and a good way to avoid any potential dissatisfied grumblings from the provincial media in the face of a Paris-only series of concerts. Thierry Suc also lets slip that tickets for the concerts will be going on sale from the 17th onwards...the very next day, in other words. After ten minutes or so, Mylène herself makes her entrance, flanked by Laurent Boutonnat, for a twenty-minute Q&A session where she again explains the unique nature of the forthcoming shows, and humbly asks the public to come to her...She also announces her new single for sometime around the end of January, although the track's name is at that point still a closely guarded secret. Also announced for a March release is the new album "Avant que l'ombre...", which Mylène points out will once again be dealing with her "zones of light and shadow", although with more guitars than usual and, as Laurent Boutonnat adds, a more acoustic feel...The press conference, the first ever in the singer's career, goes down like a bomb: overnight, radio and the press talk of little else besides Mylène's long-awaited return to the stage, and fans are instantly galvanized, not surprisingly: two days after the Bercy tickets have gone on sale, Thierry Suc announces that more than 40,000 places have already been sold. A brand new communication strategy from Mylène and her team, and an unusual one for France, too: such press conferences are usually the preserve of foreign artists. But after such a long absence from the media, it was never going to be an ordinary comeback for the singer...

Rumours quickly begin to proliferate around the new single, the delayed release date only making matters worse: initially announced for the end of January, the song won't actually be released until 14th March...in the meantime, various titles are bandied about, "Dans ma peau" being one of them. When the magazine Voici announces, a few days before the single goes out to radio, that the new song is called "Fuck them all", fans are dubious, perhaps even a little shocked: such crude language, even if it is in English, coming from Mylène? Few put any faith in this particular piece of info, and Voici's "news" is generally dismissed as ludicrous, and ignored. Which makes the shock even greater, when, at 6am on the 9th of February, NRJ plays the track for the very first time. The thousands of fans who got up especially early that morning realise with a jolt that Voici had got it right after all: "Fuck them all" it is...In the end, it is impressive to see how very little about the new single was leaked, especially in the age of internet: Voici's revelations, in retrospect, were a veritable scoop, and the only accurate piece of information pertaining to the new track. This complete information blackout, though undoubtedly hugely frustrating for many an impatient fan, nevertheless allowed for a very special moment on that early February morning: who, amongst those listening at the time, can forget the intense emotion felt as the first notes of the long-awaited new single finally rang out? New, yet somehow immediately familiar, pure Boutonnat from the very start. And as for the lyrics...well, Mylène has really outdone herself this time:

"Fuck them all" is easily one of the most complex, one of the most obscure lyrics the singer has ever come up with. On first listen, certainly, it is almost impossible to say exactly what the song is about, and the English "rap" towards the end only confuses things further: not surprisingly, the song is quickly going to give rise to myriad different interpretations as fans try to make sense of Mylène's latest musings. The meaning now most generally agreed on (though by no means definitive) is that "Fuck them all" is a song in which Mylène evokes the domination of men over women over the centuries, and imagines a society where the roles have been reversed. Of course, the one person who could shed some light on the precise meaning of the track is probably not about to do so anytime soon, so the matter must remain forever shrouded in some degree of doubt...

In a sign of the changing times, it is no longer exclusively on NRJ that the track can be heard for the first time: this time around, all the major radio networks receive the promos at the same time: an explanation, perhaps, for NRJ's diminished enthusiasm in later years, when it comes to playing Mylène's songs? In any case, airplay for the track drops off very quickly: although NRJ plays it on the hour on the first day, rotations afterwards become more and more infrequent, in a sign of things to come...In another first, the song is also made promptly available for legal download, a still relatively new development at the time, and one that will pay off handsomely, with "Fuck them all" becoming the most downloaded track in February 2005. While not afraid to embrace new technologies, Mylène nevertheless shows herself to be somewhat reluctant when it comes to engaging in any kind of promotional activity in order to support her new release: TV, radio...the singer herself will be seen or heard on none of these, her complete media absence somewhat reminiscent of the "XXL" days. Nor will she consent to giving interviews of any sort when the album is eventually released: the networks will have to make do with a short documentary showing fans running for the various album supports at midnight on the 3rd of April, during a special late-night launch event at the Champs-Élysées Virgin Megastore. And yet, in spite of her total absence and utter silence, Mylène's comeback is more than noticed, and the press speaks of little else...

The single finally lands in stores on 14th March, although even then it is only the 2-track single that is made available: the Maxi versions won't be released until April 18th. With a first week (and best) placing at number 6 followed by a swift descent down the charts, "Fuck them all" will not be a massive hit in the vein of previous glories such as "Désenchantée" or "Sans Contrefaçon": some will even say it is a flop, with sales of only just in the region of 100,000. Still, this needs to be put into context: first of all, the single sells enough to be certified silver, hardly an indication of extreme failure. What's more, the record market in 2005 is in a state of collapse, with sales down for artists across the board, in part because of the rise of illegal downloading. And on top of that, Mylène has taken on no promotion whatsoever: in view of these factors, the single's performance is more than honorable, and on a level that few others could have matched. Whatever the current circumstances, the Farmer name alone is still a huge draw...It certainly is for those 26,000 fans who rush out in the first week to buy the first support available. On 18th April, they can discover the remixes from Joachim Garraud and Y-Front (responsible for the 2003 "Libertine" remix). The reception is mixed, even if the remixers' credentials are impeccable: in any case, even if they are not overly wild about these new versions, at least the fans have a brand new video to keep them entertained by now.

Following a maddeningly short teaser on M6 on March 2, the full clip is at last shown in its entirety on the same channel from the 9th onwards. Directed by the Spanish film-maker Agustin Villaronga, the video dips its toes deep into the Farmer mythology, with the welcome return of several familiar themes: snow-covered landscapes, horses, ravens, blood, death, and not forgetting the "twins" concept, now making its third appearance after "California" and "L'Âme-stram-gram", the "Fuck them all" video is rich in symbols and nods to the singer's career. Two diametrically opposed Mylènes are presented: in the first instance, a long-haired version comes riding in on top of a black horse: as she gallops through an abandoned factory, flashback images show us her short-haired counterpart, imprisoned within a metal cage that will shortly be crushing her to death. Able to see what has transpired through the eyes of the ravens perched here and there, the long-haired Mylène picks up a stone which she hurls into the empty air, revealing an outdoor snow scene as an invisible barrier comes crashing down: and there, guarded by yet another raven, lies the shroud-covered frozen corpse of her short-haired twin. Reaching into the frozen remains, the vengeful Mylène pulls out a (possibly symbolic) sword and heads out into the cold, guided by the black birds, in the direction of a field where a congregation of strange-looking scarecrows await. Mylène unsheathes her sword, and destruction ensues: slashing and dicing, she cuts the weird scarecrows to pieces, ripping through the black cloth of their bodies, bringing black tears to the empty eye-sockets set in the bizarre bony white heads with each slash of her weapon of vengeance; black tears that fall and pool into the pure white snow, giving birth to yet more ravens. And as the woman exerts herself taking her revenge, a series of flashback shots sees her short-haired twin living out her last moments as the cage inexorably crushes down on her, with the ravens as sole witnesses. Finally, with her vengeance carried out, the long-haired twin thrusts her sword downwards one last time, deep into the snow-covered ground: the darkness and evil contained within the blade is swiftly swallowed up into the earth. Her mission accomplished, the woman gets up to her feet and stands as if to stare at the horizon: but suddenly, her body disintegrates away into a cloud of black dust, carried away on the wind in a matter of seconds. A video rich in symbols, with some of the more commonly put forward interpretations explaining the crushing cage as being a metaphor for male domination, or drawing a comparison with an earlier video: at the end of the "Pourvu qu'elles soient douces" clip, Mylène -by now some kind of angel of death- rides off on a black horse; here, she rides in on the same funeral beast, a ghost come to avenge what could very well be her own death: for as soon as she has carried out her vengeance, her spirit can finally depart, scattered to the winds.

Shot in Romania in February 2005, with the team staying at the Athénée Palace Hilton hotel in Bucarest for a week, and with an estimated budget of around €150,000, the "Fuck them all" video is an aesthetically superb, complex and highly symbolic piece of film, based on a scenario written by the singer. And yet, in spite of the obvious effort that has gone into it, the clip fails to win fans over entirely at first: perhaps disappointed because of the early rumours that announced a nine-minute epic, some feel that somehow, something is missing. In many cases, fans' opinions of the clip will improve over time, once repeated viewings have allowed for the heavy symbolism to be absorbed a little more. Equally, none can fault the visual quality of the images on offer: the scarecrow figures, in particular, are undeniably weirdly compelling. These were based on an art installation by the much-lauded Swiss artist Martial Leiter: for "Les Épouvantails", a collection of these disquieting figures was set in a field in Switzerland from June 2004 to March 2005, and allowed to remain there unperturbed amidst the passing of the seasons. The video's aesthetic qualities will indeed not go unnoticed: in March 2007, the "Fuck them all" clip wins the (perhaps a little premature) title of "Best clip of the 21st Century" after an internet vote is carried out on behalf of the MCM music channel.

On stage, "Fuck them all" will be one of the strong moments of the Bercy 2006 concerts, with a rock-out version that sees everyone on stage together, giving Mylène a chance to introduce her musicians and dancers just before the closing track. In 2009, the song comes back for the stadium dates of the tour, in a shorter version. The great reception it gets then seems to indicate that the song, although it may have divided fans like never before at the time of its release, has aged well with time, the way a good wine might do...

Two weeks after the single has been released, another event comes to join the December press conference in the list of firsts for Mylène: on 28th March, 250 lucky winners of an NRJ competition are taken by coach to a top-secret Parisian location (a theatre at the Palais Royal), to be treated to an exclusive, avant-première listen of the new album. Once past security and a thorough search, with all phones and any possible kind of recording equipment having to be left at the door, the group is shown into an auditorium. Everyone takes their seat, the lights go down...and Mylène herself shyly walks on stage, with the obvious reaction from the stunned audience. When she can finally make herself heard, Mylène says a few words of thanks, wishes everyone a happy listen, and walks off. This alone would have made anyone's day, but there is still a surprise in store for those lucky enough to be in attendance: after the preview, and as people are retrieving their belongings, each of the 250 are handed a tiny box adorned with a picture of the star and filled with various foodstuffs, and a copy of the "Fuck them all" deluxe promo, personally signed by the singer! (Some of those will be put up for sale online within hours.) A suitably amazing-sounding day, and no doubt something that none of the competition winners would have dreamed of missing for the world. And yet, gallingly, this is exactly what happened to a handful of people, who were given the wrong coordinates concerning the rendez-vous point on the day: having never been picked up by the coach that would have taken them to the secret location, and unable to get through to the radio station's constantly jammed switchboard, these poor unfortunates were then left to listen on in horror as NRJ cheerfully related how Mylène had surprised her fans with a personal appearance at the event...Understandably annoyed, the group of "winners" decided to complain and headed over to Universal's offices the very next day, only to be allegedly very shabbily treated by the unsympathetic staff on reception: luckily, Pascal Nègre, president of Universal France, happened to walk through the lobby as the group were making their case, and demanded to know what was going on: and though a personal appearance from the star was now impossible, a second preview session was improvised on the spot, in one of the offices in the building, with more deluxe promos handed out at the end. Some consolation, at least, and a timely intervention from Pascal Nègre, averting what could have been a fairly negative PR incident for the singer, even if the fault lay with the organisers, NRJ, who had somehow managed to pass on the wrong information to some of their competition winners.

French supports for "Fuck them all" consist of a 2-track single, featuring the instrumental version: this was the only support initially available on March 14. On April 18, two more formats go up for sale: the digipack Maxi CD and 12", both featuring the "Martyr" and "Mother F..." remixes that will so divide the fans. A version of the Maxi CD is also pressed and sold in Europe and Canada, with a couple of changes: a slightly different sleeve, first of all, and also a slightly different title, as the song has now chastely become "F**k them all", with a "parental advisory" sticker added on for good measure. (Another exciting first for Mylène.) Four promos will be issued: a standard monotrack CD, featuring the slightly shorter radio edit; two different 12"s: the first is pretty similar to the commercial edition, in content and appearance: they also both have the interesting particularity of playing at 45rpm on one side and 33rpm on the other. The second 12", much rarer, is a one-sided vinyl aimed specifically at DJ's and features only the "Mother F... dub mix", in a plain white sleeve with no reference or titles. The best of the lot, of course, is the deluxe edition, the very same as handed out to the album preview competition winners, although of course, in this instance, not autographed by the singer. Inside of a 53x30cm red envelope, stamped "Mylène Farmer" on one side and "Fuck them all" on the other and sealed with a red "MF" wax seal, is a fold-out cardboard object consisting of four Mylène silhouettes in different colour schemes, with the 1-track CD affixed to the blue silhouette: the first of a trio of sumptuous deluxe promos for singles issued from the "Avant que l'ombre..." album. Sadly, deluxe promos are on their way out, and will soon be a thing of the past...

With "Fuck them all", Mylène has effected what was probably the most anticipated comeback of her career, if only because of the length of time involved! Although not an out-and-out massive success, the song and accompanying video have enabled the star to renew her links with her public, who now face a year-long wait before her eventual return to the stage. Plenty of time for more singles, then: the next, coming along as early as July.

38/ Q.I.

In spite of the somewhat underwhelming performance of "Fuck them all", which was not quite the huge hit one might have wished for as the lead single from a brand new album (especially after a very long six-year wait), "Avant que l'ombre..." is nevertheless doing quite well, with 135,000 copies sold in the first week of release alone, and three consecutive weeks at the top of the album charts. Time for a new single to be put forward in order to keep sales healthy, but which one? Right from the start, whether it's 250 lucky competition winners at an exclusive preview or the general public listening to the brand new CD they just bought from the shop, most listeners seem to be in agreement: "Q.I." is one of the album's most obvious singles, a saucy little number full of naughty-sounding alliterations that sees Mylène in full-on "Libertine" mode. Rumours briefly point to "Dans les rues de Londres" or "L'Amour n'est rien..." as possible follow-ups, before the news is officially confirmed: yes, for once, the next single to be released will be the one fans were actually hoping for! Radio play for the track begins on May 13th, a little sluggishly perhaps, picking up slightly about a month later when a new mix, the "Sanctuary's radio edit" by Chris Cox, is sent out to various stations. Although the single is released physically on 4th July, it actually enters the charts a week before that, on downloads alone: its entry position in 77th place, however, is nothing to write home about, and the song jumps a massive 70 places the next week when the physical supports are made available, taking "Q.I." up to its highest chart placing at number 7. Sadly, the song fails to make much of an impact with the public at large, and once the initial wave of fan-buying has receded it quickly falls down the Top 100. With sales of around 70,000, it is one of the singer's more minor single releases. The track's chances aren't helped by the singer's continued lack of promotion: once again, there are no TV appearances, and no interviews either in the press or on the radio. Mylène remains totally invisible. Fair enough, as she can probably afford to do so, success so far being adequate enough: by the time "Q.I." is released, "Avant que l'ombre..." has sold 300,000 copies and been certified platinum, and the 13 Bercy concerts are already sold out. (It is during the forthcoming Bercy concerts that "Q.I." will be performed live for the first and so far only time, with Mylène and her female dancers putting on a "Swan Lake"-inspired choreography.) Still, in spite of her still undeniable levels of success, by the time summer 2005 comes around, some of the fans, not to mention some sections of the media, are beginning to feel more than a little bit irritated by the singer's seemingly inflexible attitude to promoting her new material: two singles in, and there still hasn't been one measly sighting of the elusive redhead. Any requests for interviews are systematically turned down. Amidst this total media blackout that only serves to feed the public's curiosity, it is then no big surprise when crazy rumours are sparked into life, seemingly out of nowhere.

On the occasion of the yearly "Fête de la Musique" festival, a tenacious rumour takes hold: Mylène will be present for the France 2 live broadcast from the Château de Versailles on June 21st, and will perform her new single "Q.I."! Strangely, the event organisers' attitude does nothing but encourage wild speculation: the host for the day, Daniela Lumbroso, refuses to answer directly when the question is put to her in press or radio interviews; a press communiqué even goes so far as saying that "Daniela will have a huge surprise for viewers on the day!" Come June 21st, the day itself, and a huge crowd has gathered at Versailles: many fans, convinced that Mylène is going to be making an appearance, have made the trip especially, coming sometimes from very far away. As the evening goes on and various acts take to the stage, one artist's name in particular is being shouted out repeatedly from the crowd, who know who they want to see. Finally, the time for the big surprise has come: and Daniela asks the audience to get ready for...a fireworks display! The initial disbelief quickly turns to anger, with the crowd raining insults on the poor host, who gets called some very nasty names: for many, the day has just turned very sour...In the end, no-one will ever get to the bottom of what really transpired on that day: was Mylène really ever scheduled to take part? Did she pull out at the last minute? Or was the whole thing just a rumour from start to finish? As she herself might say, "nobody knows"...

The "Q.I." video, like the single, will meet with mixed success. The clip is directed by Benoît Lestang, a make-up artist with work on many films to his credit, those of Laurent Boutonnat amongst them: in the early 90's, he oversees make-up and special effects on "Giorgino", returning again in 2007 for Boutonnat's second big-screen feature, the vastly more successful "Jacquou le Croquant". But his involvement in the Farmer universe dates way back to 1987, when he creates the somewhat creepy "Sans Contrefaçon" wooden marionnette. Shot in Budapest over two days in May 2005, the clip is shown on TV from 29th June, and shows a slightly domineering Mylène engaging in literary-influenced love games with her hispanic-looking companion, making her point with the help of some seriously high heels and especially probing fingers. The clip immediately divides opinion: on the positive side, some appreciate the somewhat futuristic intro, a new approach in the singer's videography. The video is felt to be in tune with the song itself, with its clear representation of the semantical pleasures Mylène is singing about, and a very picturesque interpretation of the fusion between two beings as the singer literally gets under her lover's skin...Those who like the video also point out that Mylène looks fantastic in it. The opposite, majority camp, however, is far less forgiving: to them, the video is too short, too simplistic, in dire need of a scenario, and far too bland: the risqué, saucy lyrics had them hoping for something a little more provocative. They are also not too keen on Mylène's look, feeling that the singer resembles an over-made-up doll in this latest promo. Still, at least a couple of things will be generally appreciated: the unexpected sight of Mylène's fingers exploring deep under her lover's skin, and her way with a pair of high heels as she plays dominatrix with her on-screen love interest, played by Rafael Amargo, well known in Spain as a dancer and choreographer specialising in Flamenco. But still, a lot of fans can't help but feel a little disappointed, and feel that the video could have been something more, could have taken things a little further...As it is, it is true that the clip is perfectly "safe", and not likely to encounter any problems with censorship: it is shown at any time of day, uncut. And yet, curiously, Universal Music will later be asked to remove any images showing Mylène's wandering fingers when a July TV ad for the album includes excerpts from the "Q.I." video: someone, somewhere, must have changed their mind...Apart from the creation of the "Sans Contrefaçon" puppet, the clip will be Benoît Lestang's first and last collaboration with the singer: the director commits suicide in 2008.

Mylène switches to full-on sexy mode for the "Q.I." single cover, in a Dominique Issermann shot that sees her striking a sultry pose in black stockings and suspenders while standing in front of a conveniently-placed mirror. The main support, this time, is a 3-track CD that features the instrumental version as well as the "Sanctuary's radio edit" briefly favoured by radio stations. A digipack Maxi CD carries the remixes, as well as a jigsaw-type sleeve design that plays repeatedly with close-up black and white shots of Mylène's stockinged legs. The very same shapely legs are seen again on the cover of the 12" and European Maxi CD, the sole release for foreign territories but featuring a slightly different sleeve design than the French issue. "Q.I." gets two basic and one fairly elaborate promos: as well as a monotrack CD and 3-track 12", both presented in a unique sleeve design, the penultimate Mylène Farmer deluxe promo makes its appearance. And it really is quite an elaborate object: a thick picture cardboard support that opens out in three folds, to one of which is attached the monotrack CD. With dimensions of 15x42cm when closed and 42x42cm when opened, the rather imposing item is slipped inside a tracing paper envelope sealed with a little red sticker stamped with the initials "MF". This is in turn kept inside a black leather holder with ten cut-out "windows" on its front side. Easily worth a few hundred Euros, you will need not only money for this item, but also adequate storage space.

The first two singles taken from the album so far have failed to deliver the big hit everyone was waiting for, even if success is still on the agenda for Mylène, thanks to the future Bercy concerts and relatively good sales figures for "Avant que l'ombre..." So, nothing to worry about, but a break-out hit would still be nice...will the next single do the trick? Sadly, no...but, on the plus side, it will bring the singer out of hiding at last.

39/ Redonne-Moi

The end of the year 2005 can occasionally feel like a pretty depressing time to be a Mylène Farmer fan: "Q.I.", the last single, released way back in July, has come and gone without making much of an impact. And since then, nothing. Just a continued total media absence from the singer, and an album that keeps sliding further down the charts every week. (In early November, "Avant que l'ombre..." languishes in 140th place...) In the press, various discouraging articles see the light of day: "Mylène Farmer: is she still an icon?" asks the magazine Télé Star in its November 7th edition, one of many such dispiriting pieces to be published around that time. Thankfully, the upcoming January Bercy concerts, sold out long ago, give the fans something to look forward to, and make it impossible for the media to write off the singer just yet. In the absence of any activity from the Farmer camp, rumours once again start flying around: some announce "L'Amour n'est rien..." as third single, while others, slightly more pessimistic, say there won't be any further singles at all! Enough to bring down the most enthusiastic of fans. But then, just as all hope seems lost, a breakthrough: on 13th October, a promo CD is sent out to NRJ, who play Mylène's new single for the first time at 8pm that day. Fans are obviously delighted that something -anything- is happening at last, even if the choice of "Redonne-moi" as the new single is a bit of a surprise, and one that is welcomed without much enthusiasm. A rather introspective lyric, where the singer once again enters into a dialogue with "l'autre", this undefined being that may or may not be herself, both or none, its precise meaning varying from song to song. A dialogue that this time sees the singer go in search of the missing parts of herself, in the hope of being reborn with renewed strength...Although rumoured to be much favoured by Mylène herself (some say she sees it as a new "Ainsi soit je..."), the song is a very, very slow ballad without much of a hook to speak of, and not an obvious hit...Indeed, in no time at all, airplay drops down to almost zero, the track being deemed too slow by the networks: "Redonne-moi" will never even manage to integrate the airplay Top 100. Not exactly a promising start...

But amidst all the doom and gloom, there is *some* good news: Mylène agrees to a TV appearance, finally! On November 12th, she is the star guest on "Symphonic Show", hosted by Daniela Lumbroso, a chance for the presenter to redeem herself with the singer's fans after the "Fête de la Musique" debacle. Although the show format usually dictates that guests must perform a 70's standard while accompanied by a symphonic orchestra, Mylène is exempt from such rules and allowed to perform her new single instead. She does, however, get to keep the full orchestra, and is even allowed to add her own Yvan Cassar on the piano. Not a live performance, of course, but who cares? After so long away from their TV screens, fans are happy just to see Mylène turn up somewhere, anywhere. The singer looks beautiful and classy dressed all in black, and even says a (very few) words at the end of her performance, even if those words consist mostly of "yes" and "no". Still, that's the most she's been heard to say in ages, and fans are wise enough to make the most of it: and a good thing too, as "Symphonic Show" will turn out to be both the first and last TV prestation to come from the singer for the whole of the "Avant que l'ombre..." era. She will not be seen again on TV screens until December 2008...

Mylène may have sung "Redonne-moi" on television, but that doesn't mean to say the single can be found in the shops: initially announced for a 7th November release, the track is only available as a download on the day itself. On TV, a new wave of ads for the album puts the "nouveau single" forward, and the story is pretty much the same in record stores: updated display materials alert consumers to the fact that the album "features the new single "Redonne-Moi"! But of the actual single itself, there is still no sign. Yet another rumour starts making the rounds, this one saying that Mylène has signed a number of promos, soon to be offered as prizes in an NRJ phone-in competition: seemingly without any foundation, the rumour soon fades away. Another release date for the single is vaguely bandied about, for some time in December, apparently... Yet, in the end, the release proper won't take place until January 3rd, almost three months after the first initial radio play. And even when the single does eventually come out, it is almost reluctantly: only one support is made available, and it's a limited edition too! Remixes? Forget it! An instrumental is all you get this time around. "Redonne-Moi" nevertheless manages to enter the charts at number 7, although it's quickly all downhill after that. With only around 30,000 copies sold, the song is Mylène's poorest-selling studio single ever: a figure that is perhaps not too surprising, as the one and only support to be found in stores was limited to...30,000. Of course, by the time the single eventually limps into shops, Mylène is only days away from the first date of the 13 Bercy concerts: no doubt a very busy woman by then, she can probably be forgiven for letting the single fizzle out. In any case, the fans can always console themselves with the video, about to be broadcast for the very first time.

On 19th November, "exclusive" stills from the "Redonne-Moi" video shoot surface online. Exclusive, it will turn out, by virtue of being stolen! A fan, who happened to be the girlfriend of a staffer on the shoot, saw the illicitly obtained images somehow come into her possession, and could not resist sharing them with the world: no doubt a tempting prospect, but a big, big mistake. The leak is traced, the Farmer police spring into action, and soon the law falls down hard on the bewildered fan. Taken to court by the star's management, and fined several thousand Euros (after her boyfriend has been fired from his job, obviously), the experience will no doubt be an unforgettable one for her, albeit in a *very* bad way...It is fairly easy to pass comment as an outsider, obviously, but all the same, in view of the singer's legendary degree of control over everything to do with her image, common sense would seem to indicate that messing with Ms. Farmer is never a good idea, and that any attempts to even try would result in nothing but unpleasantness...The clip is finally announced for December 7th: fans duly wait by their TV sets, but their waiting will be in vain: "Redonne-Moi" fails to materialize. Online, the rumour quickly spreads that the networks have received the video, but have been asked to refrain from broadcasting it just yet. More and more, it seems as though "Redonne-Moi" is no longer being exploited as a single in itself, but held back in order to coincide with the almost-there Bercy concerts: a logical enough approach, after all. Apart from the few stolen stills, nothing at all has leaked about the video, and there are rumours a-plenty: the new promo is a black and white film, featuring scenes of Mylène flying through the air, surrounded by ghosts, and all set in Venice. Even better, Laurent Boutonnat himself is said to be behind the camera! On the 9th, the first excerpts from the clip are shown during various mini-documentaries about Mylène's long-awaited return to the stage. And on the 11th, at last, the video is shown in full for the first time. Directed by François Hanss and shot at the Ateliers du Louvre in Paris, the video is nothing like the rumours had imagined. Laurent is nowhere to be seen, of course, and the images themselves are of a totally unrelated nature, showing a beautiful, very elegant Mylène as she moves through an artist's workshop, eventually coming across a familiar-looking statue with which she spends some time healing inner wounds. No real scenario to speak of, but a succession of beautiful and aesthetically-irreproachable images nonetheless, and, for the first time, cats make their appearance in the list of animals having starred over the years in the Farmer videography: in this instance, a black cat, an animal once believed to be the most common manifestation of a witch's familiar...

Fans and collectors won't have to dig quite so deep in their pockets this time around, what with the scarcity of supports around "Redonne-Moi": with only one item available commercially, a digipack 2-track CD that also features the instrumental version, Mylène achieves another first in her career: never before has she proposed a single available purely as a limited edition. The otherwise unavailable radio edit can be found on both the promos: the monotrack CD has a totally unique pixel-effect close-up shot of the singer's face, and is a nice enough item, but it pales in comparison with the deluxe version: a stunning, 35x49cm, thick cardboard support with, on both sides, a gorgeous picture of Mylène stepping out through half-open French doors in an impossibly sexy way, looking glamorous and very voluptuous in a see-through red dress. On one side of the item, one half of the doors lifts up to reveal the monotrack CD and artist name, while the doors on the other side fold open to reveal the song title. The whole thing is kept inside a large black envelope stamped with "Mylène Farmer" in gold lettering on one side, and "Redonne-Moi" in red on the other. The envelope is of course sealed with a red "MF" wax seal! This luxurious item is the last of the "deluxe promos", the end of an era, sadly, but at least the format went out in style. Nowadays, despite the song's low profile, this promo is one of the most sought after by collectors, and very hard to come by as only 300 copies were ever manufactured.

With Mylène just about to embark on the first of her 13 pharaonic Bercy concerts, fans are temporarily unconcerned with what the next single might be. In any case, they won't have to wait anywhere near as long this time around...

40/ L'Amour N'Est Rien...

Six months: that's how long fans had to wait for a follow-up to "Q.I." to finally come out at long last. Would it be as long again between "Redonne-Moi" and the next single? Thankfully, no: as a matter of fact, the fourth single to be taken from the "Avant que l'ombre..." album can be said to have come about surprisingly quickly. When the first of the "L'Amour n'est rien..." supports is released on 27th March, not even three months have elapsed since the last single release! Lightning quick, for a singer usually given to taking her time...In fact, the first hint of the track's potential as next single had come even earlier than that: on the 24th of January (just three weeks after "Redonne-Moi" has been released), NRJ unexpectedly include the song in their programming, just as Mylène is blowing everyone away at Bercy. (And picking up another NRJ Music Awards trophy while she's at it: on January 21st, she receives the accolade for "Best French album" in her absence, while she is on stage performing: some fans in the audience, alerted by text message, begin to shout "You've won, you've won!" at her.) And this initial NRJ broadcast, that takes everyone by surprise, takes place before any rumours about the next single have even had a chance to begin spreading around! For once, even the fans weren't quick enough to keep up with the latest Farmer developments: not a bad surprise, all things considered...The surprisingly early radio play will indeed turn out to be a very good omen for "L'Amour n'est rien...": the song will go on to enjoy far higher levels of airplay than any of the other singles taken from the album so far. On March 24th, NRJ plays the R&B-influenced "Sexually No" remix by the Bionix for the first time: a welcome foray from the singer into previously mostly unexplored musical horizons, and one that gets a very positive reception from fans overall. NRJ keeps the track on regular rotation, alternating between the radio edit and "Sexually No" versions. Even a station like Fun Radio, who has not played any Mylène songs with any regularity, and has more or less blanked her and her music since the days of "L'Âme-stram-gram", adds the track to its playlist, and spins it at fairly regular intervals.

Suddenly, and to everyone's surprise, "L'Amour n'est rien...", at least in terms of public awareness, has almost become *the* hit from the album: a gratifying development for Mylène, who, as well as writing her own lyrics as usual, co-composes the music along with Laurent Boutonnat. With sales of around 60,000, the track is a lesser commercial success than the likes of "Fuck them all", but it does come a year later, at a time when the record market has collapsed even further, this time to almost catastrophic levels. The single enters the charts at number 7 following the March 27th release of the first support, and after a temporary drop climbs back up into the Top 10, a few weeks later, when the Maxi CD is made available: overall, quite a good showing for a song not obviously thought of as being a potential future hit single. But the good fortunes of "L'Amour n'est rien..." don't stop there either: in Russia, the song becomes a huge hit, possibly even the biggest of Mylène's career in the country so far. The track will eventually be classed amongst the 10 most-played in Russia that year, and will even become the most-played track of 2006 on Europa Plus, Moscow's largest radio station! Naturally enough, the huge foreign success of "L'Amour n'est rien..." will impact on the song's presence on the stage: only performed at the 2006 Bercy concerts so far in France, the track is also integrated into the setlist for the Moscow and St Petersburgh dates of the 2009 Tour.

Mylène has never made a secret of the fact that she can't stand the tepid, the politically correct: and she says so again freely in "L'Amour n'est rien...", a carefree, playful song in which she makes clear her dislike for boring, passion-free relationships: "We moan early to make it stop", she sings at one point, deliciously naughty as always. And for such a playful song, nothing less than a playful video will do: shot in February 2006 in Paris, the clip sees Mylène performing a strip-tease that never takes itself too seriously, but yet still manages to go all the way! And quickly, too: at 3 minutes 40 seconds, it is one of Mylène's shortest clips ever. Directed by a certain M. Liberatore (Benoît Di Sabatino under a pseudonym, here working on his second pop promo for the singer, after 2002's animated "C'est une belle journée"), the video is seen by some as a cheeky, good-natured two fingers up at the paparazzi, who had recently managed to snatch some indiscreet shots of the topless singer holidaying in the Seychelles, where she was enjoying a well-earned break shortly after the triumph of the Bercy series of concerts. With "L'Amour n'est rien...", Mylène shows them all that she can show a lot more flesh than a grainy, long-distance shot when the mood takes her: she also reminds us of how good she looks doing it...she also looks radiant and undeniably happy, and certainly "liberated" as she cheerfully disrobes in front of Benoît's camera. The video is also a chance for the singer to commit her new, elaborate "flowers" hairstyle to film for the first time. Of course, the clip is not to everyone's liking, and divides the fans as always: while many welcome the sight of Mylène *au naturel*, and appreciate the touch of humour that runs throughout, some are less keen and criticize the video for being over-simplistic, and for what they feel is a blatant lack of creativity. It is true that the "L'Amour n'est rien..." budget was probably more modest than those of most of the epics that have gone before it, but at least no-one can say there isn't enough Mylène in it! The clip is shown online for the first time on 28th March, exclusively on Universal's website, before being shown on music channels from the following day onwards: this brand new way of unveiling a video is a first for the star, and quite a success too, with record viewing figures within hours. The "L'Amour n'est rien..." clip will also manage to top the charts of most downloaded music videos, after it is made available on the various legal download platforms: a sign of the times, and another first for the singer...

With the song quite the hit on TV and on the radio, it would have been easy to expect higher sales figures than the 60,000 or thereabouts that were eventually achieved: the track was never promoted on television, however, and it should also be noted that only two supports for

"L'Amour n'est rien..." ever made it into stores. One of these, the initial format released on March 27th, was also a limited edition, a 2-track digipack CD single featuring the instrumental version. Just over a month later, the second format is released, a digipack Maxi CD/CD-Rom that features the remixes as well as the clip. Both of these editions prompted some grumbling from fans over the quality of the sleeve art... No vinyl exists for the commercial issues. Three promotional items are produced: not one, but two monotrack CDs, one for the radio edit and the other for the strangely-titled "Sexually No" remix, each in a unique sleeve design. There are no more deluxe promos, sadly: sometimes, nowadays, promos are even sent out in mp3 form, a less than attractive format for collectors as they don't actually exist in a physical form. But at least, "L'Amour n'est rien" benefits from a promo-only 12" in unique sleeve art, the first time since "La poupée qui fait non" that a single sees its vinyl release limited to promotional issue only.

Four singles in already, and while none of those have been massive hits, the Bercy concerts and the moderate success of "L'Amour n'est rien..." have managed to breathe a little more life into the album, which manages to temporarily climb back up the charts, all the way up to number 15, before promptly dropping back down again. Time for a fifth, and final single...

41/ Peut-Être Toi

After four singles and still no huge hit to speak of, fans are putting their faith in one particular song to do the trick at last: "Peut-être toi" is now the track most of them pray will be released as next single. Not too encouragingly though, it is widely rumoured (to the point that it almost seems semi-official) that the fifth and final single from "Avant que l'ombre..." will be "Dans les rues de Londres". Although the track itself is a firm favourite on the album, many feel that the melancholy, mid-tempo tune is unlikely to fare too well in the charts: still, there's nothing to do but resign oneself to Mylène's choice. But then, out of nowhere, an official announcement is made on June 16th: "Peut-être toi" will indeed be the next single! Fans can hardly believe their luck: was the "Dans les rues de Londres" rumour exactly that, and nothing more? Or did Mylène give in for once and decide to give the fans what they wanted? The how and the why of it all will forever remain a mystery...In any case, not long after the unexpected announcement has been made, NRJ plays the track for the first time, on 19th June. In what is yet another great surprise, the tune has been comprehensively remixed, and now sounds more like a single than ever, punchier, more to the point, more efficient. Sadly, NRJ radio seems unimpressed, and drops the song from its playlist after a few measly rotations. Never mind: on 26th June, another remix is to be heard for the first time, the Bionix "Miss Farmer's remix": in view of the warm reception accorded to the Bionix's previous "L'Amour n'est rien..." re-working, hopes are high that their new effort will be appreciated in equal measure: unfortunately, that will most definitely not be the case. French fans, for the most part, are put off by a remix that they feel is too far removed from the singer's usual musical universe: the fact that it starts with a rap is just too much for some, who don't hesitate to call it "horrid" and "an abomination". A bit harsh, perhaps, for what is after all not such a bad version to the ears of R&B enthusiasts, and a valiant effort on Mylène's part to dip her toes in an unexpected and fairly unexplored musical genre for her. A genre that she could *almost* be said to have flirted with many years ago already anyway, with the early 90's "Mum's rap" of "Plus Grandir", even if the connection with "rap", as the term is generally understood, is perhaps a little bit tenuous in this case...But whether the fans like it or not, the R&B remix is also sent out as promo to various radio stations, in the hope of integrating their playlists: sadly, the networks won't take the bait. From the 6th of July onwards, both versions are available for legal download: initial digital sales are disappointingly average. A new remix by Chris Cox can be heard in clubs from the 27th, with a lot more enthusiasm on the fans' part this time: not too surprising a reaction, the remixer's previous work for the star (on "Q.I." and "Désenchantée") having already proved a hit with the singer's admirers.

Finally, the single itself is actually released on 21st August, more than two months after the initial official announcement. With all three supports being announced

MYLENE FARMER — THE SINGLE FILE

as limited editions, would-be buyers waste no time and rush to their nearest record store on the day of release, sending "Peut-être toi" flying in at number 3 in its first week. This is the best chart position yet for a single taken from the album, and the first time that one has made it into the Top 3, or even Top 5! And yet, after this promising early start, "Peut-être toi" quickly follows in the path of its predecessors and inexorably heads down the charts, even if it does manage to hang around in the Top 100 until early December. At around 50,000, sales are once again not what might have been hoped for, although of course this must once more be put into context: not only is she now operating in a fastly-deteriorating record market (even worse in the case of singles), but Mylène has once again enjoyed barely any radio play whatsoever, and promoted her new single on exactly zero occasions. Not only that, but no-one is really expecting miracles from what is the fifth single from an album that is by now languishing in the lower echelons of the charts...But even if "Peut-être toi" the single has failed to set the world ablaze, the song will at least be one of the strong moments of the 13 Bercy concerts: few of those present at the time are likely to forget Mylène's mind-blowing entrance, lying in her sarcophagus, as her voice ordered the crowd to "shut up!" A demand the crowd will prefer to ignore, naturally enough...

A couple of exciting rumours begin to make the rounds towards the later part of the month. First up, the admittedly tantalizing prospect of a Mylène/Madonna duet: unfortunately, it now seems like this was never on the cards at all, but had merely come about as a result of the two women providing the voices of Princess Sélénia in Luc Besson's "Arthur" movies, each in their respective language: who knows whether the two singers even actually met at all in the process of dubbing their roles...The rumour, while completely false, was nevertheless one of the most exciting to pop up around the singer, and certainly one of the easiest to want to believe in: the inevitable worldwide media exposure that would have resulted from such a duet being too fantastic a prospect not to daydream about, at least just a little...but it was not to be. The second rumour, on the other hand, was spot on pretty much from the start: Mylène would apparently have recorded a song with an international male artist of considerable stature. The name Moby starts to float around very quickly: indeed, fans have no idea just how soon they'll be able to hear the finished product.

But in the meantime, the spotlight, dull as it may be, is still on "Peut-être toi", and the accompanying video that sees Mylène exploring new visual ground. Although the clip is her second animated video, after 2002's "C'est une belle journée", this is the first time that the singer turns to the world of manga and anime for inspiration. Her collaborators for the occasion certainly have impeccable credentials: the director, Naoko Kasumi, was behind the 2004 anime classic "Innocence (Ghost in the shell II)", while the scenario comes from none other than Katsuhiro Otomo, who was part of the creative team responsible for the all-time anime and manga classic "Akira". For anyone both a Farmer *and* manga fan, the collaboration was nothing less than a match made in heaven...After a captive cartoon Mylène is freed by her blond male companion from some dank forgotten cell, the pair make their escape through a ravaged, post-nuclear-Armageddon-type subterranean city, fighting malevolent robots along the way with the use of some serious sword skills. But the cornered heroine falls from a great height into a vast body of water and almost drowns, saved only by her rescuing lover's underwater kiss of life. Fighting their way ahead, the couple eventually reach the city's highest levels, where a trapdoor at last allows them to exit onto the surface and into the sun's welcoming rays. Finally free, the couple momentarily lose themselves in a loving embrace, but their inattention will prove fatal: a fierce-looking spear promptly comes flying in through the air in their direction, impaling the couple on the spot. Ouch! But at least their love will now remain eternal, as symbolized by the moss-covered statue they will eventually turn into...Many have pointed out the ending's similarities to that of previous clips such as "Désenchantée", with the recurring theme of a hard-gained freedom that is, in the end, only in vain. The thematic is also somewhat reminiscent of "Beyond my control" and its notion of death being the only guarantee of ever-lasting love: as such, the collaboration between Mylène and the anime I.G. production company can be said to have produced a video that is faithful to and consistent with the singer's complex universe. Which is not to say that everyone is happy with the video, far from it: while most fans love the concept of a manga Mylène, some find the scenario lacking and the animation not the best it could have been. For Mylène, in any case, the experience seems to have been a pleasant one: allegedly a fan of "Ghost in the shell", the singer was said by the video director to have put great faith in the creative team, and to have been "enchanted" by the end result. The clip's artistry will also be recognized professionally on two occasions: in 2006, "Peut-être toi" is voted best animated clip of the year on the Yahoo Music France website, beating videos by Jamiroquai, Gorillaz and Eminem along the way. In 2007, it is selected for inclusion in the 15th Anima Mundi International animation festival, which takes place in July in Brazil. In a manner that is fitting for the times, the clip is initially revealed on 7th July as a 20-second excerpt available exclusively on mobile phones through I-mode, followed by a full-length broadcast the very next day only on the Orange network! It can be viewed for free online from the 13th, with pre-historic television having to wait until the 19th. "Peut-être toi" then goes on to reach first place in the iTunes music video download charts when it is made available digitally on the 29th. Despite the occasional grumblings, the animated promo still succeeds in creating something of a little buzz overall: and while it hasn't managed to become one of the Farmer video classics, it is nevertheless fair to say that the clip remains, for many fans, one of the favourites from the "Avant que l'ombre..." era.

In the shops, three manga-tastic supports are on offer: a 2-track digipack single features the single and instrumental versions, with the remixes coming courtesy of the digipack Maxi CD and vinyl 12", a format which makes a welcome return. A deluxe promo for "Peut-être toi" would no doubt have been a beautiful object, but alas, it was not to be...Of the three promos to be found, the most desirable must be the 2-track CD (featuring the much-despised "Miss Farmer's remix") that comes with a unique black and white manga-style depiction of the singer on its sleeve. The European promo CD (issued although the single will eventually be released within France only) features the radio edit and no cover art at all, as it comes in a clear plastic sleeve: not the most interesting of items. As for the promo 12", it is completely similar to the commercial issue, bar the mentions on the sleeve and label.

"Peut-être toi" marks the end of the "Avant que l'ombre..." era. It has been a long time since a Mylène Farmer studio album failed to reach the million mark, but here it is. Of course, Mylène can't escape the collapsing record market, and it is also true that her media absence and lack of promotional activity around this period are at their highest level ever, often frustratingly so for fans and the media alike; still, the album cannot be so easily dismissed, both in artistry and in terms of commercial success. It may not have generated any huge hits, it's true, but "Avant que l'ombre..." is nevertheless a rich and rewarding record, one that has subsequently gone on to become a favourite for many fans. With the title track, Laurent Boutonnat delivers one of his finest compositions, and there is no denying the sublime beauty of Mylène's voice on tracks such as "J'attends" or "Et pourtant..." Many also appreciate the album's overall warm tone and rich colours, even if others are perhaps less keen on the over-representation of ballads on this particular opus. Inevitably, by now, the weight of expectation that lies on Mylène's shoulders is so great that it would be impossible for her to release an album that pleases everyone anyway: indeed, one of the reviews around the time of the album's release will pick up on the fact, noting that "in the end, Mylène Farmer's latest album suffers from only one major flaw: it is the sixth studio album by an artist from whom everyone expects too much." Commercially, while not as big a success as its predecessors on pure sales alone, the album still can not be said to be a failure, having shifted around 500,000 units, and earning itself double platinum status. Not quite the million we were used to, but the internet and sickly record market have inevitably made their mark. Originally released as a limited "cruciform" edition (limited to 200,000), the album will also be edited in several European countries, reaching the number one spot in Belgium, number 2 in Switzerland and 5 in Greece. "Avant que l'ombre..." is also made available in the Ukraine, Russia, Canada, Taiwan, Japan...no doubt gaining the singer many new overseas admirers at the same time. The collectors' box set, in its luxurious heavy velvet packaging, is amongst the best: inside the box, an LP-sized replica of the limited CD sleeve folds out to measurements of almost 1x1m, with a beautiful glazed-paper booklet that includes some daring shots of the singer posing in very little as she wanders the rooms and corridors of an empty castle. Limited to 7,000, this item was the object of much desire amongst fans, and caused some heavily chaotic scenes when it first appeared in stores...

With the "Avant que l'ombre..." era behind her, it is almost time for Mylène to move on to the logical next step and "Avant que l'ombre...à Bercy". But not just yet though, for there is still the question of that Moby duet first, and it will be coming surprisingly quickly.

42/ Slipping Away (Crier La Vie)

Internet rumours have begun to circulate as early as June: it is whispered that Mylène has hooked up with Moby in New York, and that the two artists have recorded one -or possibly even two- brand new tracks together. The rumour doesn't sound too far fetched: Moby is said to have been in the crowd for at least one of the January Bercy concerts, and it is already known that there exists a friendship between the two, with Moby's name having come up on several occasions in the past already, as a possible collaborator for some future hypothetical Boutonnat-free album. The collaboration, apparently, would have come about just a month before, in May, with the singers hitting on the idea of recording a new version of Moby's own "Slipping Away", from his "Hotel" album, originally a solo song, with Mylène adding French lyrics (her own, of course) for her parts. Fans won't be kept waiting too long wondering, as the track is played on the radio for the first time as early as September 5th. For once, NRJ will miss out on the exclusive: a provincial station somehow beats them to it by a good few hours, forcing NRJ to bring forward the time of their initial broadcast, in case any more stations should get there first: bad news for the usually Mylène-shy broadcaster, but a sign of great things to come for the song itself. The version chosen to act as radio edit is markedly different from Moby's original: remixed by the

British duo Manhattan Clique towards the end of July in London, with Mylène in attendance, the new production is faster, more polished, and right away, on very first listen, it sounds like a hit. The reaction from the public and fans alike is also immediately very positive, with great enthusiasm and many openly expressing thanks that Mylène has, at last, seemingly opened herself up to new musical horizons. After the so-so performance of the "Avant que l'ombre..." singles, many fans, a little disappointed by the album as a whole, are delighted to hear their idol coming back with such an obvious and potent smash. It is, obviously, an almost sacrilegious thing to say, but it is an undeniable fact: after "Avant que l'ombre...", the idea has begun to float amongst some fans that, maybe, just maybe, it might be time for the singer to try new things, perhaps even, shock horror for some, to start working with different people...

But of course the time for that hasn't quite come yet, even if "Slipping Away (Crier la vie)", as it is now known, quickly gives rise to a rumour that Mylène's next album will be composed and produced entirely by Moby. The rumour is false but, as we now know, not without a grain of partial truth concerning future endeavours...Another rumour that comes back around this time is that of the infamous "duets album": a compilation of the singer's existing duets, plus new collaborations with the likes of Brian Molko, David Bowie, Kate Bush...clearly a pleasing concept, but sadly nowhere near true. In any case, in September of 2006, the Moby duet -the fourth of Mylène's career- is off to a great start: radio play keeps on building up, with Fun Radio and NRJ both including the track in their playlists, and playing it several times a day: Mylène hasn't known airplay like this since, well, a long time ago. As well as sustained radio play, "Slipping Away" also benefits from a strong advertising campaign on TV and in the press: Mylène, as is her way, may not actually be taking part in any of this herself, but the fans are delighted anyway, as the singer's name is suddenly everywhere again, and once more associated with an unqualified success. The song is initially made available as a download across the various legal platforms, taking only a few hours to become a best-seller. And when it is eventually released as a physical single on 25th September (only just over a month after "Peut-être toi" first hit the stores!), "Slipping Away" goes straight in at number 1: for the singer, this is her fourth visit to the top of the singles charts, after the triumphs of "Pourvu qu'elles soient douces", "Désenchantée" and "XXL", and it also happens to be her first number 1 single in eleven years! The song will be a huge hit in France, spending eleven consecutive weeks inside of the Top 10 and selling close to 200,000 copies (yet another gold certification), a sales figure reminiscent of the good old days and a genuine triumph in an age where the singles market is looking decidedly unhealthy. "Slipping Away" also does great business in Belgium, Greece, Switzerland and Quebec, as well as being a huge smash on Russian radio. Even those sections of the media not usually given to praising the star have to concede that her latest offering is right on target: to those who were already getting ready to prematurely bury her, gleefully convinced that she was "finished" as a relevant musical force, "Slipping Away" is a timely reminder that Mylène Farmer is still a name to be reckoned with...

The video, directed by Hugo Ramirez, remains the same as Moby's original promo, with the exception of the inclusion of French text and, also, of one or two shots of a *very* young-looking Mylène, although these are not overtly easy to find and can easily be missed. Available to view on the Yahoo website from September 15th, and on television from the 20th, the video puts together a succession of "slice of life" images from photographs taken over the last few decades, the shots being linked together in neat and inventive ways as the song lyrics drift by across the screen. The same concept will be used again when yet another version of the duet, featuring a local artist, is released for the Spanish market. As well as having no original video of its own, the single "Slipping Away (Crier la vie)" does not feature on any of Mylène's studio or compilation albums to date: it will, however, be included on the French version of Moby's own "Go- very best of", although sadly *not* on the English or American editions: it will be replaced by his own solo version for these markets. (In England and America, it is not "Slipping Away", but "New York New York" featuring Debbie Harry that will act as lead single for the American musician's hits compilation.) And strangely for such a huge hit, it will never appear on hit singles compilations of any kind, or if it does, it is then only under the guise of Moby's original solo version: this is, of course, in keeping with the tradition of Mylène's work never appearing on any compilations (other than her own) since 1989.

Some of the promotional materials for the single promised "an unseen Mylène" on the cover, and they weren't lying: when "Slipping Away" becomes available to buy from the shops, fans can discover their idol sharing the front sleeve with Moby...as babies. (A surprisingly well-built baby, in Mylène's case.) In France, there are no less than three different CD editions to choose from, including a 2-track single as well as two Maxi CDs with varying content, in addition to a 12" that will also be distributed in some European countries. The only Europe-specific release is a Maxi CD that will be issued slightly later on, in January 2007. French promos consist of a monotrack CD in a blue titles sleeve, as well as a 5-track CD-R in a translucent plastic picture sleeve. Unusually, there are also promo CDs for normally neglected territories such as Greece and Italy, and even Lithuania! A UK "white label" 12" is also pressed, in a plain black sleeve with no mentions whatsoever.

Having punctuated the end of the "Avant que l'ombre..." period with a massive hit single (even if it did not come from the album itself), Mylène is now ready to move on by looking back to the early part of the year, and the amazing triumph of the 13 Bercy concerts: time for a couple of live singles to remind us of those glorious days...

43/ Avant Que L'Ombre...(live) - 44/ Déshabillez-Moi (live)

In accordance with Mylène's wishes, it is "Avant que l'ombre..." that is chosen to act as first single to be taken from the forthcoming live album "Avant que l'ombre...à Bercy". Easily one of the best tracks off the original studio album, possibly even one of Laurent Boutonnat's finest-ever compositions, the song serves as closer for the live shows and benefits from one of the most astounding moments in the singer's stage career: Mylène calls on the talents of the Aquatic Show team to create what is possibly her most moving and elaborate stage exit to date. A gigantic water curtain, an incongruous yet magical sight within the cavernous Bercy space, opens and closes on the singer as she performs, the water sending a wave of freshness settling over the stunned audience; more magical still, the water is cleverly manipulated into spelling out, in huge, fleeting letters, the word "passé", and then the singer's silhouette, with fans looking on open-mouthed as Mylène makes her slow ascent up the stairs, at the top of which she will shortly be making her goodbyes in her own inimitable fashion. An innovative, breath-taking spectacle that makes use of burgeoning techniques, with computers regulating the water output into complex sequences in order to achieve the desired effect. And if the desired effect was to astonish, well, mission accomplished: it's enough to take a look at the fans' shocked, overwhelmed expressions at the end of the show to realise that the moment was of a profoundly moving and magical nature: Mylène certainly can't be faulted for grandeur, and none will even try. Farmer fan or not, the never-before-seen water effects make a huge impression, and may well have caused as much ink to flow as there was water in the original curtain itself, with countless press articles reporting breathlessly on the singer's latest scenic wonder.

The track is played on the radio for the first time on October 20th, with a provincial station once more managing to somehow snatch the exclusive from NRJ by just a few hours. Sadly, these sneaky tactics won't bode as well for this track as they previously did for "Slipping Away (Crier la vie)": after a few initial broadcasts, airplay quickly becomes non-existent. The track, admittedly, is not exactly radio-friendly, even in its (cruelly) truncated edit; as for playing the full-length version, few stations are prepared to commit to a running time of almost eight minutes. The same fate will befall the clip when it is sent out to TV: few networks bother to broadcast the full-length version, or even the shorter edit that is also made available, past a few initial showings. Nevertheless, this is a great day for the fans, who get to see the first filmed images of the soon-to-be released concert, their first opportunity to re-live those magical January days. The single is released on 27th November, on one support only, a two-track CD that features the live edited version as well as the "version album", actually an edited mix of the album original.

Entering the charts at number 10, it is down all the way after that for the song, although it will not leave the Top 100 until mid-May of the following year, with cumulative sales of around 25,000: a low number, but fairly representative for a live single release, and still comparatively impressive. A solitary promo is pressed, a 2-track CD with identical tracklisting and a unique "giant closed doors" sleeve. Although "Avant que l'ombre…" has only been performed in full during the Bercy concerts so far, its musical theme will be used again for the interlude section of the 2009 shows: at the Stade de France, the haunting melody soundtracks the singer as she takes the long slow walk back to the stage under the cheers of the adoring crowd, as blue spotlights open the way before her: who can even begin to imagine what she must have been feeling at the time?

"Avant que l'ombre…à Bercy" has been in the shops since December, and a real triumph it is too, not too surprisingly: 100,000 copies of the DVD are sold in just one week. In just a few days, it becomes the best-selling musical DVD by a French artist, ever. In view of its already resounding success, few were hoping for a second single release, and yet a promo CD is sent out to radio stations in early February 2007 for "Déshabillez-Moi". A cover of Juliette Gréco's 1967 classic, which originally outraged 60's French society with its then-shocking lyrics, the song has a long history with Mylène. Included on her "Ainsi soit je…" opus, the singer performs the song live for the first time at the televised "Oscars de la Mode" in 1987: a revealing performance, as one of Mylène's breasts makes a bid for freedom and is briefly broadcast live to the nation. It has often been said that "Déshabillez-Moi" almost made it as a single back in the 80's: when another artist released their own version of the song around the same time, however, any plans for release were abandoned. On the stage, Mylène first performs the track during the '89 Tour, showing an undeniable sense of irony as she does so while wearing a straitjacket. The restraints are gone for the 2006 Bercy version, as is clear from Mylène's sensual performance and rather enthusiastic emphasis on the word "doigté"...There is a lot of humour in the 2009 performances, too: on the first night, she messes up the words and sings "Je me suis trompée..." instead; and on the 22nd, she is overcome with laughter after screaming her famous "Déshabillez-Moiiiiiiiiiiii!!!" On the 27th, the song is dedicated to Juliette Gréco, the track's original performer, who is in the audience: Mylène does her justice with a sizzling prestation. After the radio stations have received their promos, however, not much happens, and the song is barely played, if at all: the same goes for the clip, a straight excerpt from the concert, when it is shown for the first time on February 15th. This is not overly surprising though, with this being another live release; and what's more, it is generally felt that the single release of "Déshabillez-Moi" is not so much a commercial endeavour as a little gift from Mylène to her fans. So no-one is overly disappointed when the single ends up selling just 20,000 copies, the lowest score so far of Mylène's career. Once again, only one support is available in stores when the song is released on March 5th: a 2-track CD that features live versions of the single as well as "Porno Graphique", in a picture sleeve by Claude Gassian. Mylène's faitfhul fans nevertheless manage to purchase enough of the support to give her another Top 10 hit the following week. Collectors don't have much to choose from this time around either, as once again only one promo sees the light of day, a monotrack CD in titles sleeve (minus Claude Gassian photograph) that features the live version.

And so the "Avant que l'ombre...à Bercy" era comes to an end. 13 dates, almost 200,000 spectators, one of the most visually and emotionally rich live shows ever: often described, quite appropriately, as "pharaonic", the 2006 Bercy shows, sold out a year in advance, represent, for many, Mylène Farmer at her scenic pinnacle. A grand entrance, multiple stages, a suspended bridge, Mylène flying above the audience's heads, a gigantic water curtain...The kind of spectacle never before seen in France, and, arguably, not very often seen anywhere else either. A number 1 album in its first week of release, the "Avant que l'ombre...à Bercy" live recording will go on to sell over 150,000 copies, and is certified gold two weeks after its December 4th release. A faithful record of the concerts, although the song "Ainsi soit je...", performed on three occasions during the early dates, is missing. An elaborate collectors' item is issued: limited to 7,000, a 38x18x16cm box slides open to reveal a plastic replica of the sarcophagus in which the singer makes her entrance, inside of which are included the double CD and double DVD, as well as an oversize booklet. The accompanying DVD will achieve even more spectacular sales figures: with 400,000 units shifted, it is certified diamond later on in the month. In another sign of the changing times, "Avant que l'ombre...à Bercy" is the first of the singer's albums not to be released in cassette form!

And so begins another period of silence. Who knows how long the singer will keep us waiting this time? Thankfully, it won't be quite as long as six years, and when Mylène does return, she will be doing so with quite some style, once again managing to make a rather big impression...

Part 7: Point De Suture / No 5 On Tour

45/ Dégénération

To everyone's complete and utter surprise, Mylène's return is announced by Pascal Nègre, head of Polydor, as early as January 2008: an unexpectedly rapid comeback, as it has only been just over a year since her last album, "Avant que l'ombre...à Bercy"! An unusually swift turnaround for the singer, but still, no-one is complaining...But the best is yet to come, and an announcement on February 28th causes an instant sensation with fans and in the media: Mylène is coming back to the stage with a concert at the Stade de France on 12th September 2009, her birthday, with tickets going on sale from March 28th! The following week, another stadium date is revealed, this time in Geneva: any fears that this would be another Paris-only series of concerts are quickly dismissed. Come the day, and the 80,000 Stade de France places are sold in a record two hours, with the internet going into meltdown, and many frustrated fans unable to get their hands on the precious tickets. To satisfy those who were unlucky first time round, another date is added for the 11th, and Mylène goes on to beat her own record: this time, the stadium is sold out in just over an hour! Another stadium date is then added, this time for Brussels. This rush for tickets, and the speed with which they disappeared would be amazing in any case, but even more so when one considers that the concerts are at the time still more than a year and a half in the future! Shortly afterwards, a full-scale tour is announced, bringing about record ticket sales once again: 100,000 sold in the first day alone. And all this, before a single note of the singer's new material has even been heard...

It is the daily newspaper Ouest-France that carries the very first piece of information concerning said material: on May 21st, an interview with Thierry Suc reveals that the new single will be called "Dégénération", with an initial first radio play on June 19th. Immediately, countless fans everywhere are reminded of the "Génération Désenchantée": Mylène will indeed later confess to deliberately "amusing" herself by playing with the words in this self-referential way. Meanwhile, fans also "amuse" themselves online: mere days after the Ouest-France article, the first supposed "leaks" make their appearance on the net, prompting endless speculation in forums dedicated to the star. Is it real? Is it a fake? While some are clearly and obviously not the real thing, some of the more inventive efforts at least have the merit of keeping us guessing, and are a good way to kill time until the real thing is revealed...The single visuals are presented for the very first time on June 7th, on the music.me website: naturally, the sleeve, featuring a brand new shot by Simon Hawk (a.k.a. John Nollet, Mylène's long-time personal hair artist), is immediately considered from all angles and dissected to within an inch of its life. The most common observation is that the photograph is reminiscent of the "L'Histoire d'une fée, c'est..." cover artwork. Another reference: the photographer Man Ray and his early 20th century work "Violon d'Ingres". And to those who look closer, another seemingly significant detail is revealed: a close inspection of the scar running across Mylène's back appears to show the letters IY/H, or "With God's will" in Hebrew. Another religious reference from the star? It would seem so, although this has of course never been confirmed, and could -just could- be mere coincidence: although, given that Mylène is very much aware that everything to do with her and her work is immediately put under the microscope, coincidence never seems too likely...Surprisingly, not everyone is convinced that this is the real deal: this woman, ony half-seen from the back, doesn't look like Mylène at all, some say. This photograph is a fake!

In retrospect, such disbelief may come across as somewhat amusing, but it is worth remembering that skepticism seemed to be the order of the day, as far as "Dégénération" was concerned: for as well as making public the single cover art, the website also proposes two 30-second excerpts from the track itself. And there, the fans' reaction is unlike anything that has come before: the cold, electronic sounds, the lack of a classical verse/chorus structure, not to mention the lack of words, all of these factors polarize opinion and leave everyone feeling slightly confused. Is this the original version, or some kind of remix? What has happened to Mylène's way with words? Some are now convinced, more than ever, that it is indeed just some kind of fake: how could this possibly actually be Mylène Farmer's new song? And yet, it won't be long until their doubts are irreversibly cast aside: in the early hours of June 14th (incidentally, Laurent Boutonnat's birthday), the Ecompil website unexpectedly offers the full track for legal download, albeit for only a few hours before it is mysteriously withdrawn, with Thierry Suc said to be "furious" over the leak. And yet, in spite of Mylène's manager's protestations, some begin to put forward the hypothesis that the leak was, in fact, totally voluntary and intended to create a buzz...In the end, however, this doesn't seem to be a very likely scenario: although it was promptly taken down, many on-the-ball fans nevertheless managed to download the track that night, with the inevitable result that "Dégénération" quickly became available, for free, to anyone determined enough to look for it on the net...With an official online release date only days away, this wouldn't make any commercial sense, and it is more likely that the slip happened as the result of some kind of programming error. As for the suggestion that the "leak" was meant to generate a buzz, it could be argued that the buzz could harldy have been any bigger than it already was anyway!

On 17th June, the DJ Martin Solveig is named by "Le Parisien" as one of the remixers: his version is unique in the Farmer remixography as being the only one to ever go by two different official names: and indeed, the "Comatik Club" and "Dégénérave" remixes are one and the same. Two days later, from noon on the 19th, "Dégénération" is available for legal download at last, with radios able to download it slightly earlier, at 6am, from a dedicated platform: most of the major stations have, in any case, received a copy of the monotrack promo CD by then, and NRJ duly plays the track from 7.30. The very next day, the song sits pretty at the top of the digital charts, and with impressive sales figures to boot: close to 5,000 (4,998, to be precise) downloads in three days, an unheard-of achievement in France at the time. As Polydor don't fail to point out, this is yet another record for Mylène Farmer...On 26th June, the first clip teaser, 22 seconds long, is shown on the musique.sfr.fr website, with two further teasers announced for the 30th and the full video to come later in July, on the 10th! The first, all too brief images immediately send fans into ecstasies: it's going to be a long two weeks...The following day, it is Tomer G who is in turn revealed to be one of the "Dégénération" remixers: a 1-minute excerpt from his "Tomer G Sexy Club Mix" gets an immediately enthusiastic reception. The wait becomes even more unbearable when, on July 1st, Polydor issue a communiqué informing the public that "the first single "Dégénération" will be illustrated by the talented Bruno Aveillan. The clip, shot in Prague, fits in with the great Farmer tradition and renews the link with the cinematographic genre of the early days. Mylène Farmer plays the role of a character with powers as exceptional as her musical career!" After a build-up like that, it even gets hard to sleep, waiting for this new video...Paris-Match magazine eases the pain a little on the 3rd, with an article that features new exclusive Claude Gassian photographs from the video shoot. "Only" a week to go...and finally, on the 10th, it is here at last: the brand new "Dégénération" video is shown in full for the first time from 12.45 on the SFRmusic website. What happens next is of course no surprise: untold thousands rush the site, which promptly crashes. Luckily, the (understandably) frustrated fans don't have to wait too long for their chance to see Mylène's new video at last, as it is soon made available on other websites, and on various TV music channels later on that same day, to their great relief...

When the single is finally released on 18th August, success is once again on the cards: "Dégénération" goes straight to the top of the charts, with 27,401 copies sold in the first week alone: the best first-week sales for any other single that year so far. The number 1 is Mylène's fifth: she now holds the joint record with Céline Dion for most number 1 singles (although Céline will quickly be left to eat dust in Mylène's wake in the coming months.) All in all, "Dégénération" will go on to achieve sales of around 80,000: a figure that includes both physical formats and downloads, and a great tally, not only in view of the current singles market, but also for a song that is so structurally atypical that it initially left many fans feeling confused. On the radio, on the other hand, the song cannot be said to be an outright hit: airplay drops considerably after the initial first few weeks, and the song will never get any higher than number 51 in the airplay charts. "Dégénération" cannot truthfully be said to have been a hit with the public at large either, and once the initial wave of fan-buying has passed, the single heads down the charts fairly quickly. On TV and online, at least, things are a little bit better, if only temporarily: but that's no surprise, what with all the fans wanting to see, again and again, *that* video...

Shot in the Czech republic, near Prague, the "Dégénération" video opens to the clinical sights and sounds of some forbidding secret medical laboratory, set in a fantasy-universe whose location is somehow vaguely reminiscent of Eastern Europe, without ever being too specific on the subject. The "laboratory" is in fact an old psychiatric hospital, the Bonice Asylum on the outskirts of Prague. Mylène is introduced as an otherworldly creature dressed in tightly-bound white strips of cloth: perhaps, as has often been pointed out, a visual reference to the Fifth Element's heroine Leeloo, as imagined by her friend Luc Besson and played by Milla Jojovich. Or maybe, as others have also said, a bandage-wrapped Mummy coming to life after a centuries-long sleep (but better preserved.) According to the storyboard, however, Mylène was initially supposed to be wearing a long dress: this will eventually be replaced by an original creation by Patricia Aveillan, the director's sister. Another commonly-evoked possible visual reference is the film "Perfume", in which the murderous "hero" puts a whole angry crowd under his spell with a simple wave of his hand, turning the mob into one huge copulating mass by wafting an irresistible perfume over their heads... Strapped down onto an examination table, the red-haired creature effortlessly breaks free of her bonds before the assembled, sinister-looking medical staff have a chance to probe her from all angles. Confusion and panic ensue, with medics shouting orders as heavily-armed soldiers rush to the scene, ready to subdue the escaped creature. But the strange, beautiful being has a few tricks up her sleeve, or thereabouts: before any of her captors can apprehend her, she shoots out a strange, benign-looking fluid from her palms. The effect of the curious wave as it settles over the medical staff and soldiers is soon apparent, as they forget all about law and order to give in to their loving urges instead (girl, boy, anyone nearby will do.) Soon the whole place becomes one big (tasteful) orgy, Mylène lovingly covering everyone in the now much-desired blue light...Some of these scenes, eventually deleted, made use of an X-ray machine in order to show the embracing bodies in their skeletal form, but this was dropped when it was felt that the scenes didn't fit in with the rest of the images. Having thereby neutralised her jailors' crueller instincts, and having delivered them into more agreeable ones, the creature makes her exit, unbothered... The video is, in fact, a fairly close imagining of the song's central message: though its meaning was not immediately evident, thanks to fairly cryptic lyrics, it was eventually concluded that with "Dégénération", Mylène urges the listener to wake up from their cold, frigid "coma", and give in to the only possible salvation: sex! This may be a little over-simplistic, of course, and the song may not be solely about the pleasures of the flesh, but also about the redemptive power of love in a more general way. In any case, the symbols of evil and unhappiness (guns, control, clothing) are soon banished by loving feelings and replaced with the more relaxed ways of French-kissing, sexual free-for-all and nudity.

Originally, during the pre-production stages, there was some hesitation as to which part of the supernatural creature's anatomy the love waves should be emanating from: eyes, mouth, hands? Eventually, Mylène will settle for the latter (imagining the other two possible versions is a little weird, but fun.) In order to get the best-looking slow-motion shots possible, the director, Bruno Aveillan, used a "Phantom" camera, which is able to film at a rate of a thousand images per second instead of the usual 25: a technique previously employed in his work in television advertising to beautiful effect, and enough to attract the singer's professional interest. After she contacted him, Aveillan came up with the idea of the extra-terrestrial creature, a concept the singer immediately embraced. Auditions for the figurants were held in Prague, in the presence of the production team, with Mylène and Bruno eventually settling on 14 dancers, all Czech and almost all from the same dance troupe, "Preljocacj". The choreographed sections of the video alone will require three days of filming, for what is Mylène's first choreographed video since 1991's "Je t'aime mélancolie".

Of course, at the time, as the alien Mylène makes her leisurely way out of the laboratory, leaving her former tormentors to their lustful passions, no-one realised that "Dégénération" was in fact part of a larger project, the "Farmer Project" to give it its full name: the truth would not be coming out for a while yet, the surprise perfectly maintained right to the end. A blessing, really, in view of the fairly large number of leaks that surrounded "Dégénération" around the time of its release: in addition to the track's premature (if fleeting) availability for legal download, an even more alarming leak had taken place just a few days before when, on the 9th of August, 30 seconds of each track from the not-yet-released album, apart from "Ave Maria", were made available online! A leak that, supposedly, originated from the German factory where the CDs were pressed. Even worse, on the 12th, a Russian website has the full album, with sleeve artwork, available for full legal download, when it hasn't officially been released yet: somehow, the site quickly becomes temporarily "unavailable", and when it is eventually restored, there is of course no trace of the album...A Simon Hawk photoshoot, featuring a large quantity of brand new pictures of the star (all fantastic) is also inadvertently made available online, without being validated by Mylène first: of course, the pictures will quickly be withdrawn, but not fast enough, and plenty of fans have enough time to copy every single one of them. The video itself will also suffer from leaks, as Jiri Maria Sieber, one of the clip's Czech dancers, posts photos taken from the set on her blog, no doubt earning herself a big slap on the wrist very soon afterwards...

In shops, "Dégénération" is available as a 3-track CD, featuring the instrumental version, as well as a digipack Maxi CD and 12" both carrying the remixes. Five promos are issued, a fair number: there is of course a good old monotrack edition, but this also exists, unexpectedly, in a "deluxe" edition, a format thought dead since the days of "Redonne-Moi"! It isn't *quite* as luxurious as that particular item, but very welcome nonetheless, and a very, very nice piece, unfortunately rather hard to find: it consists of a copy of the monotrack CD inside a gatefold, LP-style sleeve. A "remixes" CD is also pressed, featuring the "Comatik club mix", while the promo 12" has the differently-named but identical "Dégénérave" mix. The final promo is a second 1-track "New Remix" CD featuring the "MHC Future

Generations club mix": limited to just 120, this is the among the rarest and dearest of the lot.

More than ever, Mylène has shown herself to be a master at the art of creating a buzz: each new development in the "Dégénération" saga has been avidly followed by fans and media alike, with unreal levels of interest in every single new twist and turn. Mylène Farmer certainly knows how to make a comeback, even after all this time... Soon, she will take us once more into the "Dégénération" universe, but not just yet: for now, with the next single up ahead, Mylène seems to be waiting on a phone call...

46/ Appelle Mon Numéro

No sooner has the "Point de Suture" album come out on 25th August that rumours and speculation begin to circulate about the second single to be issued from it: some are hoping for "C'est dans l'air" (they will get their chance later), but most are banking on either "Je m'ennuie" (to go with the theme of the brand new "Lonely Lisa" website, a recently created online community to the glory of boredom) or "Appelle mon numéro". In the end, it is the latter that is sent out to radios on 12th September, first in mp3 form and then as a 1-track promotional CD, just a few days later. Right away, radios take to the new single a lot more than they did to "Dégénération": no surprise there, the new track being a lot more radio-friendly than its predecessor, perhaps deemed too unusual and not "normal" enough to warrant sustained airplay. While not exactly a runaway success, "Appelle mon numéro" will nevertheless manage to climb up to 38th place in the airplay chart, and will indeed become the album's most radio-played track overall. Released on November 3rd, the single shoots straight up to the top of the charts, giving Mylène her 6th number 1 hit! This is another very significant milestone for the singer, as she now stands in a class totally her own: no other artists, whether French or international, have ever notched up this many chart-toppers within France at the time. And, for once, the single is in no mad rush to take its leave of the charts and maintains its high position quite well, remaining in the Top 10 for three weeks before making its leisurely way downwards. It also becomes a hit on Belgian radio, and even starts making a few waves in Russia as well...Sales figures will eventually reach the 60,000 mark: by then, not a triumphant, but certainly respectable amount. Of all the singles to be taken from the "Point de Suture" album, "Appelle mon numéro" can probably be said to be the one to have made the most memorable and lasting impression: if not always with the fans, then certainly with the general public.

The relatively higher levels of success enjoyed by "Appelle mon numéro" with the public at large, when compared to other single releases of the same era, can be mostly attributed to two factors: the song itself, of course, is easy on the ear, with an easily remembered melody and carefree, not too challenging lyrics that ensured its radio success. (Indeed, this was generally the received idea about the single: "It will do well on the radio".) But, perhaps more significantly, "Appelle mon numéro" will also benefit from its moment under the prime-time spotlight: on 13th December 2008, Mylène makes a welcome and long overdue return to French television when she takes part in "ça ne finira jamais" on France 2, her first TV show appearance in three years. The programme is dedicated to Johnny Halliday, that other giant of French music, who once famously declared Mylène to be his "female alter-ego". At Johnny's invitation, the singer has agreed to play a role in what is more of a film than a regular TV show: Johnny Halliday can be seen wandering a hotel's corridors, coming across a few familiar faces here and there. At one point, a pair of stockinged feet in killer high heels are seen coming up to a halt in front of a door, and Mylène is briefly glimpsed before she disappears inside room 7021. Back in his own room, after he has hung up the "do not disturb" sign, Johnny says a few appreciative words about Mylène and his own career, while an ethereal rendition of "The first time ever I saw your face" plays softly in the background. Cut back to Mylène, sat in the window bay of her hotel room, looking out over the New York cityscape (actually a film studio near Paris), her shapely legs displayed to fine effect inside some ultra sexy barely-there mesh tights. "Appelle mon numéro" begins to play, and Mylène manages to give a seductive, sultry performance while remaining sat down the whole time, looking sublime as ever, occasionally reading from a book which she eventually tosses away as if bored. The song ends, and the singer exits her room to be greeted by Johnny standing in the corridor: he gives her an appreciative glance, with Mylène looking back coquettishly as if to say "why, thank you" before walking away to the strains of "Blue Moon". The heavily scenarised prestation is filmed by Mylène's long-time collaborator, François Hanss, who manages to inject an atmospheric feel into the proceedings: not since the days of "Je te rends ton amour" has a TV prestation been recorded under such video-like conditions. And indeed, the whole thing almost feels like a brand new, second clip for "Appelle mon numéro".

But before Johnny and Mylène's brief encounter in a hotel corridor, there was of course the video proper. In early October, the first rumours talk of a clip filmed just the previous weekend in a Saint-Ouen studio, with Benoît di Sabatino once again behind the camera. The whispers are spot on first time: the clip has indeed only just been shot, over a period of two days, on the 3rd and 4th. Another rumour, less accurate, predicted a return from Marcus Niespel, the "XXL" and "Comme j'ai mal" video director. On the 17th, three photographs from the video shoot emerge on some websites, shortly followed by the exclusive first online showing of the full clip on the 20th: Mylène can be seen lazing about on a huge bed, initially asleep before waking up to mess around with an assortment of varied implements (including an umbrella, a hammer, and, naturally enough, a phone) as the four seasons come and go all around her until, after a high-speed rewind of the "action", Mylène goes back to sleep, with a content expression on her face... No real scenario to speak of, and a bright, fluffy visual aesthetic: certainly, no tragic deaths or rolling around in a pool of your own blood are to be found here! The reception from the fans is mixed: some miss the edgier side of previous videos, feeling little connection to the humorous, at times almost goofy Mylène larking about on her Queen-sized bed, while others appreciate seeing the singer so smiling and playful. Clearly, "Appelle mon numéro", with its light-hearted and easy-going feel, was never going to bring about a "California"-style video, and none but the most wildly optimistic of fans would have been hoping for a 17-minute epic: so, even if some complain of a video without any real meaning, no-one is really overly disappointed. And whatever may be said of the clip's other qualities, most agree that it is aesthetically pleasing, with Mylène looking pretty fine in it...

In mid-December, Mylène carries the "Appelle mon numéro" video imagery out into the real world as part of her collaboration with the mobile giant Sony Ericsson, in what is one of the first operations of its kind within France. For the very first time, Mylène agrees to associate her image with that of a brand, at least temporarily. The first phase of the collaboration, back in August, saw 175,000 mobile phones, pre-loaded with the "Point de Suture" album, being put on the market, but it is really the second phase, on 12th December, that will make its mark with committed fans: on that day, a collectors' box-set of a different kind is made available, in very limited quantities: only 2070 copies are manufactured. (2000 are to go on sale; the remaining 70 are intended for the singer's friends and associates.) The contents include a specially-engraved mobile phone on which can be found the pre-loaded album, an exclusive "MHC Disconnected remix" of "Appelle mon numéro" not available anywhere else (and which happens to be one of the better remixes, too), the "Dégénérave" remix of "Dégénération", five "Point de Suture" ringtones, the "Dégénération" clip *and* an exclusive making-of (called "Born Again" and over five minutes long), and six Mylène-themed wallpaper screens. The whole thing comes packed inside a very desirable "Point de Suture/Sony Ericsson" numbered black box: not wanting to miss out, dozens of fans are standing by the doors outside the SFR studios venue on the Rue Tronchet in Paris from 8am, some having been there since even earlier, from five in the morning! (And in freezing temperatures, too.)

It has all been worth it once the doors open though, as the space inside has been transformed into Mylène-land for the occasion: past a white corridor with "Point de Suture"-style scars on the floor and walls, the early-rising fans discover a room that has been carefully decorated to bring to mind the "Appelle mon numéro" video. Almost everything inside is white: there is no gigantic bed with Mylène lying on it, sadly, but plenty of big fluffy white pillows scattered about the floor, all bearing the scar print. Suspended under the white drapes that hang from the ceiling, three pillows serve as projection screens for alternating pictures of Mylène and of the album sleeve. Feathers, leaves and rose petals are artfully strewn here and there, bringing a touch of colour and a nod to the four seasons. Five TV screens play the "Dégénération" and "Appelle mon numéro" videos non-stop, without the sound as the album is being played on repeat through hidden speakers. On one side of the room, sitting silently like a black and silver mountain, a huge pile of box-sets waits to be assaulted: in the very center of the room, under a glass display cabinet surrounded by security guards, an open box proudly displays its contents, lit from above by a solitary spotlight and looking like it should really be sitting in a museum. In a brilliant touch, a digital screen suspended above the display case counts down the number of box-sets left, one by one, as they are being sold off at two "Point de Suture" emblazoned counters. A brilliant and very elaborate set-up, fully overseen and approved by Mylène herself and requiring more than a week's worth of preparations, with the final touches still being added as late as 6.30 that very morning! A real treat for Parisian fans, and those willing to travel from further afield: any collectors based outside of France, however, could expect to pay around €500 for the box-set, the only price available to those wanting to get hold of the item without having to take on a mobile contract...

Thankfully, there were cheaper ways to mark the release of "Appelle mon numéro", thanks to the various formats sold in stores from November 3 onwards. A 2-track single featuring the instrumental, a digipack Maxi CD featuring the remixes and a 12" were all made available commercially, all illustrated with a John Nollet photograph of a smiling Mylène sat on top of a piano. Promotionally, there were no less than three different CDs to be issued: a regular, basic monotrack edition, a 5-track "Club Remixes" CD that includes the "Manhattan Clique x-directory dub" (the only CD edition for this particular remix), and a 2-track CD with Greg B and Manhattan Clique radio edits. A 12" also exists, in a similar sleeve but easily recognizable as being a promo thanks to its slightly different colour scheme. Sadly, there are no "deluxe" editions this time around: the "Dégénération" revival of the format was apparently a one-time only affair...

After another number 1 hit (her second consecutive chart-topper of 2008) and a brand new approach to marketing, the time soon comes to hang up on "Appelle mon numéro", and move on to the next single. And when it eventually comes, something about it is going to be quite the surprise...

47/ Si J'Avais Au Moins...

After the first two singles, fans are now hoping to see a release for "C'est dans l'air" or "Sextonik", so it is a considerable surprise when, in mid-December, word gets out that a promo CD for "Si j'avais au moins..." has been sent out to radio. No-one had seen this coming, and the initial response is far from enthusiastic: fans are puzzled, at best. Although the song is reputed to be Mylène's personal favourite off the album, the same cannot always be said for her admirers in general: in various online polls, the least popular choice for third single is always "Si j'avais au moins...", which invariably manages to pull in the least votes, if any. But, it seems Mylène has made her choice: nothing to do but go along with it. A choice that is not without bringing to mind the selection of "Redonne-Moi" as third single from the preceding album: another ballad, without any obviously immediate commercial appeal. Fans console themselves by reasoning that Mylène has elected, for this release, to go with her heart and favour the artistic over the commercial, surely a commendable intention for an artist of her stature. Still, even with the best will in the world, it is hard for some not to feel at least *a little* disappointed...On the plus side, NRJ put a little more effort into playing the song than is usual for them: surprising, perhaps, but it isn't so much that they have fallen in love with "Si j'avais au moins...", and more to do with the fact that their annual Music Awards are just a few weeks away, and the radio station had better play the game if they want to welcome Mylène on the night itself...

It won't be long, however, until interest in "Si j'avais au moins..." spikes up considerably, and for good reason: on December 18th, Bruno Aveillan, the "Dégénération" video director, is named as also being at the helm of the forthcoming clip. What's more, it is revealed that both clips were shot back to back in June '08, in the same Prague location. Interesting enough, and yet an official communiqué on December 22nd still comes as a huge surprise: for the first time, it is revealed that the video for "Si j'avais au moins..." is actually part of a larger enterprise, the "Farmer Project", which also includes the "Dégénération" clip. Fans may have a little trouble with visualizing how the two are going to fit together, but one thing is for sure: Mylène has once again managed to take everyone by surprise. No-one saw this coming. Hard not to be impressed at the singer and her team's success in keeping the whole thing under wraps for so long in this age of internet, especially when one considers the numerous leaks around the time of "Dégénération", in particular those that emanated from one of the on-set dancers. Clearly, Mylène's grip on her image is as tight as ever...The "Farmer Project" is shown for the first time exclusively on the Allociné website, on 9th January. Or, at least, *almost* for the first time, as a programming error means the clip is available for viewing a few days earlier, for a brief period of time only. Still, only a few were quick or lucky enough to catch it back then, and it is still more or less an unknown quantity that fans can discover on the official launch date: and when they do, it suddenly all makes sense. The reason for the unexpected release of "Si j'avais au moins..." as third single now becomes abundantly clear: the supernatural Mylène with the busy hands wasn't quite done yet as she made her exit from the laboratory-turned-orgy, oh no. There was still a whole lot of action to come...Things kick off with an aesthetically superb introduction (we never did get to see how Mylène ended up getting strapped to that table, after all), in which two vaguely dodgy-looking cops sat in their patrol car are rudely yanked out of their drunken stupor by a sudden and unexplained thunderous flash that blows discarded newspaper pages all over their windows. Getting out to investigate, the two men are confronted by an unbelievable sight: an entity of light, slowly coalescing into a human shape, topped off with a familiar-looking mane of red hair. Although the creature appears to be benign and hasn't even fully materialized yet, one of the freaked-out cops gets a little trigger-happy and sends two electric darts flying into the pale, almost translucent flesh: the creature collapses (with a few familiar-sounding cries), blacks out, and eventually comes to on the table to which she is strapped..."Dégénération" kicks in, Mylène turns everyone into a sex beast with a wave of her hands, and makes her exit, which is where we had left her back in July...

And now, as the alien Mylène, having neutralized her captors, walks through a door and into another room, the second half of her adventures gets underway. At first, the room is dark, and the alien can see little beyond a sea of twinkling lights set against the dark background, in a scene with echoes of Snow White's first terrifying night alone in the forest. Luckily, her hands are wonderfully adaptable, a kind of cosmic Swiss-army knife with more settings than just "uncontrollable lust", and the alien uses them to light up the space around her, revealing a cruel and heartbreaking sight: all around, animals of many diverse species are being kept prisoners inside cages and tanks, unwilling test subjects for no doubt gruesome experiments. Wandering around the room, the red-haired extra-terrestrial casts her eyes over each of the cages in turn: snakes, birds, cats with electrode caps attached to their tiny heads...Bringing forth yet another benign power, she goes about healing the animals, lifting a half-bald kitten out of its enclosure and taking away its scars with a stroke of the healing blue light. With the animals in good shape once more, the alien uses her hands to manifest yet another power, of a destructive kind this time: blasts of electric light shatter the cages everywhere, setting the animals free. Rabbits, mice, cats, birds, all run away and down a long corridor, towards their freedom. A couple of shots show Mylène lovingly cuddling a monkey, prompting fans to wonder whether this could be E.T.'s first appearance in one of her owner's videos: but the monkey, as it turns out, is just a hired actor, and not Mylène's own pet at all. The alien pushes open the doors at the far end of the corridor, and the animals spring free, in what is a strangely touching and affecting scene: it is hopefully not too shameful to confess to a few tears on the first viewing...With the animals -and herself- free once more, the extraordinary creature once again becomes pure energy, in a stunning scene that makes great use of state-of-the-art special effects. With a smile on her face, the alien turns into pure light once again and departs the earth, in a final shot of a light-beam heading out into space...The clip is an immediate hit with the fans, delighted by the beauty of the images as well as the ambitious scale of the "Farmer Project": an aesthetically and conceptually stunning short-film, worthy of the mind-blowing Boutonnat epics of the "good old days". In the media too, the reception is great, with music channels featuring the clip heavily, or often, like in the case of M6, making it their "clip of the week": a more than deserved accolade for what could arguably be called the "clip of the year".

On January 17th, Mylène performs "Si j'avais au moins..." on television during the 10th annual NRJ Music Awards on TF1. The singer is nominated in two categories: French album and French female artist of the year. She is triumphant in the first category; the prize for the second will go to Jenifer. Reading out the nominees' names and opening the envelope is none other than Seal, who gets to hand over the trophy himself. Tellingly, by the time the winner of the best French female artist award is announced, Mylène is already no longer in her seat next to Pascal Nègre, Jenifer having taken her place... For her performance, pre-recorded for TV as usual although she performs live in front of the Awards studio audience, Mylène is backed by a full philarmonic orchestra: just like the singer, all nine musicians are dressed all in white. After her performance, the singer is briefly interviewed by the host Nikos, but unfortunately he has forgotten that the star only likes to show her good profile: stubbornly, he stands on the wrong side of her, wondering why Mylène lowers her head so much with every one of his questions, until he finally realises his mistake (or is told through his earpiece, as seems more likely from the recording) and moves to stand to her other side. After Mylène has expressed a few words of gratitude, Nikos awkwardly attempts to guide her towards the front of the stage with him as he goes into his next link, but the singer is having none of it and walks off backstage, all smiles, leaving the host looking slightly foolish: "Stay with me, Mylène...", he calls out half-heartedly, but the star has by then already disappeared from view...This somewhat ramshackle 10th edition of the NRJMA constitutes the only televised performance in existence for "Si j'avais au moins...", and while fans obviously welcome any and all of Mylène's rare TV appearances, some will talk of it in terms of a missed opportunity: maybe as a result of the Awards' somewhat bumbling feel that year (somehow, they manage to forget to include the shots of Mylène walking up the steps in the pre-show sequence), or, perhaps, as some have pointed out, because Mylène hasn't performed an uptempo track on TV since 2002, thus a feeling, perhaps, of déja-vu as she performs yet another slow number... On the stage, however, the song will be used to powerful effect, making for a highly emotional closer during the indoor dates of the 2009 Tour, although it will be dropped for the stadium concerts in favour of the far more upbeat "Désenchantée" conclusion.

The single's physical release, which was originally announced for February 9th, is put back to the 16th, two whole months after the track first went out to radio: nevertheless, "Si j'avais au moins..." effortlessly flies into the charts straight in at number 1, selling 12,000 units in its first week, twice more than the next best-seller, Lady Gaga and her "Poker Face" at number 2. This gives Mylène her 7th chart-topper, and her third consecutive number 1: the singer beats her own record, once again. This is even more amazing considering that the single is only released on two supports, one of which is a limited edition. After the initial high entry, however, the song very quickly drops down the countdown, not helped by a level of airplay that is by now non-existent: indeed, "Si j'avais au moins..." will never get any higher than 60th place in the airplay charts. Total sales for the single will eventually amount to around 35,000, a fairly modest amount.

The two supports available to record-buyers consist of a 2-track CD and 12", both featuring the instrumental version: the vinyl is issued as a limited edition. There is only one promo in existence, a 1-track CD of the radio edit (a rare version) that comes in an awesome sleeve (better than that of the commercial single's sleeve, some have said): a red-tinted, close-up shot of the stitched-up doll's face from the album artwork. Tantalizingly, rumours briefly flew about a super-limited promo 12" as well as a promo CD featuring...remixes! Sadly, it was not to be...

While the choice of "Si j'avais au moins..." as third single may have disappointed and confused some at first, its awesome video, a totally unsuspected two-parter, has more than made up for it on surprise factor alone. But Mylène isn't done with surprises yet: just when fans are getting themselves resigned to the idea that it will never happen, the singer, when the time for the next single comes around, is going to give them exactly what they want.

48/ C'Est Dans L'Air

Ever since the release of the "Point de Suture" album way back in August of the previous year, one song in particular has been getting fans hot under the collar: "C'est dans l'air", a fast-paced, whimsical little number that sees Mylène listing, in an ironic, almost blasé tone of voice, all the transgressions of the world as if to better denounce them. A darkly humorous track, heavy on the second degree, with a deep voice delivery for the verses that is slightly reminiscent of the earlier "Je t'aime mélancolie" in terms of dry wit and irony. Of course, as is usually the case with any track generally favoured by fans and hoped for as a single release, a nice long wait is in order: Mylène, more than any other artist, seems to have understood that expectation only heightens the eventual pleasure...And, when it does come, it must be admitted that the surprise is all the sweeter for it. It is on 27th March 2009 that the news breaks: "C'est dans l'air" will be the album's fourth single. Amazingly, the announcement is unspoilt by any leaks whatsoever, and the track is on radio before anyone has a chance to know what's happening, with the web radio NRJ All French first with the exclusive. Other radio stations promptly follow suit but sadly, as has more or less become the custom by now, airplay soon dwindles to next to nothing...Just a few days later, on the 31st, promos featuring a variety of remixes are sent out to the various stations and, surprise surprise, one of those is an "Extended Club mix" from the maestro Laurent Boutonnat himself: a pleasant surprise for countless fans, and a sweet reminder of the "good old days". This is Laurent's first remix contribution to a Mylène single in a very long time: his last recorded effort being, technically, the "Dark side of the mix" produced for "Pardonne-Moi" in 2002, with remixes proper dating to even further back, the last instance being "Comme j'ai mal", way back in 1996!

The single is released digitally and as a 2-track CD on 27th April, and enters the charts at number 2, a shockingly low placing by Mylène standards by now: can her unprecedented run of consecutive number 1 singles really be over so soon, after a mere three? Thankfully, no: the 4th May release of the Maxi CDs and vinyl sees "C'est dans l'air" hitting the top spot in its second week. Yet another triumph for the singer, who relentlessy keeps on beating records. Her own, in any case, as, with an incredible eight number 1 singles under her belt so far, Mylène is now way ahead of all and any competition, and is left to compete with none but herself...For what is already the fourth single to be taken from the album, the song does fairly well, with sales figures reaching a more than respectable 55,000 units shifted: a decent showing in a by now comatose singles market. Clearly, extra enthusiasm is no doubt generated, at least in part, by the fact that "C'est dans l'air" gets its single release just as the 2009 Tour gets underway: a canny move from Mylène and her team, as the song is an immediate and huge success in its live incarnation, getting the crowd on their feet just as much as the all-time classic "Désenchantée" does! Not to mention the "C'est laid!" sing-along opportunity, which the fans clearly aren't going to miss: next to last on the setlist, both in the indoor and stadium dates of the tour, "C'est dans l'air" sets the place on fire each time. It is such a success, indeed, that the year won't even be out before it is released once more, this time in its live version: an unusually early repeat performance for any of the singles so far, and another first in the singer's discography.

The clip is shot in two parts in February, in studios in Saint-Ouen and Paris, and directed by Alain Escalle, responsible for the "Avant que l'ombre...à Bercy" synthesis images, as well as the short film that preceded the same concerts, the troubling "Le conte du monde flottant". In Saint-Ouen, Mylène spends a very long day in front of a green screen: images for use in the future concerts are shot on the very same day, with the team working on until four in the morning...During the Paris section of the shoot, the choreography is recorded for motion capture purposes, in order to bring the dancing skeletons to life, with Mylène and Christophe Danchaud doing the honours. The video concept was decided on in early February, when Mylène's interest is caught by the images Alain Escalle has created in order to accompany the song on stage. From this early concept of the "singing skull", the singer hits on the idea of animated skeletons as backing dancers; later on, in order to counterbalance the darkly comic images of Mylène and her bony dancers, footage of various nuclear testing operations is added, bringing in a somewhat darker, more disquieting tone to the clip. Work on the short film, from start to finish, takes about a month, and will eventually result in a video that manages to keep a certain degree of continuity with the visual universe of the soon-to-be-performed live version. Surprisingly, just as was the case with the single, there were practically no leaks, on the net or otherwise, around the time of the "C'est dans l'air" video: only a single image, showing Mylène with skeletons in the background, managed to make it online (possibly even on the singer's own initiative), and even the director's name wasn't revealed until shortly before the actual first broadcast. In a now unusual turn of events, the clip is shown for the very first time on television, and the net will have to wait (although, admittedly, a very short time): another nod to the days of old, along with Laurent Boutonnat's unexpected return to remixing duties...The music channel M6 is first with the exclusive on April 15th, with an initial broadcast as early as 6.20: other channels soon follow suit, and play the clip with some consistency. In fact, the "C'est dans l'air" video will go on to achieve some considerable success, eventually becoming the 47th most broadcast clip on French music channels in 2009, Mylène's best placing in the video charts since "C'est une belle journée" in 2002. A small consolation, at least, for the almost non-existent radio airplay earned by the song (and just as well, as Mylène will not be performing the track on television a single time: but, with a tour just started, she can hardly be taken to fault on the issue). But, in spite of its success on TV networks, the video inevitably goes on to divide the fans: while some think it's ok, many are those who think differently. In forums, there is some criticism that the whole affair looks a little cheap, in particular the skeleton sequences. Some decree the clip to be "atrocious", or even one of the singer's worst. Mylène is also criticized over her hairstyle...but, then again, the amount of criticism the singer has to endure with every single new release nowadays is but an indication of the fascination she still exerts over so many, to this day, and of the sky-high expectations we all have of her: what other artist in the world today can boast of having every single aspect of their career scrutinized to such a degree, every single move or utterance immediately dissected as if under a microscope? Who else in the world of pop can invite such heated debate as to the aesthetic qualities of a clip, a sleeve, a haircut, or even the use of a particular type of font?

The "Point de Suture" era has so far been a great one for remixes, and "C'est dans l'air" is no exception: after the initial release of the 2-track CD single on 27th April, fans can then choose from two different "Remixes" digipack CDs: the first time since "Optimistique-Moi" that a Mylène single receives such dedicated treatment, if one excludes the Moby duet "Slipping Away (Crier la vie)", which wasn't technically two CDs of remixes anyway. Across the two "C'est dans l'air" CDs, both issued as limited editions, the song is reworked into a dancefloor stomper thanks to the likes of Greg B, or transformed into a weird, dreamy aural landscape after Fat Phaze and Wize have worked their magic on it. And of course, as a great, nostalgic bonus, Laurent Boutonnat is also represented with an "Extended Club mix", also available as an instrumental: a precious treat for fans, and one not yet repeated since. A vinyl 12" is issued as well, also in a limited edition: a situation that causes a certain degree of frustration in some quarters, the limited availability of most of the formats sometimes making it hard to get hold of a copy! Promotionally, "C'est dans l'air" only exists in CD form, although there are admittedly three distinct editions, a monotrack CD as well as two separate "Club Remixes" discs. A skull-shaped "promo luxe" edition would have been a dream...

From the 2nd of May, Mylène embarks on her fifth ever tour, with a première in Nice at the Palais Nikaia: it isn't long before the latest concerts are widely acclaimed in turn. The indoor dates, which end with a moving and theatrical "descent into hell" performance of "Si j'avais au moins...", will eventually lead the singer to two nights at the Stade de France in early September. "Point de Suture" was, by the star's own admission, written with the stage specifically in mind: fittingly, a fifth and final single taken from it will mark yet another milestone in the singer's career, just as the 2009 Tour is about to reach its triumphant conclusion.

49/ Sextonik

When the "Point de Suture" album is first heard in August 2008, one track in particular immediately sets tongues wagging: the ode to vibrators that is "Sextonik". Easily the most sexual lyric on the album, even if Mylène never directly refers to the item by name, the track is a daring, tongue-in-cheek allusion to those trustworthy toys that never have an off day... Of course, this being Mylène, the toys in question are evoked in a poetic and elegant manner, with many a picturesque turn of phrase, but still, there is no mistaking her meaning: indeed, the lyric is probably one of her most straightforward, and just in case anyone didn't quite get it, the singer hammers the point home with a few well-placed suggestive moans... Needless to say, the press and the net quickly get all hot and steamy over the song, with countless articles appearing overnight: clearly, Mylène the Libertine isn't a spent force just yet...The song, set to a fast-paced electro backing, is widely thought to be a dead cert for the stage, but, surprise, when the indoor setlist is revealed in May 2009, "Sextonik" is nowhere to be seen! It will be, along with "Réveiller le monde" (another one of the album's great electro stompers), one of the most unexpected stage omissions of the 2009 Tour, and missed by many.

But never mind: stage or no stage, "Sextonik" is still going to manage to generate a huge "buzz", and quite literally too. On May 15th, before Mylène's concert at the Zénith de Toulouse, there is a new arrival over by the merchandising stands: the "Sextonik" sex-toy. Clearly, Mylène is fully committed to thoroughly satisfying her audience! Sleek and smart-looking, the vibrator is adorned with 24 replica precious stones at its base, and comes housed inside a beautiful coffin-shaped box that plays a few notes from the chorus when the lid is opened (just so everyone knows what you're up to when you're trying to use it discreetly.) The link between sex and death has been made before in the course of the singer's career, but perhaps never quite so forcefully: but this is understandable, the item inside the coffin being likely to bring you to what many have often termed "the little death", after all. The item was initially rumoured to be limited to 1,000 copies: whether this was ever accurate is unclear, but in any case the sex-toy will later go on to be manufactured in much larger quantities, in order to cope with increasing demand. Nowadays, with the item still widely available on the merchandising website, it would seem most people have had their fill already...

On June 22nd, lucky concert-going fans get another sizeable surprise: just before the Gayant Expo show in Douai, the last of the French indoor concerts, a brand new remix of the song is unexpectedly played to the crowd, who go absolutely nuts over it. The remix will also be played before the St Petersburgh concert in Russia on June 28th, as well as before the two Stade de France shows, sending the audience wild each time. Soon, Tomer G, who had previously remixed the track "Dégénération" to such great effect, announces on myspace that he is the author of this, and another remix of "Sextonik". From then on, it seems obvious that the song will be the next single to be taken from the album. Many are those who also believe that its single release will guarantee a live prestation at the Stade de France dates: sadly, it was not to be, and the song remains, so far at least, a stranger to the stage. On July 7th, the "Sextonik" radio edit is available for download by the media from a dedicated platform, with a monotrack promo CD being sent out shortly thereafter. And on the 17th, a 2-track CD featuring the Tomer G remixes, both pretty similar but of high quality nevertheless, is sent out to the major radio stations.

When the single does land in the shops on 31st August, however, only one support is made available: a 2-track CD single that features the single and instrumental versions. Curiously, the Tomer G remixes will never be made available commercially, despite an early summer announcement on a Swiss website about a forthcoming Maxi CD and 12"! As for a video, fans will wait and wait and then wait some more, but it will all be in vain: in the end, "Sextonik" will turn out to be the third and (so far) last of the "orphan" Mylène songs, after "On est tous des imbéciles" and "L'Histoire d'une fée, c'est...". Whether there ever really was a clip for "Sextonik" must, it seems, forever remain shrouded in mystery. Some rumours categorically state that such a video was indeed filmed, but no evidence has ever surfaced to support the theory. Although some captures, supposedly from the clip, did emerge online, it didn't take a magnifying glass to quickly ascertain that the woman in the pictures was not, in fact, Mylène at all. The mystery thickens with the photograph featured on the single's cover, which appears to show Mylène peeking out from under a bedsheet: a capture from the hypothetical clip? A Benoît di Sabatino picture? As it is not credited anywhere, it is impossible to determine its provenance...In the end, with all the rumours of cancelled supports and video, something about "Sextonik" screams out "aborted project". Or does it really? Perhaps there never was a video, and perhaps the single was never intended to benefit from anything more than the limited release it did receive: but then why commission the Tomer G remixes? Who can say? Maybe we'll get a huge surprise when Mylène releases her next video compilation...or, more probably, maybe not...Still, all the mystery and confusion cannot stop "Sextonik" from crashing straight in at number 1 in the charts, thereby giving Mylène her 5th consecutive chart-topper, and the 9th number 1 single of her career! Which isn't to say that the song is a huge hit, far from it: with first-week sales of just 4,500, "Sextonik" is actually the worst-performing single to be taken from the album. What's more, with no promo, hardly any airplay, and of course no video, the song quickly plummets down the charts, with eventual sales figures estimated at a measly 15,000. Still, there's no arguing with the figures, and "Sextonik", by reaching pole position, has enabled Mylène to send all the singles taken from "Point de Suture" to number 1: an unequalled feat. Of course, with the singles market in complete collapse, getting a chart-topper is no longer automatically the sign of a huge hit: this is no longer 1986...But the symbolic is strong in any case, and just as Mylène is about to triumph at the Stade de France, yet another number 1 is an undeniably nice touch...Also of note on the 31st of August: on the same day as the single "Sextonik" is released, Mylène's entire back catalogue (minus live albums) is re-released in digipack CD form, and also on limited, numbered vinyl! The 2003 compilation "Remixes" gets its first-ever vinyl edition in the process. Almost enough to assuage any collectors disappointed by the ultra-limited number of supports for this new single...

"Sextonik", fifth and final single, brings the "Point de Suture" era to a close. Mylène's seventh studio album, while not particularly innovative, at least gave the fans what they wanted: after the mostly ballad-led "Avant que l'ombre..." opus, many were hoping for a fresher, more upbeat sound, and that is exactly what they got. As Mylène herself says at the time, "Faut qu'ça bouge!", and "Point de Suture" doesn't disappoint in that respect, with only two ballads out of an (admittedly few) ten tracks, not counting the hidden track "Ave Maria", where Mylène takes on one of the all-time classics with great results. (Potentially a great opener for the concerts, as many fans had hoped: but, understandably, the technically super-hard song was not to be included as part of the setlist.) The album also brings about a first for the singer in terms of promotion: on 20th August, Mylène grants an exclusive interview to the gay monthly "Têtu", in a gesture much appreciated by the community who has supported her so much through the years. The usual bare-chested hunk on the cover is exceptionally replaced by the red-haired icon, with one condition which the singer happily agrees to: for the occasion, Mylène must dress up as a man. Not a huge problem for the "Sans Contrefaçon" performer: razor in hand, shaving foam all over her face, she plays the game with gusto, in what has become one of her most iconic magazine covers of recent years. In another first, "Point de Suture" gets a simultaneous release in both France and Russia: a clear indication of the singer's ever-growing levels of popularity in the country...In 2009, the album is certified triple platinum, for sales of over 600,000: still short of the million of bygone days, but Mylène remains France's biggest-seller still, and one of the country's undisputed pop icons, not to say "the" icon. A strange thing about "Point de Suture" is that it cannot technically be said to have given birth to any major hit singles: a bizarre thing to say, perhaps, when all five singles taken from it have managed to reach number 1 in the charts. And yet it is true: of the five tracks released, none have made a lasting impression on the general public at large, with the possible but disputed exception of "Appelle mon numéro". It is of course a different matter with the fans, but casual listeners would no doubt be hard-pressed to hum any of the tracks in question, certainly not with as much ease as they would recall the melody to a "Désenchantée" or "Libertine". Now, does this in itself make the album a failure? Clearly not: aside from the impressive sales figures, "Point de Suture" has now become a firm favourite with many fans, with songs like "Paradis Inanimé" or "Dégénération" even going on to acquire an extra dimension on the stage; not to mention "C'est dans l'air", often said to be a new "Désenchantée" in the context of a concert, and this after only one tour! If anything, the album has cemented the singer's success even further, by offering eleven tracks of pure vintage Farmer/Boutonnat sound that somehow managed to sound contemporary and relevant. Of course, when you have a musical universe as rich and diverse as Mylène's, the trends of the day are never going to be a huge preoccupation to you anyway...An intriguing rumour around the album, never officially confirmed or denied, concerns the song "Looking for my name": Mylène's second recorded duet with Moby was, allegedly, initially intended to feature a different male vocalist altogether. Unfortunately, David Bowie's health problems at the time prevented him from taking part...No-one can say for sure whether the rumour has any truth to it, but it would certainly have been a mind-blowing prospect! As per the usual custom, "Point de Suture" is also released as a limited collectors' box-set, with only 7,000 copies in existence. Inside of a flat metallic box in the style of an early 20th century first aid kit, the limited edition CD album nestles above a copy of the "promo" CD for "Dégénération": although it is not technically a promotional item, as it differs in terms of reference and legal mentions (and, of course, it was sold commercially.) The box -which gives off a strong, slightly compelling medicinal smell from the dense protective foam inside when opened- also contains a pair of surgical instruments, a scalpel and a pair of scissors (the scalpel perhaps not as sharp as the real thing, but that is understandable enough.) On 25th August 2008, when the album is released, including in this collectors' version, "La Chasse aux Supports" can begin...

Indeed, "Point de Suture" will be for me an opportunity to experience first-hand my very own "Chasse aux Supports", for the very first time in my life: previously, not too keen on putting myself through the chaotic and possibly somewhat traumatic experience, I had favoured the internet as a way of getting hold of the latest collectors'. But, on the 25th of August 2008, I stand outside "Le Furet du Nord", a bookstore cum record store in the northern French town of Lille, along with a good ten or so other people. It is still very early: the store isn't due to open for another 45 minutes, at 9am, but this is surely a very clear case of "the early bird gets the worm"...The small group congregates as close as can be right in front of the still locked doors, as if huddling for warmth: we are, of course, really jostling for position. Even an inch or so extra at the starting block can make all the difference...It wasn't easy getting up super early that morning, but as more and more people start to arrive and mass up behind us, I feel thankful that I did: it already seems clear that not everyone here is going to manage to get hold of one of the box-sets...especially as a rumour is going round the small crowd, saying that the store have only received twenty copies. At quarter to nine, the pressure goes up a notch: shapes can be glimpsed moving about inside the store, and everyone presses in even tighter towards the front in anticipation. Advantageously positioned only inches away from the doors, I resist any attempts by late-comers to take over my spot, and refuse to budge an inch: I travelled from abroad for this, I am *not* leaving empty-handed. Five to nine: you can feel the tension in the crowd by the way it has suddenly gone silent. Faces are tense, concentrated. Someone's phone rings: the ringtone is "Dégénération". This lightens the mood somewhat, but only for an instant: the final few minutes go by, ever so slowly, with the push from the crowd behind getting steadily stronger and stronger. My heart is beating like crazy, my body is getting ready to run: the same story is written on every face all around me. 9:00: the metal gate over the doors slowly begins to lift up, the doors behind are wide open. Me and the others at the front crouch down and squeeze under as soon as is humanly possible, even if it means crawling on all fours: then we're in, the first few of us. We all stop, as one, scanning the room for the precious collectors': wherever they are, they cannot be seen from here, and blindly running away in the wrong direction would be fatal...A sales assistant, who obviously knows what we're here for, takes pity on us: "They're upstairs!" He points to the escalator. Go! The whole group rushes up the moving stairs. Amazingly, I'm almost at the front, with just a handful of fellow enthusiasts before me, and I run like crazy, a small crowd of hungry people at my heels. At the top of the stairs, one of my competitors takes herself out of the race in what must have been a painful experience: perhaps overcome by her own momentum, she loses her balance and goes crashing into a large display stand which topples over, sending CDs and DVDs flying out everywhere. The security staff are not amused. Not that I spare more than a second in observing this: that collector still ain't mine just yet... The upstairs level is quite spacious, and once again the group stops, like a single organism, until a silver mini-mountain is spotted on the main sales counter on the far side: someone actually shouts out "Over there!" I race to the counter: by now, it's more than every man for himself, it's all-out war. Run or miss out. I don't quite get there in first position, and the collectors are almost all gone by the time I finally grab one of the very last few, snatching it from amongst a sea of outstretched hands. And just like that, in less than maybe twenty, thirty seconds, it's all over: the collectors' are all gone, every last one of them. I can hardly believe I managed to get a copy, and the rush of adrenalin combined with my successful expedition puts a huge smile on my face. Empty-handed people are scanning the room desperately: a couple comes up to me and ask "Où sont les Collectors?". But it's clear by the look on their faces that they know they're too late. "Ils sont tous partis", I answer, as sympathetically as I can. Still, I can't help but hold on to my box-set a little tighter...To this day, I thank my lucky stars: sure, I could probably have got hold of the item in some other way, eventually. But I did not have to experience the cruel disappointment I saw written on the couple's anxious faces that morning, and my one and only "Chasse aux Supports" was a success: I shamelessly ran for Mylène, and she didn't let me down. Anyone with the opportunity (and a strong enough heart) should try and experience this situation like no other for themselves, at least once in their lives: failure may be devastating and will probably leave you suffering from post-traumatic stress for the rest of your life, but a positive outcome will be a rush like you've never known before, guaranteed.

Mylène drives her fans crazy (in a good way) like no other pop star, that much is plain to see. It isn't only in how fans throw themselves on anything stamped with the Farmer name, but also in the intensely moving, almost transcendental experience that being at one of her concerts can constitute, even for the non-initiated. Once again, with the 2009 Tour, Mylène is going to put on one hell of a show: two singles will mark the occasion, including a surprisingly recent number...

50/ C'Est Dans L'Air (live) -
51/ Paradis Inanimé (live)

After a triumphant tour that saw the singer embark on a series of 29 concerts throughout France (not including the foreign and stadium dates), and the provinces being taken care of first this time around (perhaps as a way of making up for the Paris-centric 2006 shows), the album of the concert is released to great publicity on 7th December 2009, bearing the name "No 5 On Tour". Some discussion promptly ensues about the possible meaning of the title: a reference to a favoured brand of perfume? Not very likely. The most logical explanation is that this simply alludes to the 2009 Tour being the fifth time Mylène has graced the stage so far, although no official interpretation has ever been forthcoming. In any case, regardless of exactly what the enigmatic name may or may not mean, the album is off to a great start: "No 5 On Tour" is certified double platinum in its first week of release, with over 200,000 copies sold and a number 1 placing in the charts to show for it. A superb collectors edition, limited to 10,000, opens up onto a pop-up of a scene from the concert and, as well as two CDs and a bonus DVD, also includes an "eye" flipbook for hours of fun getting Mylène to wink at you and 21 picture cards showing dancers and musicians. A 3-disc gatefold vinyl, much sought after and also limited to just 10,000 copies, comes with stunning picture insets and fabulously heavyweight vinyl: a great representation overall for the "No 5 On Tour" album.

The first single to be taken from it is on radio from November 30th, and, surprise surprise, "C'est dans l'air" is back again under the spotlight! Never before has Mylène re-released a single within such a short amount of time: it was almost a whole five years between the original "Plus Grandir" in 1985 and its subsequent live release in 1990, while nine years elapsed between the original "Ainsi soit je..." single and its 1997 live counterpart. But this time around, with the original studio release of "C'est dans l'air" dating no further back than April of the very same year, it is only just about eight months before the track gets its second outing, and the two are only separated by one single, "Sextonik". Rather amazingly, "C'est dans l'air live" is Mylène's 50th single, a milestone the singer will mark with a couple of firsts: apart from its unexpectedly early reappearance, the single is also the first not to be released on any commercial supports whatsoever, ensuring that it does not chart or sell a single copy! The track does, however, benefit from a brand new Tiesto remix, available in its full length only on a mp3 promo and a "Remixes" CD sent out to radio: the first editions of the promo CD may have left buyers feeling somewhat short-changed, with a sleeve tracklisting of 6 different remixes, but actually only one to be found on the CD itself! A mistake that will no doubt push the price of the item even higher over time... The only official release for fans to get their hands on is the "Tiesto remix radio edit", available solely as a download. There is, naturally, some puzzlement as to why a single would be put forward when there are no formats subsequently made available to buy. And, inevitably, a fair amount of disappointment in the collectors' camp. Unfortunately, it would seem that the market for physical singles issued from a live album was no longer viable by this point. Which is fair enough, when one considers the sales figures of previous live single releases "Avant que l'ombre..." and "Déshabillez-Moi": at what point does the whole thing become a loss-making enterprise? It's a shame for fans and collectors, true, but it is probably true also that not even Mylène can escape the laws of economics, or the changing times...Instead, we most probably now have to accept that live single releases will be symbolic, rather than actually taking on a physical form, from now on: essentially, nothing more than a showcase for the parent concert. And in that respect, "C'est dans l'air live" certainly does a great job, perfectly capturing the show's electric energy, especially in the accompanying video, first shown online from November 27th.

On 12th April 2010, the long-awaited DVD and Blu-Ray are released at last, a record of the two dates at the Stade de France, on 11th and 12th September of the preceding year. Finally, fans can discover or re-live those magical few hours, that had taken so long to finally come around, only to fly by in what seemed more like minutes! Selling over 100,000 in its first week, the film is a complete success, commercially as well as artistically, with a satisfyingly comprehensive amount of bonus material. It *is* unfortunate that no indoor version of the concert was ever released, but given the overall quality of "Stade de France", it seems a little churlish to complain.

The magic is undeniable in the images of 80,000 people singing a happy birthday to the emotional singer, or of her long walk back to the stage to the strains of the "Avant que l'ombre..." instrumental interlude. Almost two and a half hours of an incredible show, with an achingly beautiful "emotion section" and the madhouse atmosphere of the "Dégénération/C'est dans l'air/Désenchantée" end trio. Some will express a slight disappointment at the singer's relatively low-key entrance and exit, when compared to the 2006 Bercy shows: of course, the infrastructure then was on a totally different level, to the extent that the show was simply untransportable, and the comparison is a little unfair. It is true that the 2006 entrance, in a glass sarcophagus carried across a bridge by six muscle-bound men, was more elaborate, but this minor issue surely takes nothing away from what is, in the end, yet another hell of a show from everyone's favourite redhead. With the promise of such spectacle, and traditionally strong sales for any Mylène Farmer live show extravaganzas anyway, "Stade de France" wasn't exactly in desperate need of further promotion, but Mylène decides to mark the occasion with a second live single "release" regardless.

Officially coming out in April, the live version of "Paradis Inanimé", like "C'est dans l'air" before it, is released essentially on a symbolic level. No physical supports, and even less promo editions than before: just a simple monotrack CD featuring the live radio edit version, sent to (and not much played by) radio stations. The clip, rather than a straightforward capture of Mylène's performance, is a compilation of the show's best moments, and will hardly be shown at all anywhere. With yet another single not available in any physical form, some fans begin to worry and speculate that this might mean the end of singles as we know them altogether...In forums, collectors express their frustration: how can you collect something that does not actually exist? Thankfully, the future will show that studio singles, that we can touch and hold, still have a place to occupy on our specially dedicated Mylène shelves...

Another live album reaches the end of its exploitation period. No doubt Mylène is now about to go into hibernation mode: no point in expecting any new material for a good two, maybe even three years, at least...Any new music is a long time away. Well, that's what we think, anyway. And yet, before very long, Mylène is going to pull another one of her surprises on her public, and her fans: and this time, more than merely surprised, they will be completely blown away.

Part 8: Bleu Noir

52/ Oui Mais...Non

September 2010. Unsuspecting Mylène Farmer fans discover two new duets from the singer: a collaboration with American singer Ben Harper on a cover of "Never Tear Us Apart": the Ben Harper-heavy version is planned for inclusion on an INXS tribute album, with Mylène being the only French artist featured. The second, and totally unexpected collaboration sees Mylène teaming up with "Grande Dame" of French song Line Renaud: "C'est pas l'heure", written by Mylène and composed by Laurent Boutonnat, is the last track on "Rue Washington", Line's first album in 30 years. It is also Mylène's first duet with another female singer. A photograph of the two artists sat side by side in a recording studio is soon released and creates a veritable polemic amongst fans, who could swear that the picture is actually a montage: the matter will never be fully resolved but will, in any case, soon be forgotten. Anyhow, in this month of September, Mylène's activity on the musical front is pretty much limited to those two collaborations: and, given the fact that her "Stade de France" DVD was only released in April, the two new songs, if anything, seem like a bonus. At least this time the singer hasn't disappeared off the face of the earth between albums! What's more, her spectacular (but yet elegant) fall on the Élysée Palace steps earlier in the year on 1st March, as she was making her way to a state dinner held in honour of Russian president Dimitri Medvedev, has seen the singer's picture appear in a variety of publications worldwide: in England, Mylène's slip is documented in the legendary tabloid "The Sun" as well as in the London daily "Metro", where the singer gets a half-page article with three colour pictures all to herself, under the heading "A Gaul heads for a fall". The story also runs in countless other countries, generating a huge buzz and thrilling both French and international fans. So, while the singer may find herself in a period of inactivity, there are at least signs of life, and two brand new duets is more than anyone could have hoped for: clearly, any further new music is a long way off yet, especially in view of the long-gestating "L'Ombre des Autres" film project, rumoured to be underway at last, and likely to be taking up a large chunk of Mylène's time for the foreseeable future. Rumours of a Stade de France concert in September 2011, in order to mark the singer's fiftieth birthday, are also still going strong in some quarters (as they have been, in fact, since September 2009), but the generally accepted wisdom is that there will be no new album before 2012, possibly even 2013, if not beyond...

Which is why so many of us then go on to fall off our chairs when, on September 27th, Polydor officially issue the following simple-worded communiqué: "Mylène

Farmer -Oui Mais...Non- New single written by Mylène Farmer -Composed and produced by RedOne -On radio 29th September- First single from the forthcoming album". Ben and Line were a convenient diversion! To say that everyone is taken by surprise is something of a major understatement: Mylène had surprised us in the past, but this...Never before has the secrecy around a new album been successfully maintained to such a degree: until that thunder-like communiqué, not a single rumour, not even a hint of a leak had managed to filter through: the surprise is utmost and total, and all the more thrilling for it! Especially when no-one could possibly have anticipated such a quick return to the fold from the singer, usually given to taking her sweet time between studio albums...Even Pascal Nègre, Universal MD, gets caught up in the rush of it all, enthusiastically sharing his feelings on Twitter: "Énooormeeee!" is how he qualifies the news. It would seem that Universal themselves were just as taken aback as everyone else: apparently, the entertainment giant only got to hear the track for the first time in the afternoon of the very same day that their earth-shattering announcement was made! Within minutes of the communiqué's release, the various forums go into meltdown, with much talk of "a fantastic present from Mylène" and general expressions of disbelief: can it really be true, is Mylène really back with a new album already? The relative speed with which the singer is making her return is of course totally unexpected, but the biggest shock, surely, really comes courtesy of the five words "Composed and produced by RedOne": the names "Laurent" and "Boutonnat" are nowhere to be seen...It is as if a bomb has just gone off amongst the fans: "But where's Laurent?" is a sentiment much expressed on forums that day. Indeed, after more than a quarter of a century of a faithful and unchanging collaboration, the news is nothing less than revolutionary: with the exception of "Slipping Away" (which was really an original Moby song on which Mylène eventually featured, rather than a track properly her own), this is the first time that the singer is working with someone who is not Laurent Boutonnat. And that someone isn't just anybody either: RedOne is, at the time, arguably the hottest producer on the planet, thanks in large part to his work with the emerging pop sensation that is the amazing Lady Gaga, and her subsequent monster hits including "Just Dance" and "Poker Face". The prospect is enough for any fan to go into meltdown, although sometimes possibly from opposite perspectives: for those who had been dreaming of a day when Mylène would be "unfaitfhul", as it were, to her long-time collaborator in order to explore new musical horizons, the upcoming "Oui mais...Non" seems like a thousand Christmases come all at once, even more so if the RedOne sound and/or Lady Gaga were already your cup of tea. For those more "traditional" fans however, the idea is a little alarming: Mylène without Laurent? Can it still be the same? And, fair enough, the change is indeed of seismic proportions, and no doubt a little bit terrifying: after all, the singer's musical identity is so closely entwined with her early days collaborator that it can be understandably difficult to get your head around the news, and most of all to accept it...This fear is reflected in many of the comments made on forums and websites that day: surely Laurent will still be a part of the new album, he must be! But, for the time being at least, such information is not known, and the only thing that can be done is to speculate wildly. That, and, of course, eagerly anticipating the first radio play of the new single, only two days away now...

Objectively, two days isn't really such a long time. But sometimes, it can feel like an eternity, and that is certainly the case for the many fans now counting down the hours until "Oui mais...Non" gets its first radio play. In the meantime, Mylène is stubbornly not letting any leaks through, and it isn't long before the first fakes appear online. Not just supposed excerpts of the track, but also a full set of lyrics: all slightly intriguing, they will nevertheless turn out to be complete fabrications. Still, it only adds to the fun, and gives us all something to do besides posting innumerable "I can't wait any more!" messages in various forums...Finally, after what is, for many, a next to sleepless night, the single finally debuts on NRJ at 7.30 on the morning of Wednesday 29th: many around the world will get up at an even more punishing hour, according to their own time zones, simply to catch the event in real-time. And it must be said that it is an undeniably genuine pleasure, in this day and age, to be able to discover your favourite artist's latest single on the radio first, knowing that thousands of others around the world are living the exact same thing simultaneously: the moment is unquestionably more memorable as a result, and all the more special for it. The response is, of course, immediate, and, for the most part, very positive: as many go on to point out, "Oui mais...Non" sounds like a huge hit on first listen, with its devilishly catchy melody combined with a simple and easy to remember lyric. Of course, this being Mylène Farmer, the lyrics are anything but straightforward, and to this day their interpretation remains slightly ambiguous at best. The general consensus seems to be that the singer, at least in some parts of the song, comments on the cheap and ready culture of today, although even this is by no means certain. What is quite clear, however, is that "Oui mais...Non" is one of those tracks that instantly and permanently take residence inside your brain: a processus helped, no doubt in many, many cases around the globe, by repeated plays after *that* initial broadcast. Naturally, initial reactions cannot be 100% positive, and there are those who think the song is rubbish, that it will be a complete flop. Others find it hard to get past the fact that this is not a Boutonnat production. And -it was only to be expected- Mylène finds herself accused of "trying to be Gaga": but as practically every other female singer in the world has had the same accusation levelled at her at some point or other in recent times, this is fair enough. In view of Mylène now working with the same producer as the Gaga one herself, especially, it would have been naive to expect otherwise. A common criticism of the song on that first day is that, compared to other RedOne productions, it comes across as rather simplistic, almost minimalist in its instrumentation: but it could be argued that this is indeed just another example of RedOne's genius when it comes to producing tracks that appear throw-away and forgettable at first glance, and yet go on to make a lasting impression. Certainly, the subsequent chart history for "Oui mais...Non" will support the theory...On an individual level, there were no doubt many listeners who, like this very one here, were not completely bowled over on the first listen, and yet could not stop themselves from playing the track over and over and over...just because something about it compelled them to, until, finally, they had no other option but to admit that, yes, "Oui mais...Non" + their ears = love...

One famous pair of such ears belongs to Kylie Minogue who, soon after the song is first heard on the radio, tweets RedOne to say "Am LOVING your Mylène Farmer track "Oui mais...Non"!!!! Oui...Oui...Oui!!!!" Kylie's impeccable taste is a clear indication of the buzz that surrounds the track: it would appear that Mylène has yet another huge hit on her hands. This is soon confirmed when "Oui mais...Non" becomes available for download on 11th October: in no time at all, the song is number 1 across most platforms, including Itunes France, and sets new records in the country with over 9,200 downloads in the first week alone. On the same day, Pascal Nègre returns to Twitter to announce the clip for sometime in early November: a long, long time away. Still, there will be plenty in the meantime to keep fans occupied: on the 15th, the German producer and DJ Klaas reveals on the omnipresent Twitter that he is currently working on a remix of the song, adding that "I'm in love with the melody!" Another remixer soon joins the party: on the 19th, Chew Fu, who has created remixes for the likes of Gaga and Rihanna, is announced to be at work on a "Re-Fix" of the song. On the 21st, a second official communiqué reveals the album title: just in time, as an online leak the previous evening had correctly predicted this to be "Bleu Noir". As well as the name of the album, the communiqué also gives information on Mylène's musical partners for the occasion: RedOne is on board, obviously, as are Moby and the hip English band Archive. One name in particular shines by its absence...it is just as some fans had feared, and as others had hoped: "Bleu Noir" is a Boutonnat-free zone. Once again, it's utter pandemonium in the online forums, with many fans clearly distressed by the obviously major change, while others welcome what they see as a long-overdue overhaul. Of course, feelings about music are clearly never objective, and there is no right or wrong on this issue: some may lament Mylène's decision to work with other producers, feeling that Mylène without Laurent doesn't quite add up to Mylène Farmer. After over 26 years of the incomparable duo, it is easy to see where they're coming from...At the same time, many others, while clearly in awe of Boutonnat's talents, were desirous to see Mylène in a different light, set to a different beat after singing just one man's melodies for so long: both points of view are valid. Indeed, sometimes it is even possible to hold them both at once...In any case, the news is unequivocal, and must either be deplored, or rejoiced at. On the 29th, Tomer G tweets: "Mylène Farmer- The new remixes by Klaas, Chew Fu and Tomer G- soon to be released!" In fact, some of these remixes are going to be made available even sooner than could have been anticipated: on the 4th of November, in what is a brand new avenue of marketing for the singer, the "ephemeral" website mylenefarmer-bleunoir.com opens its doors, with a Jérémy Hills remix available for listening to right away. The following days will no doubt be memorable for many fans across the world, as various elements around the single and album are progressively revealed on the site once a sufficient number of visitors has been registered. A bit of a tease, but we love it and it works ever so well, probably too well, even, as the counter at the bottom of the page seems to have a tendency to mysteriously freeze at random times: no doubt this was intended to keep the momentum going over the course of several days, rather than have to reveal everything at once as each successive plateau was reached in record time! Thus, no matter how furiously we click, our pleasure is delayed for us and divided into small morsels here and there: the first part of the album tracklisting, the other, another remix, a song lyric (not forgetting the album cover visual, that goes on to generate a huge amount of tenacious debate as to its quality)...admittedly, this constitutes more of an opportunity to savour the moment: left to their own devices, would fans have been able to save anything for the following days? Personally, I very much doubt I could have, especially once it became clear that the next element to be revealed would be the clip teaser, followed by the full video itself...

On November 1st, a rumour goes around to the effect that the "Oui mais...Non" video is being shot somewhere in London that very day, and directed by Chris Sweeney, a late-twenties UK-born and based director once described as "a new Spike Jonze", with videos for Sophie Ellis-Bextor and the band Friendly Fires under his belt. As well as being accurate, the rumour is also very much happening in real time: at some point in the preceding days, the information had been posted online that Mylène had just been seen boarding a London-bound Eurostar train. Though the idea was quickly rejected as being a little too extreme, I did happen to come across that information soon after it had been posted, and, living not too far from the Eurostar terminal, it did cross my mind very quickly that it was perfectly possible to cycle over in the hope of getting a glimpse of the star as she came out at the other end...But this was too unsettling somehow: some more clicking on the Bleu Noir website instead, building up those figures for the next element, seemed more preferable. Two weeks later, the site has been visited a sufficient number of times, and a brief teaser is shown for the first time on the 15th: a single unedited shot, that will not feature as such in the video, showing Mylène and her dancers mostly immobile as the first notes of "Oui mais...Non" play in the background. Immediately after the teaser -all ten seconds of it- has been revealed, there are innumerable cries of "Gaga!", although the end result will in no way be reminiscent of -and certainly not "copy"- the American superstar. The full-length video, available on the site from the next day onwards, sees a fairly static Mylène on a white chair, surrounded by male and female dancers wearing some fabulously exotic headgear (the men, in particular) while performing an innovative choreography all around her. The scenes are intercut with shots of Mylène writhing sensually under flashing neon lights or hugging the wall as she sings into camera, as well as a fair amount of potentially highly symbolic shots, such as a fist punching through a pane of glass, or a hand or dancer treading through a milky substance, giving rise to a multitude of interpretations as to their possible meanings. These are still fairly uncertain, in spite of having been discussed at great length...What is obvious on first viewing, in any case, is that the "Oui mais...Non" video is a stylish, contemporary piece of work that fits the songs to a tee: indeed, the clip will be much appreciated and will go on to enjoy considerable success both online and on French TV networks, topping the chart of most-requested videos, an incredibly renewed level of success for the singer.

"Oui mais...Non" is initially released in physical form on the 29th of November, when the basic 2-track CD single is available in stores: that is enough, of course, to send it flying straight in at number 1 in the singles charts, and the song becomes Mylène's tenth chart-topper! But more than that, unlike a "Sextonik" also at number 1 before it, the track goes on to become a genuine popular hit: indeed, it becomes a massive smash for Mylène, who hasn't experienced this kind of singles success since the days of "Slipping away (Crier la vie)", or even, purely as a solo artist, since "C'est une belle journée". "Oui mais...Non" will go on to remain in the pole position for three weeks running, with a total of twelve consecutive weeks spent inside the Top 10, reaching eventual sales estimated at around 125,000. What's more, the radio stations have, at least temporarily, given in to the song's huge popular appeal and revoked their usual "no Mylène" airplay guidelines: a hit is a hit, regardless of who sings it...The following week sees the release of the remaining commercial supports, a digipack Maxi CD and a 12" both featuring the remixes. Rumours of a second CD of remixes will briefly make the rounds, encouraged by the late appearance of yet another version, the "Glam As You" remix by Guéna LG: sadly, this will not come to pass, and "Oui mais...Non" will have to make do with a single disc of remixes, the Guéna LG versions never being released commercially. (This, at least, goes some way towards disproving the often stated assumption that Mylène treats her fans as cash cows: if there ever was a single that could have been "milked", "Oui mais...Non" was it, and yet no such thing happened.) There is a little bit more choice on the promotional front, however, with three different versions available: as well as a 1-track CD featuring the single version, the "Club Remix" promo offers two Jérémy Hill remixes, while the "Remixes" CD features no less than six different versions of the song, and some mixes not available anywhere else. Early on in the following year, Mylène performs the song at the NRJ Music Awards on the 22nd of January. On the night, she also loses out to Jenifer in the "French female artist of the year" category, a much-disputed result that sees the organizers' true motives come under close scrutiny; as for Jenifer, she finds herself the target of some fierce, angry criticism -some of which, regrettably, takes the form of extremely nasty verbal abuse- from disgruntled Farmer fans: not one of the best, or most edifying editions of the NRJMA to have ever come about. Mylène's performance is, not too surprisingly, one of the highlights of the evening: a prestation that is faithful to the clip, with the dancers all in attendance and the singer's white chair back in action too. No sign, however, of the rumoured acrobats. Mylène's performance for broadcast has been recorded beforehand as usual, although she is present on the stage and performing at the same time, in spite of some crazy rumours that insisted she was never even anywhere near the building on the night...

With a huge hit as lead single, the album is off to an amazing start: "Bleu Noir" is released on 6th December (a week after the earlier digital release) and promptly hits the number 1 spot with 139,176 copies sold in its first week: a better score than both of Mylène's last two studio albums. Not only that, the album also becomes December's best-seller in France, and the 10th best-selling album of the year 2010 overall with only one month of exploitation time! As early as December, "Bleu Noir" is certified triple platinum for over 300,000 copies sold. A few months later, in March 2011, it will receive a diamond certification for sales of over 500,000. Of course, with such levels of success, the album's exploitation must continue apace. With "Oui mais...Non" having most definitely done the business, attention soon turns to the second single...

53/ Bleu Noir

"Oui mais...Non" having scored a huge hit for the singer -easily her biggest in years- the time soon comes to consider the matter of the follow-up single. In forums, the two tracks most favoured as possible choices are "Lonely Lisa", the *other* RedOne produ tion, or the title track "Bleu Noir", an anthemic, sing-along Moby composition to which Mylène has added her own particular brand of fatalistic yet hopeful lyrics, the very first few lines setting the tone perfectly: "I walk towards the darkness, towards the funeral horizon..." Once again, death and its inevitability are the central preoccupation here, even if the overall tone is far from being merely pessimistic: indeed, over the very next lines, the singer makes it clear that, "still, it's worth it". A more serene approach to the inevitable, perhaps, than on occasions past: certainly, "Bleu Noir" broaches the issue in a far more upbeat fashion than previous tracks such as "Et si vieillir m'était conté" or even "L'Horloge", where Baudelaire's terrifying, nightmarish vision of the inexorable passing of time is set to the disquieting tick-tock of the clock that counts down the remainder of man's season. The end result will, of course, still be the same, but "Bleu Noir" at least puts the emphasis on the "beautiful battle" to be fought in the meantime, a battle which is that of "long, long days...": the raw, unadultered fear of the void now being tempered by the singer's comforting words of encouragement, of hope against hope.

With "Oui mais...Non" still doing the business in the charts, there is no question of rush-releasing the follow-up: although "Bleu Noir" may have been sent out to radio as early as January 28th, its actual release will come about in a most leisurely fashion, with almost a full three months elapsing between the first radio play and the physical release of the various supports on 18th April. Sadly, although not too surprisingly, NRJ and other stations have quickly reverted to their "no Mylène" airplay policies, and the build-up for the new single, such as it is, will have to come from other sources. (Incidentally, as far as NRJ radio is concerned, it is interesting to note that, just as was the case for "Si j'avais au moins..." and its subsequent performance at the NRJ Music Awards 2009, the station somehow managed to make room on their airwaves for Mylène and her "Oui mais...Non", also due to be performed at the 2011 Awards edition: clearly, NRJ know enough to play the game when they need the singer to put in an appearance at their little annual televised event.) But with no awards ceremony on the horizon just yet, "Bleu Noir" is on its own, with predictable results: airplay that is sporadic at best, non-existent at worst. But that, by now, is pretty much par for the course, and no particularly great cause for concern amongst the fans who, for the most part, are pleased with the choice of second single: though opinion is of course not unanimous, many feel that "Bleu Noir" is one of the album's strongest tracks, and well worthy of a single release. A couple of new remixes of the track are soon sent out to radio stations, in an effort to boost rotations: on March 10th, a Jérémy Hills re-working is heard for the first time, while the club-friendly Guéna LG "Glam As You" radio mix is sent out in promo form on the 31st: sadly, this doesn't help matters much, and airplay remains far from enthusiastic for the new single, with most stations ignoring it completely...But never mind: more importantly, a new single means, of course, a new clip: naturally, many fans are anxious to find out just what Mylène is going to come up with this time...

Their questions are first answered on February 18th, when a 15-second teaser (apparently not released in an official capacity) is somehow leaked on youtube: a moody, atmospheric shot of a somber-looking Mylène making her slow way under what appear to be weeping willows, to a soundtrack of sparse, intriguing sound effects. An undeniably beautiful teaser that quickly engenders very positive reactions: the dark, slightly ominous tone finds much favour with fans, always up for a bit of moody Mylène. This is shortly followed by the unexpected but welcome re-opening of the mylenefarmer-bleunoir.com website on March 7th, when an ever so slightly different teaser is presented. For the first time, the forthcoming video's director's name is revealed: Olivier Dahan, to whom we owe the fantastic Édith Piaf biopic "La Môme", released as "La Vie en Rose" in English-language territories. A beautiful, stunning-looking movie: hopes are high for the clip to come. But "Bleu Noir" is certainly taking its sweet time, and fans will have to wait until the 16th to see it in full at last, when it is broadcast for the first time exclusively on the newly-reopened website. The response from fans is huge and generally speaking very positive: in a clip that is light-years away from "Oui mais...Non" in terms of style, Dahan delivers a simple, mostly black and white short film that consists of almost one single continuous take. Mylène is seen making her way through a succession of landscapes, going from forest to snowy plain to starlit sky, the seasons changing in the background (*à la* "Appelle mon numéro"), with a touch of explosions and fireworks here and there to distract her as she sings her song. In a great touch, Mylène adopts a relaxed approach to lip-synching, frequently missing out words or entire lines altogether: this works a treat, in a way almost allowing the singer to "jump out" of her own song and adding another layer of intrigue to what is a deceptively straightforward-looking video. Mylène's deliberate lyrical omissions immediately give rise to much questioning amongst fans as to their precise meaning: what is the singer trying to tell us? Another element of the clip soon prompts further debate: what could be the significance of the three mysterious stars or points of light glimpsed early on at the start, and then much more clearly in the very last shot, when the film has switched to colour? Interpretations vary, with some seeing in it a nod to lost loved ones, or an allusion to the Holy Trinity, while others detect a possible pictorial reference to the Freemasons; little green men are obviously mentioned too, if only briefly. A definitive explanation anytime soon seems very unlikely, of course, and the strange lights' exact meaning must undoubtedly remain fairly obscure. What is beyond doubt, however, is that the singer looks positively beautiful and radiant in her new video: interestingly, many will comment on the felt similarities between some of the shots and scenes from the "Plus Grandir" clip, all the way back in 1985. Mylène, at times, is strangely reminiscent of her past self, not only in her stance but also in her facial expressions, and varying sources will talk of the "Bleu Noir" video as a "return to the source": and it is true that there is something vaguely troubling about the clip, even if it is in a most pleasing manner, in the way that the Mylène on screen is occasionally spookily reminiscent of the "Mylène of old". Not just a grovelling compliment to the singer's legendary age-defying beauty, even if it is undeniably so (how many times, already, has it been said that "Mylène Farmer doesn't age"?), the observation is also in tune with a theme picked on by keen-eyed viewers, the theme of rebirth: the scarab beetle brooch as worn by the singer in the video is significant because of its highly symbolic connotations. In Egyptian mythology (something Mylène has already flirted with in the past with the Mylènium Tour Isis statue, for instance), the scarab beetle represents the Sun God Ra, who is reborn every morning and is thus a symbol of resurrection and renewal. And the idea of change, of renewal, is indeed very strong in Olivier Dahan's images: the singer, herself perpetually in motion, never static (in another change from the previous video), is surrounded by a constantly shifting landscape, through the varying seasons, as she herself appears renewed and rejuvenated, singing about the approaching darkness, perhaps in itself the ultimate rebirth. Of course, these somewhat mystical interpretations of the video don't always sit well with everybody, and it is fair to say that some fans are perhaps not as impressed by what they see as being not much more than Mylène taking a long walk in front of a green screen. There is also a commonly-heard complaint, running along the lines of "whatever happened to the teaser"? True, the 15-second original teaser may have led many to anticipate a darker, perhaps more scenarised final product. In retrospect, however, Mylène's early wander through the weeping willows can perhaps be viewed as the prelude to what was to come, especially as the opening scenes of "Bleu Noir" do see the singer gradually emerging from a forest-like environment: perhaps a future edit for an as of yet unreleased video compilation?

In a slightly surprising development, it is revealed on March 22 that the song "The Day", first single to be taken from Moby's latest album "Destroyed", is in fact the English version of "Bleu Noir". Not only is it sung in a different language, with a completely unrelated lyric, but the track has also undergone a drastic rearrangement, and is markedly different from Mylène's version. An unexpected instance of "recycling", perhaps, but after the earlier success of "Slipping Away (Crier la vie)", one that seems like something of a fair trade too..."Bleu Noir" -as sung by Mylène- is physically released on 18th April 2011, on three different commercial supports: a CD single featuring the instrumental version, a limited edition vinyl and a digipack Maxi CD featuring the Jérémy Hills and Guéna LG remixes, both remixers having worked on the previous "Oui mais...Non" versions. Poor Henry Neu's ears are no doubt ringing a fair bit by now, as once again the quality of the sleeve art is debated at length in online forums: a similarity with the "C'est dans l'air" cover artwork is also pointed out, perhaps justifiably so as the images are indeed very similar. But it is the promo editions, in particular, that come under sustained fire over their graphic design qualities, or the perceived lack of. To this day, no-one appears to have been able to make out just what the weird squiggle on the promo covers is supposed to represent, with many a negative comment passed as a result. Nevertheless, no less than three different editions are pressed, one each for the radio edit, Jérémy Hill and Guéna LG radio remixes, with the disputed cover art defiantly remaining in place on each occasion. In any case, any displeasure at the single's artwork will in no way harm the chart performance of "Bleu Noir": when the figures are revealed on April 27th, Mylène's 53rd single becomes her seventh consecutive number 1, bringing her total tally so far to an amazing and unequalled eleven chart-toppers: an incredible, unbeaten record, one that is likely to remain unchallenged for a long while yet. A triple record, in fact, as "Bleu Noir" also happens to be Mylène's 40th Top 10 single. Not only that, but with 9,743 copies sold in its first week, the song is also the best start for any 2011 single yet! She may have her detractors, forever looking out for the least perceived weakness in order to proclaim "the end", but the truth is, the singer just keeps getting better and better: by now, any single that failed to make it to number 1 would probably be declared "a flop" by them, for want of any other more obvious signs of failure. Still, as far as Mylène is concerned, that isn't such a bad problem to have...

With the single "Bleu Noir" already in the past, the time will soon come to move on to the next release: indeed, if rumours are to be believed, it looks like the next single may arrive far sooner than could have been anticipated...

54/ Lonely Lisa

And so, here we are: as I write these last few words in the first few days of May 2011, rumours as to the next single, strongly pointing to a quick release for "Lonely Lisa", have only just been definitely confirmed, with the first promo visual having only just been made available. This lightning-quick single release, for what is the second RedOne production off the album, is something which apparently was the plan all along, should "Bleu Noir" fail to meet with sustained chart success. Although it could be argued that the song has hardly even been given a chance! In fact, there has already been some talk on the various forums of the previous single being more or less prematurely buried, in spite of its number 1 placing, which, lest we forget, only came about a week ago! Interestingly, the French remixer Romain Curtis has very recently revealed that he was working on a Mylène Farmer remix, although he wouldn't be drawn on the exact song, saying simply that it is a track off the album. In view of today's announcement, it is tempting to jump to conclusions and assume that the track in question is indeed "Lonely Lisa". What is also *very* tempting, at least from a personal point of view, is to wonder at the reasons behind this incredibly fast-moving new single release: of course, this is nothing but the wildest speculation, but could Mylène be keeping to some kind of schedule here, with a view, perhaps, to putting on a concert or series of concerts later on in the year? On the occasion of her 50th birthday, perhaps?

Ok, I admit it: this is nothing more than wishful thinking and the wild rantings of an over-excitable fan. It is not for me to try and out-guess Mylène Farmer: doing so is a risky business indeed, and nothing could be more doomed to failure...

55: ???

What is more probable, on the other hand, is that by the time you read these words, this book will already be out of date: one, or perhaps more, further singles will have come along, too late for me to include them here. Does that bother me? Not in the slightest: on the contrary, I hope this book is still missing many, many chapters. May there be twice, three times as many again; may the story never end, and may Mylène continue to enchant us and make us dream like only she knows how: because, as she so rightly says, "Le monde est triste sans imagination". And our world is undoubtedly a brighter place for her being in it.

Thank You

First and foremost, I would like to dedicate this book to all international MF fans: if it wasn't for you, it would never have been written in the first place.

Thank You to Claude Christian for friendship and sound advice (and movies!) through the years.

Thank You to Paul Jarvis and Ian McInnes for their invaluable advice on the technical aspects of putting together a manuscript, but more importantly for their friendship.

Thank You to Paul Gayle for computer and hugs expertise.

Julian Williams (R.I.P.), Gavin Smith, Paul Oremland, Charles Adesina...

Thank You to MFInternational.com and all its members: this book would never have come about if it wasn't for you. Big shout out to all Mylène fans worldwide.

Thank You to Mylène.net, Innamoramento.net, Sans Logique.com and many more: I don't know what I'd do without my daily fix.

Thank You to White Lions (Indonesia) for some bitchin' cover artwork: you guys are incredibly talented, and real friendly with it too. Commission your very own MF artwork! Get in touch at: socceripoy@gmail.com

For my family, and anyone who's ever been in my heart, in particular my sister Nathalie and my beautiful nieces and nephew Léa, Manon and Noa.

Mamie, Pépé: vous me manquez toujours, vous me manquerez toujours.

For Spike, the definition of a cool cat.

And of course, a huge Thank You to Mylène Farmer and Laurent Boutonnat: in this life, I couldn't have asked for a better soundtrack.

Enjoyed this book? Hated it? Feel free to let me know at: farewell_to_Aeris@yahoo.com

Mylène Farmer, the singles:
a crazy bonus French "poem"

Mylène Farmer, espace fumeur, une autre époque et
d'autres moeurs

Maman a tort changea l'décor, on l'aura jouée
jusqu'au rebord

My mum is wrong was the same song, so we'll just
move swiftly along

Deuxième single, pas très facile, on était tous des
imbéciles

Puis plus grandir, et quel délire, déja elle parlait de
mourir

Vint libertine, perverse comptine, Jeanne devint
"out", Mylène fut "in"

Cours loin de là, pure Tristana, Tellier revient, une
deuxième fois!

Le carton sans contrefaçon, échange les filles et les
garçons

Le premier slow, que se nomme-t-il, ainsi soit-je, doux
et subtil

Elles ont l'air douces, pourvu qu'elles soient,
entièrement rousses, châtain j'aime pas

Toréador un peu sadique, sur belles images, conte sans
logique

A part écrire ces stupides vers, quelqu'un peut m'dire,
à quoi je sers?

Une p'tite pause live, et que c'est beau, d'avoir comme
sujet monsieur Poe

Puis de rev'nir, sur plus grandir, avant le top, de
conquérir

Courir est vain, vous n'échapperez, au raz d'marée
désenchantée

Les snobs riaient, comme on aimait, une chose est
sure, y'a pas d'regrets

Mélancolie que tu nous donnes, il est évident qu'elle
résonne

It's in our hearts, it's in our souls, beyond any kind of
control

Et Luc Besson, que tu r'verras, que mon coeur lâche,
il filmera

My soul is slashed, ça j'en dis quoi, oui non en fait, là
je sais pas

Alors je passe à l'xxl, et te cueille une fleur de poubelle

Pour l'instant x où l'on s'ébat, dans de la mousse aux
usa

J'ai beau courir, tu n'es plus là, t'es partie en
California!

Et comme j'ai mal, tu le pensas, quand de la scene, tu
t'expulsas

Ce soir à Lyon, ou envoutés, nous reprenions tous sur
rêver

Ainsi soit-je...fait un retour, j'peux d'mander si c'est
pas trop lourd

Quand tu chantais de la poupée, c'est pas Khaled qui
t'a poussée?

Sur une muraille reconstituée, des jumelles déja
condamnées

Nous rendent un regard étriqué, tel un tableau d'Egon
Schiele

Puis d'un hôtel en incendie, tu te souviens de jours
  maudits
Avant de faire un tour au cirque, où tu r'deviens
  optimistique
Les yeux et le coeur vers le haut, c'est là
  l'innamoramento
J'ose pas d'mander, je sais qu'c'est con, mais dis tu
  m'dessines un mouton?
Les Razmokets l'ont mérité, si de ta main ils furent
  fessés
C'est pas Seal dans la vidéo, celui que tu vires du
  radeau
Mais tu t'en fous, tu vas t'coucher, encore la fin d'une
  belle journée
Pardonne-moi pour ces vers tarés, là j'ai encore du
  trop fumer
J'entends des djs qui remixent, trois titres classiques,
  dont l'instant x
Victoires? Musique? You don't play ball. Et ça les
  pique, tu fuck them all!
Qi pointu, aussi perçant, que ces doigts fins dans ton
  amant
Un atelier, statues en blanc, pour redonner le gout
  d'avant
Parfois une statue se dévoile, avec Benoît, tu t'mets à
  poil
Mon sang était bien chaud déja, en plus après, tu
  d'viens manga!
Tu te rhabilles avec Moby, même s'il te fait crier la vie
Avant que l'ombre tombe sur Bercy, pour un retour
  live inoui
Encore une fois, déshabillée? Mais tu viens juste de les
  enlever!

Extraterrestre, descends sur terre, pour qu'en partouze ça dégénère

J'ai bien essayé de t'appeler, mais ton numéro a changé

Si j't'avais au moins contactée, la SPA veut t'honorer!

Mais t'es r'partie, tu es dans l'air, mode de propulsion nucléaire?

J'ai bien besoin d'un p'tit tonique, alors je sors ton jouet magique

Dans l'air déja, remix nouveau? J'veux bien vibrer, pas sur Tiesto

On touche la fin, pour ton entrée, voici l'eden inanimé

Hey tu dis oui, ou tu dis non? Avec RedOne, c'est trop canon

Alors on finit sur Bleu Noir, juste temps de dire au revoir...

Mais attendez, qu'on l'oublie pas, sinon elle s'ra Lonely, Lisa...

Lightning Source UK Ltd.
Milton Keynes UK
UKHW010806110123
415170UK00001B/205